Standards Practice Book

For Home or School

Grade 1

INCLUDES:
- Home or School Practice
- Lesson Practice and Test Preparation
- English and Spanish School-Home Letters
- Getting Ready for Grade 2 Lessons

HOUGHTON MIFFLIN HARCOURT

CRITICAL AREA

Operations and Algebraic Thinking

COMMON CORE

Critical Area Developing understanding of addition, subtraction, and strategies for addition and subtraction within 20

1 Addition Concepts

Domains Operations and Algebraic Thinking
Common Core Standards CC.1.OA.1, CC.1.OA.3, CC.1.OA.6

2 Subtraction Concepts

Domains Operations and Algebraic Thinking
Common Core Standards CC.1.OA.1, CC.1.OA.6, CC.1.OA.8

5 Addition and Subtraction Relationships

Domains Operations and Algebraic Thinking

Common Core Standards CC.1.OA.1, CC.1.OA.6, CC.1.OA.7, CC.1.OA.8

 **CRITICAL AREA**

Number and Operations in Base Ten

 COMMON CORE **Critical Area** Developing understanding of whole number relationships and place value, including grouping in tens and ones

 6 ## Count and Model Numbers

Domains Number and Operations in Base Ten
Common Core Standards CC.1.NBT.1, CC.1.NBT.2, CC.1.NBT.2a, CC.1.NBT.2b, CC.1.NBT.2c, CC.1.NBT.3

7 ## Compare Numbers

Domains Number and Operations in Base Ten
Common Core Standards CC.1.NBT.3, CC.1.NBT.5

Two-Digit Addition and Subtraction

Domains Operations and Algebraic Thinking
Number and Operations in Base Ten

Common Core Standards CC.1.OA.6, CC.1.NBT.4, CC.1.NBT.6

 **CRITICAL AREA** **Measurement and Data**

COMMON CORE **Critical Area** Developing understanding of linear measurement and measuring lengths as iterating length units

 Measurement

Domains Measurement and Data
Common Core Standards CC.1.MD.1, CC.1.MD.2, CC.1.MD.3

10 **Represent Data**

Domains Measurement and Data
Common Core Standards CC.1.MD.4

© Houghton Mifflin Harcourt Publishing Company

CRITICAL AREA Geometry

COMMON CORE **Critical Area** Reasoning about attributes of, and composing and decomposing geometric shapes

11 Three-Dimensional Geometry

Domains Geometry
Common Core Standards CC.1.G.1, CC.1.G.2

12 Two-Dimensional Geometry

Domains Geometry
Common Core Standards CC.1.G.1, CC.1.G.2, CC.1.G.3

End-of-Year Resources

Getting Ready for Grade 2

These lessons review important skills and prepare you for Grade 2.

School-Home Letter

Dear Family,

My class started Chapter 1 this week. In this chapter, I will learn to add numbers up to ten, to write addition sentences in different ways, and to use pictures to help me add.

Love, _____

Vocabulary

plus (+) part of an addition sentence that means "to add to"

$$plus$$
$$1 + 3 = 4$$

sum the answer to an addition sentence

$$2 + 4 = ⑥$$

zero a number that means none; if you add zero to any number, the number does not change

$$1 + 0 = 1$$

Home Activity

Use 10 checkers, crayons, or other small objects. Work with your child to show all the ways to make 10. ($1 + 9$, $6 + 4$, and so on.) Together write addition sentences for each way to make ten.

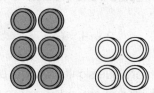

Literature

Look for this book in a library. Ask your child to count how many objects are on each page.

How Many Snails?: A Counting Book
by Paul Giganti. Greenwillow Books, 1994

Carta
para la casa

Querida familia:

Mi clase comenzó el Capítulo 1 esta semana. En este capítulo, aprenderé a sumar números hasta diez, cómo escribir oraciones numéricas de suma de distintas maneras y cómo usar ilustraciones para aprender a sumar mejor.

Con cariño, _____

Vocabulario

más (+) parte de una oración numérica de suma que significa "sumar a"

$$\text{más}$$
$$1 + 3 = 4$$

suma la respuesta a una oración numérica de suma

$$2 + 4 = ⑥$$

cero un número que significa nada; si sumas cero a cualquier número, ese número no cambia

$$1 + 0 = 1$$

Actividad para la casa

Use 10 fichas, crayolas u otros objetos pequeños. Trabaje con su hijo para mostrar todas las maneras de formar 10. (1 + 9, 6 + 4 y así sucesivamente). Luego escriban juntos oraciones numéricas de suma para cada manera de formar diez.

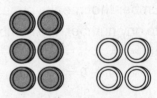

Literatura

Busque este libro en una biblioteca. Pídale a su hijo que cuente cuántos objetos hay en cada página.

¿Cuántos caracoles?: Un libro para contar
por Paul Giganti.
Greenwillow Books, 1994

Algebra • Use Pictures to Add To

COMMON CORE STANDARD CC.1.OA.1
Represent and solve problems involving addition and subtraction.

Write how many.

1.

5 horses   and   3 more horses   ____ horses

2.

3 dogs   and   2 more dogs   ____ dogs

3.

4 cats   and   1 more cat   ____ cats

PROBLEM SOLVING REAL WORLD

There are 2 rabbits. 5 rabbits join them. How many rabbits are there now?

There are ____ rabbits

Lesson Check (CC.1.OA.1)

1. How many birds are there?

2 birds	and	6 more birds	_____ birds
4	6	8	9
○	○	○	○

Spiral Review (CC.1.OA.1)

2. How many goats are there? (Lesson 1.1)

2 goats	and	4 more goats	_____ goats
2	6	8	10
○	○	○	○

3. How many rabbits are there? (Lesson 1.1)

5 rabbits	and	1 more rabbit	_____ rabbits
2	4	5	6
○	○	○	○

4. How many ducks are there? (Lesson 1.1)

5 ducks	and	4 more ducks	_____ ducks
9	8	5	1
○	○	○	○

Name _____

Model Adding To

COMMON CORE STANDARD CC.1.OA.1
Represent and solve problems involving addition and subtraction.

Use 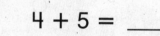 to show adding to.
Draw the 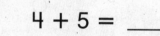. Write the sum.

1. 5 ants and 1 more ant

$5 + 1 =$ ____

2. 3 cats and 4 more cats

$3 + 4 =$ ____

3. 4 dogs and 4 more dogs

$4 + 4 =$ ____

4. 4 bees and 5 more bees

$4 + 5 =$ ____

PROBLEM SOLVING REAL WORLD

Use the picture to help you complete the addition sentences. Write each sum.

5. ____ + ____ = ____ in all

6. ____ + ____ = ____ in all

Lesson Check (CC.1.OA.1)

1. What is the sum of 4 and 2?

| 2 | 4 | 6 | 8 |
| ○ | ○ | ○ | ○ |

Spiral Review (CC.1.OA.1)

2. How many butterflies are there? (Lesson 1.1)

5 butterflies   and   2 more butterflies   ____ butterflies

| 2 | 3 | 6 | 7 |
| ○ | ○ | ○ | ○ |

3. What is the sum of 2 and 3? (Lesson 1.2)

| 1 | 2 | 5 | 6 |
| ○ | ○ | ○ | ○ |

4. How many birds are there? (Lesson 1.1)

6 birds   and   1 more bird   ____ birds

| 8 | 7 | 6 | 5 |
| ○ | ○ | ○ | ○ |

Model Putting Together

COMMON CORE STANDARD CC.1.OA.1
Represent and solve problems involving addition and subtraction.

Use ◯ to solve. Draw to show your work. Write the number sentence and how many.

1. There are 2 big dogs and 4 small dogs. How many dogs are there?

   ____ dogs

   __ ◯ ___ ◯ ___

2. There are 3 red crayons and 2 green crayons. How many crayons are there?

   ____ crayons

   __ ◯ ___ ◯ ___

3. There are 5 brown rocks and 3 white rocks. How many rocks are there?

   ____ rocks

   __ ◯ ___ ◯ ___

PROBLEM SOLVING REAL WORLD

4. Write your own addition story problem.

   _____
   _____
   _____
   _____

Lesson Check (CC.1.OA.1)

1. There are 3 black cats and 2 brown cats.
   How many cats are there?

   6   5   1   0
   ○   ○   ○   ○

2. There are 4 red flowers and 3 yellow flowers.
   How many flowers are there? (Lesson 1.3)

   1   3   7   8
   ○   ○   ○   ○

Spiral Review (CC.1.OA.1)

3. How many turtles are there? (Lesson 1.1)

   6 turtles   and   3 more turtles   _____ turtles

   2   5   8   9
   ○   ○   ○   ○

4. What is the sum of 2 and 1? (Lesson 1.2)

   4   3   2   1
   ○   ○   ○   ○

Problem Solving • Model Addition

COMMON CORE STANDARD CC.1.OA.1
Represent and solve problems involving
addition and subtraction.

Read the problem. Use the bar model to solve. Complete the model and the number sentence.

1. Dylan has 7 flowers.
   4 of the flowers are red.
   The rest are yellow.
   How many flowers are yellow?

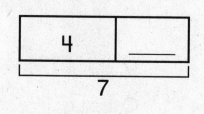

$4 + \_\_\_\_ = 7$

2. Some birds are flying in a group.
   4 more birds join the group.
   Then there are 9 birds in the
   group. How many birds were in
   the group before?

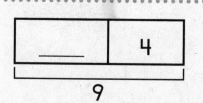

$\_\_\_\_ + 4 = 9$

3. 6 cats are walking.
   1 more cat walks with them.
   How many cats are walking now?

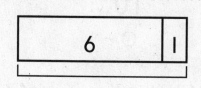

$6 + 1 = \_\_\_$

Lesson Check (CC.1.OA.1)

1. 3 ducks are in the pond.
6 more ducks join them.
How many ducks are in the pond now?

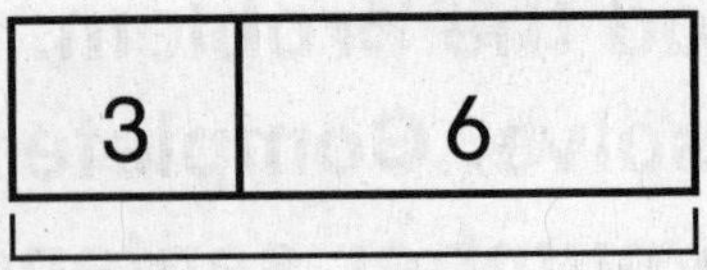

3	6

9   6   3   I

○   ○   ○   ○

Spiral Review (CC.1.OA.1)

2. There are 4 green grapes and 4 red grapes.
How many grapes are there? (Lesson 1.3)

I   5   8   9

○   ○   ○   ○

3. What is the sum of 7 and 3? (Lesson 1.2)

10   9   7   4

○   ○   ○   ○

4. What is the sum of 6 and 2? (Lesson 1.2)

9   8   7   4

○   ○   ○   ○

Algebra • Add Zero

COMMON CORE STANDARD CC.1.OA.3
Understand and apply properties of operations and the relationship between addition and subtraction.

**Draw circles to show the number.
Write the sum.**

1.

$3 + 0 =$ ___

2.

$0 + 5 =$ ___

3.

$1 + 3 =$ ___

4.

$5 + 1 =$ ___

PROBLEM SOLVING REAL WORLD

Write the addition sentence to solve.

5. 6 turtles swim.
No turtles join them.
How many turtles are there now?

___ + ___ = ___

___ turtles

Lesson Check (CC.1.OA.3)

I. What is the sum for 0 + 4?

6	5	4	0
○	○	○	○

Spiral Review (CC.1.OA.1)

2. There are 3 goats are in the barn.
4 more goats join them.
How many goats are in the barn now? (Lesson 1.4)

5	6	7	8
○	○	○	○

3. There are 7 blue crayons and 1 yellow crayon.
How many crayons are there? (Lesson 1.3)

4	6	7	8
○	○	○	○

4. What is the sum of 3 and 3? (Lesson 1.2)

3	4	5	6
○	○	○	○

Name _____

Algebra • Add in Any Order

COMMON CORE STANDARD CC.1.OA.3
Understand and apply properties of operations and the relationship between addition and subtraction.

Use 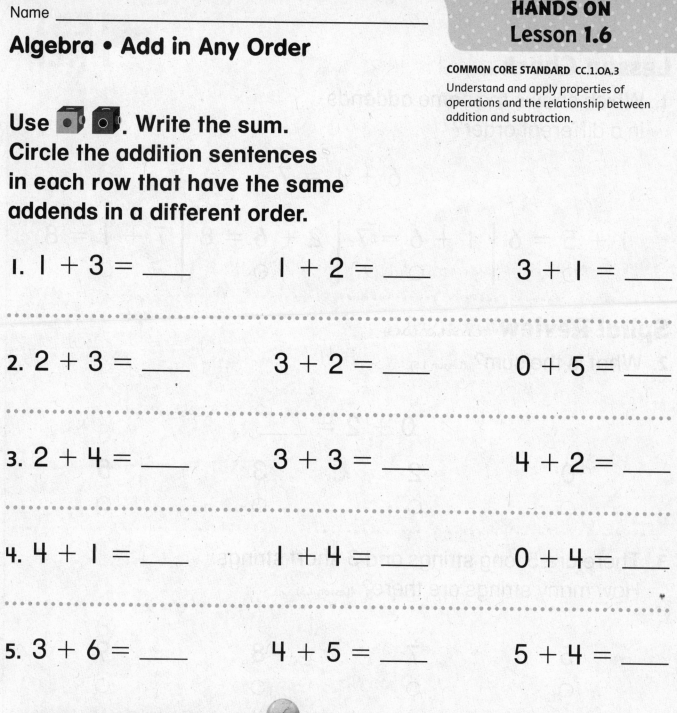 . Write the sum.
Circle the addition sentences
in each row that have the same
addends in a different order.

1. $1 + 3 =$ _____ $1 + 2 =$ _____ $3 + 1 =$ _____

2. $2 + 3 =$ _____ $3 + 2 =$ _____ $0 + 5 =$ _____

3. $2 + 4 =$ _____ $3 + 3 =$ _____ $4 + 2 =$ _____

4. $4 + 1 =$ _____ $1 + 4 =$ _____ $0 + 4 =$ _____

5. $3 + 6 =$ _____ $4 + 5 =$ _____ $5 + 4 =$ _____

PROBLEM SOLVING REAL WORLD

Draw pictures to match the addition sentences.
Write the sums.

6. $5 + 2 =$ _____

   $2 + 5 =$ _____

Lesson Check (CC.1.OA.3)

1. Which shows the same addends in a different order?

$$6 + 1 = 7$$

$1 + 5 = 6$	$1 + 6 = 7$	$2 + 6 = 8$	$7 + 1 = 8$
○	○	○	○

Spiral Review (CC.1.OA.1, CC.1.OA.3)

2. What is the sum? (Lesson 1.5)

$$0 + 2 = \underline{\quad}$$

0	2	3	5
○	○	○	○

3. There are 5 long strings and 3 short strings. How many strings are there? (Lesson 1.3)

5	7	8	9
○	○	○	○

4. What is the sum of 6 and 2? (Lesson 1.2)

10	8	6	4
○	○	○	○

Name _____

Algebra • Put Together Numbers to 10

Use 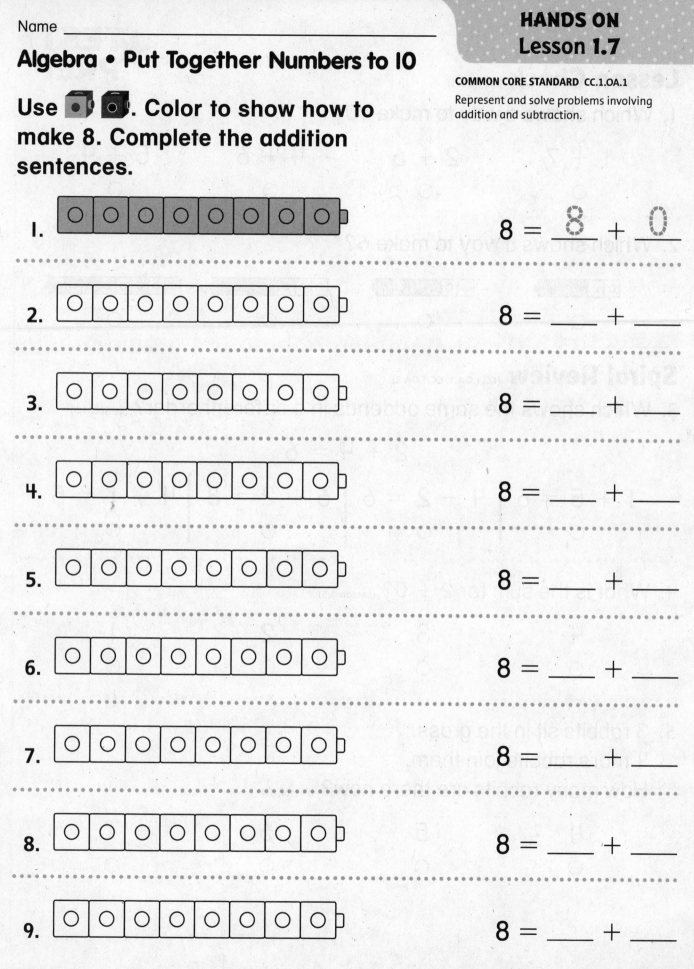. Color to show how to make 8. Complete the addition sentences.

COMMON CORE STANDARD CC.1.OA.1
Represent and solve problems involving addition and subtraction.

1. $8 = \underline{8} + \underline{0}$

2. $8 = \underline{} + \underline{}$

3. $8 = \underline{} + \underline{}$

4. $8 = \underline{} + \underline{}$

5. $8 = \underline{} + \underline{}$

6. $8 = \underline{} + \underline{}$

7. $8 = \underline{} + \underline{}$

8. $8 = \underline{} + \underline{}$

9. $8 = \underline{} + \underline{}$

Lesson Check (CC.1.OA.1)

1. Which shows a way to make 10?

$1 + 7$ ○ $2 + 6$ ○ $4 + 6$ ○ $5 + 4$ ○

2. Which shows a way to make 6?

○   ○   ○   ○

Spiral Review (CC.1.OA.1, CC.1.OA.3)

3. Which shows the same addends in a different order? (Lesson 1.6)

$$2 + 4 = 6$$

$1 + 5 = 6$ ○ | $4 + 2 = 6$ ○ | $6 + 2 = 8$ ○ | $4 + 1 = 5$ ○

4. What is the sum for $2 + 0$? (Lesson 1.5)

4 ○   3 ○   2 ○   1 ○

5. 3 rabbits sit in the grass.
   4 more rabbits join them.
   How many rabbits are there now? (Lesson 1.4)

4 ○   5 ○   6 ○   7 ○

Addition to 10

COMMON CORE STANDARD CC.1.OA.6
Add and subtract within 20.

Write the sum.

1. 4
   + 1
   ___

2. 2
   + 6
   ___

3. 3
   + 4
   ___

4. 5
   + 1
   ___

5. 8
   + 0
   ___

6. 2
   + 3
   ___

7. 0
   + 0
   ___

8. 5
   + 2
   ___

9. 5
   + 5
   ___

10. 0
    + 6
    ___

11. 3
    + 1
    ___

12. 2
    + 4
    ___

PROBLEM SOLVING REAL WORLD

Add. Write the sum. Use the sum and the key to color the flower.

13.

2 + 5

4 + 5 = ___

7 + 1

KEY

6 YELLOW
7 RED
8 PURPLE
9 PINK

Lesson Check (CC.1.OA.6)

1. What is the sum?

$$\begin{array}{r} 5 \\ + 3 \\ \hline \end{array}$$

2   4   7   8
○   ○   ○   ○

Spiral Review (CC.1.OA.1)

2. Which shows a way to make 9? (Lesson 1.7)

2 + 7   2 + 6   4 + 3   5 + 3
○   ○   ○   ○

3. There are 8 large stones and 2 small stones. How many stones are there? (Lesson 1.3)

11   10   8   6
○   ○   ○   ○

4. What is the sum of 2 and 2? (Lesson 1.2)

2   3   4   5
○   ○   ○   ○

COMMON CORE STANDARDS CC.1.OA.1, CC.1.OA.3, CC.1.OA.6

Chapter 1 Extra Practice

Lessons 1.1 - 1.2 (pp. 13–20)

Use ⬚ to show adding to.
Draw the ⬚. Write the sum.

1. 4 dogs   and   3 more dogs   ____ dogs

$$4 + 3 = \underline{}$$

Lesson 1.3 (pp. 21–24)

Use ◯ to solve. Draw to show your work.
Write the number sentence and how many.

1. There are 5 large rabbits and
   3 small rabbits. How many
   rabbits are there?

____ rabbits   ____ ◯ ____ ◯ ____

Lesson 1.5 (pp. 29–32)

Draw circles to show the number. Write the sum.

1.   2.

$$0 + 3 = \underline{}$$ $$3 + 1 = \underline{}$$

Lesson 1.6 (pp. 33–36)

Use 🎲🎲. Write the sum.
Circle the addition sentences
in each row that have the same
addends in a different order.

1. $5 + 1 = \underline{}$ $2 + 1 = \underline{}$ $1 + 5 = \underline{}$

2. $4 + 3 = \underline{}$ $3 + 4 = \underline{}$ $2 + 2 = \underline{}$

Lesson 1.7 (pp. 37–40)

Use 🎲🎲. Color to show how to make 10.
Complete the addition sentences.

1. ⬜⬜⬜⬜⬜⬜⬜⬜⬜⬜ $10 = \underline{} + \underline{}$

2. ⬜⬜⬜⬜⬜⬜⬜⬜⬜⬜ $10 = \underline{} + \underline{}$

Lesson 1.8 (pp. 41–44)

Write the sum.

1. $\begin{array}{r} 2 \\ + 2 \\ \hline \end{array}$ 2. $\begin{array}{r} 5 \\ + 2 \\ \hline \end{array}$ 3. $\begin{array}{r} 3 \\ + 0 \\ \hline \end{array}$ 4. $\begin{array}{r} 1 \\ + 1 \\ \hline \end{array}$

5. $\begin{array}{r} 1 \\ + 4 \\ \hline \end{array}$ 6. $\begin{array}{r} 3 \\ + 5 \\ \hline \end{array}$ 7. $\begin{array}{r} 8 \\ + 0 \\ \hline \end{array}$ 8. $\begin{array}{r} 2 \\ + 3 \\ \hline \end{array}$

School-Home Letter

Dear Family,

My class started Chapter 2 this week. In this chapter, I will learn different ways to subtract. I will learn to write subtraction sentences.

Love, _____

Vocabulary

minus (−) part of a subtraction sentence that means "to take from"

minus
6 − 5 = 1

difference answer to a subtraction sentence

3 − 2 = ①

fewer smaller number of something 3 books and 2 bags, you have 1 fewer bag than books

Home Activity

Show your child two groups of household objects, such as spoons and forks. Have your child use subtraction to compare how many more or fewer. Use different amounts and different objects every day.

5 − 2 = ?

Literature

Look for these books in a library. Have your child compare groups of items using *more* and *fewer*.

More, Fewer, Less by Tana Hoban. Greenwillow Books, 1998.

Elevator Magic by Stuart J. Murphy. HarperCollins, 1997.

Carta
para la casa

Querida familia:

Mi clase comenzó el Capítulo 2 esta semana. En este capítulo, aprenderé distintas formas para restar. Aprenderé a escribir enunciados de resta.

Con cariño, _____

Vocabulario

menos (−) parte de un enunciado de resta que significa "quitar de"

$$\text{menos} \atop 6 - 5 = 1$$

diferencia respuesta a un enunciado de resta

$$3 - 2 = \textcircled{1}$$

menos un número Cantidad menor de algo. Si tienes 3 libros y 2 carteras, tienes 1 cartera menos.

Actividad para la casa

Muestre a su hijo dos grupos de objetos que haya en la casa, como cucharas y tenedores. Pídale que use la resta para comparar cuántos objetos más o menos hay de cada tipo. Use distintas cantidades y objetos diferentes cada día.

$$5 - 2 = ?$$

Literatura

Busque estos libros en una biblioteca. Pídale a su hijo que compare grupos de cosas usando *más* y *menos*.

More, Fewer, Less por Tana Hoban. Greenwillow Books, 1998.

El ascensor maravilloso por Stuart J. Murphy. HarperCollins, 1997.

Use Pictures to Show Taking From

COMMON CORE STANDARD CC.1.OA.1
Represent and solve problems involving addition and subtraction.

Use the picture. Circle the part you take from the whole group. Then cross it out. Write how many there are now.

1.

3 cats   1 cat walks away.   _____ cats now

2.

5 horses   2 horses walk away.   _____ horses now

3.

7 dogs   3 dogs walk away.   _____ dogs now

PROBLEM SOLVING REAL WORLD

Solve.

4. There are 7 birds. 2 birds fly away.
   How many birds are there now?

_____ birds

Lesson Check (CC.1.OA.1)

1. There are 4 ducks.
   2 ducks swim away.
   How many ducks are
   there now?

   6   5   3   2
   ○   ○   ○   ○

Spiral Review (CC.1.OA.1, CC.1.OA.3, CC.1.OA.6)

2. What is the sum for $2 + 0$? (Lesson 1.5)

   0   1   2   4
   ○   ○   ○   ○

3. How many birds? (Lesson 1.1)

   5 birds   and   2 birds   ____ birds

   7   5   3   2
   ○   ○   ○   ○

4. What is the sum? (Lesson 1.8)

$$\begin{array}{r} 6 \\ + 2 \\ \hline \end{array}$$

   9   8   6   4
   ○   ○   ○   ○

Model Taking From

COMMON CORE STANDARD CC.1.OA.1
Represent and solve problems involving
addition and subtraction.

Use 🎲 to show taking from.
Draw the 🎲. Circle the part
you take from the group. Then
cross it out. Write the difference.

I. 4 turtles I turtle walks away.

2. 8 birds 7 birds fly away.

$$4 - 1 = \underline{\hspace{1cm}}$$

$$8 - 7 = \underline{\hspace{1cm}}$$

3. 6 bees   2 bees fly away.

4. 7 swans 5 swans swim away.

$$6 - 2 = \underline{\hspace{1cm}}$$

$$7 - 5 = \underline{\hspace{1cm}}$$

PROBLEM SOLVING REAL WORLD

Draw 🎲 to solve. Complete
the subtraction sentence.

5. There are 8 fish.
   4 fish swim away.
   How many fish
   are there now?

$$\underline{\hspace{1cm}} - \underline{\hspace{1cm}} = \underline{\hspace{1cm}}$$

_____ fish

Lesson Check (CC.1.OA.1)

1. What is the difference?

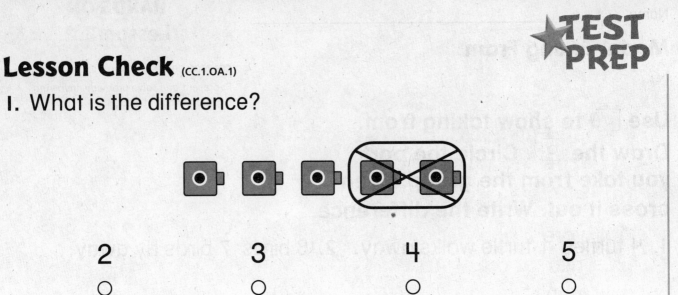

2	3	4	5
○	○	○	○

Spiral Review (CC.1.OA.1, CC.1.OA.3)

2. How many snails? (Lesson 1.1)

7 snails   and   I snail   ____ snails

5	6	7	8
○	○	○	○

3. Which shows the same addends in a different order? (Lesson 1.6)

$$6 + 2 = 8$$

$7 + 1 = 8$ $2 + 6 = 8$
    ○   ○

$8 - 6 = 2$ $8 - 2 = 6$
    ○   ○

Model Taking Apart

COMMON CORE STANDARD CC.1.OA.1
Represent and solve problems involving
addition and subtraction.

Use 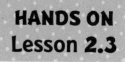 to solve. Draw to show your
work. Write the number sentence
and how many.

1. There are 7 bags. 2 bags are
   big. The rest are small.
   How many bags are small?

   _____ small bags   ___ ◯ ___ ◯ ___

2. There are 6 dogs. 4 dogs are
   brown. The rest are black.
   How many dogs are black?

   _____ black dogs   ___ ◯ ___ ◯ ___

PROBLEM SOLVING REAL WORLD

Solve. Draw a model to explain.

3. There are 8 cats. 6 cats
   walk away. How many cats
   are left?

                                       _____ cats left

Lesson Check (CC 1.OA.1)

1. Which number sentence solves the problem? There are 8 blocks. 3 blocks are white. The rest are blue. How many blocks are blue?

$3 + 3 = 6$ | $5 - 3 = 2$ | $8 - 3 = 5$ | $2 + 8 = 10$
○ ○ ○ ○

Spiral Review (CC.1.OA.1)

2. There are 4 green grapes and 5 red grapes. How many grapes are there? (Lesson 1.3)

10   9   8   5
○   ○   ○   ○

3. 3 ducks swim in the pond. 2 more join them. How many ducks are in the pond now? (Lesson 1.4)

1   2   3   5
○   ○   ○   ○

4. What is the sum of 1 and 4? (Lesson 1.2)

5   4   3   2
○   ○   ○   ○

Problem Solving • Model Subtraction

COMMON CORE STANDARD CC.1.OA.1
Represent and solve problems involving addition and subtraction.

Read the problem. Use the model to solve. Complete the model and the number sentence.

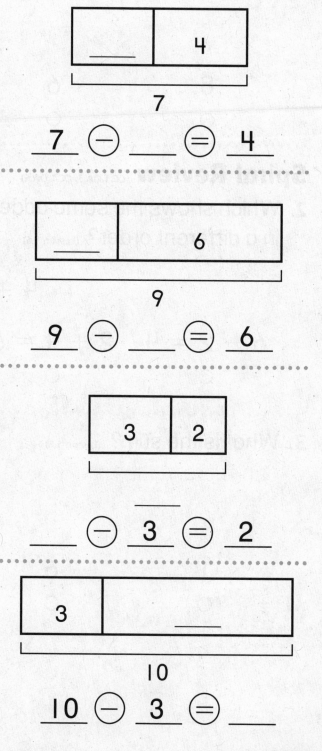

1. There were 7 ducks in the pond. Some ducks swam away. Then there were 4 ducks. How many ducks swam away?

$$\underline{}\;7\;\ominus\;\underline{}\;\circleq\;\underline{}\;4$$

2. Tom had 9 gifts. He gave some away. Then there were 6 gifts. How many gifts did he give away?

$$\underline{}\;9\;\ominus\;\underline{}\;\circleq\;\underline{}\;6$$

3. Some ponies were in a barn. 3 ponies walked out. Then there were 2 ponies. How many ponies were in the barn before?

$$\underline{}\;\ominus\;3\;\circleq\;2$$

4. There are 10 puppies. 3 puppies are brown. The rest are black. How many puppies are black?

$$\underline{10}\;10\;\ominus\;\underline{3}\;3\;\circleq\;\underline{}$$

Lesson Check (CC.1.OA.1)

1. There are 8 shells. 6 shells are white. The rest are pink. How many shells are pink?

6	

8

    8   6   3   2
   ○   ○   ○   ○

Spiral Review (CC.1.OA.3, CC.1.OA.6)

2. Which shows the same addends in a different order? (Lesson 1.6)

$$4 + 2 = 6$$

$6 - 2 = 4$ $2 + 4 = 6$ $2 + 2 = 4$ $6 - 4 = 2$
    ○   ○   ○   ○

3. What is the sum? (Lesson 1.8)

$$\begin{array}{r} 4 \\ + 3 \\ \hline \end{array}$$

    1   6   7   8
   ○   ○   ○   ○

Name _____

Use Pictures and Subtraction to Compare

COMMON CORE STANDARD CC.1.OA.8
Work with addition and subtraction equations.

Draw lines to match.
Subtract to compare.

1.

8 − 5 = ____   ____ more

2.

9 − 4 = ____   ____ fewer

PROBLEM SOLVING REAL WORLD

Draw a picture to show the problem.
Write a subtraction sentence to
match your picture.

3. Jo has 4 golf clubs and
2 golf balls. How many fewer
golf balls does Jo have?

____ − ____ = ____   ____ fewer

Lesson Check (CC.1.OA.8)

1. How many fewer 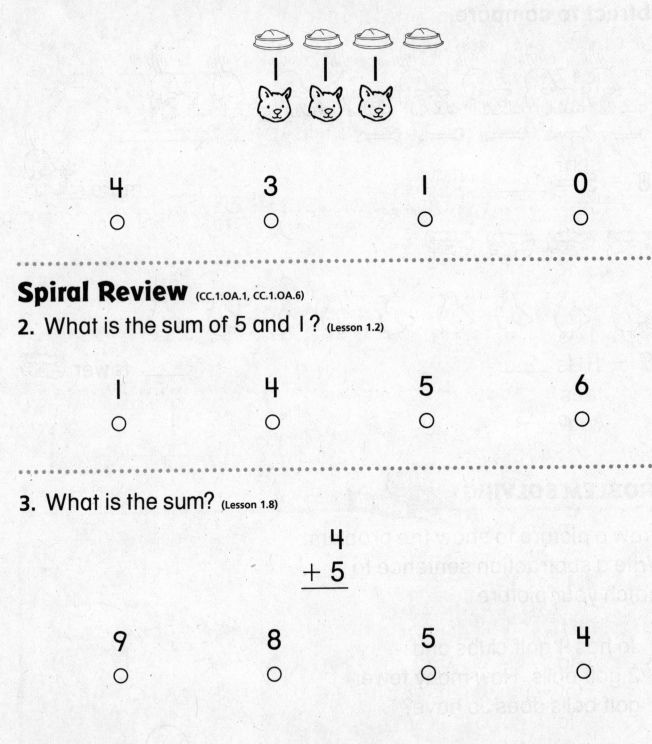 are there?

4   3   1   0
○   ○   ○   ○

- -

Spiral Review (CC.1.OA.1, CC.1.OA.6)

2. What is the sum of 5 and 1? (Lesson 1.2)

1   4   5   6
○   ○   ○   ○

- -

3. What is the sum? (Lesson 1.8)

$$\begin{array}{r} 4 \\ + 5 \\ \hline \end{array}$$

9   8   5   4
○   ○   ○   ○

Subtract to Compare

COMMON CORE STANDARD CC.1.OA.1
Represent and solve problems involving
addition and subtraction.

**Read the problem. Use the bar model
to solve. Write the number sentence.
Then write how many.**

1. Ben has 7 flowers. Tim
   has 5 flowers. How many
   fewer flowers does Tim have
   than Ben?

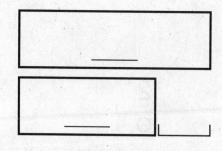

_____ fewer flowers

_____ ◯ _____ ◯ _____

2. Nicky has 8 toys. Ada has
   3 toys. How many more
   toys does Nicky have
   than Ada?

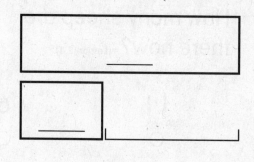

_____ more toys

_____ ◯ _____ ◯ _____

PROBLEM SOLVING REAL WORLD

Complete the number sentence to solve.

3. Maya has 7 pens. Sam has 1
   pen. How many more pens
   does Maya have than Sam?

_____ − _____ = _____

_____ more pens

Lesson Check (CC.1.OA.1)

1. Jesse has 2 stickers. Sara has 8 stickers. How many fewer stickers does Jesse have than Sara?

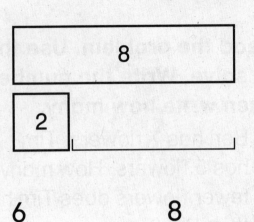

2 ○   4 ○   6 ○   8 ○

Spiral Review (CC.1.OA.1)

2. There are 6 sheep. 5 sheep walk away. How many sheep are there now? (Lesson 2.1)

11 ○   6 ○   5 ○   1 ○

3. 5 cows stand in a field. 2 more cows join them. How many cows are in the field now? (Lesson 1.4)

7 ○   5 ○   3 ○   2 ○

Subtract All or Zero

COMMON CORE STANDARD CC.1.OA.8
Work with addition and subtraction equations.

Complete the subtraction sentence.

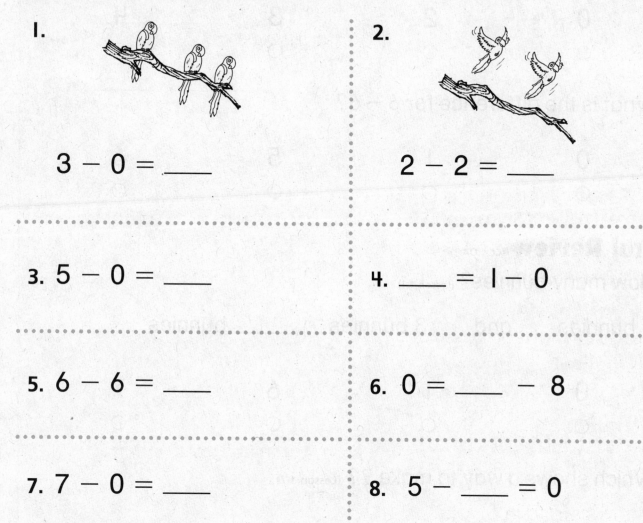

1. $3 - 0 =$ ____

2. $2 - 2 =$ ____

3. $5 - 0 =$ ____

4. ____ $= 1 - 0$

5. $6 - 6 =$ ____

6. $0 =$ ____ $- 8$

7. $7 - 0 =$ ____

8. $5 -$ ____ $= 0$

PROBLEM SOLVING REAL WORLD

Write the number sentence
and tell how many.

9. There are 9 books on the shelf.
   9 are blue and the rest are green.
   How many books are green?

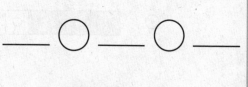

____ green books

Lesson Check (CC.1.OA.8)

1. What is the difference for 4 − 0?

    0   2   3   4
    ○   ○   ○   ○

2. What is the difference for 6 − 6?

    0   1   5   6
    ○   ○   ○   ○

Spiral Review (CC.1.OA.1)

3. How many bunnies? (Lesson 1.1)

3 bunnies   and   3 bunnies   ____ bunnies

    0   1   6   7
    ○   ○   ○   ○

4. Which shows a way to make 9? (Lesson 1.7)

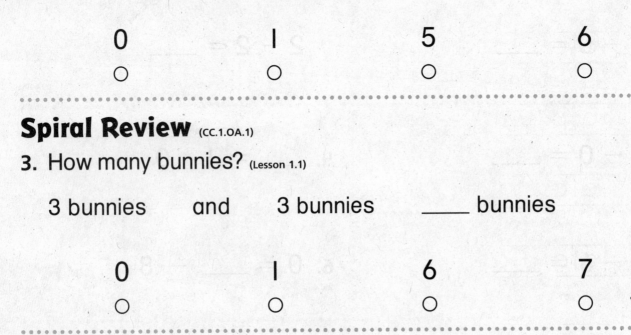

Algebra • Take Apart Numbers

COMMON CORE STANDARD CC.1.OA.1
Represent and solve problems involving addition and subtraction.

Use 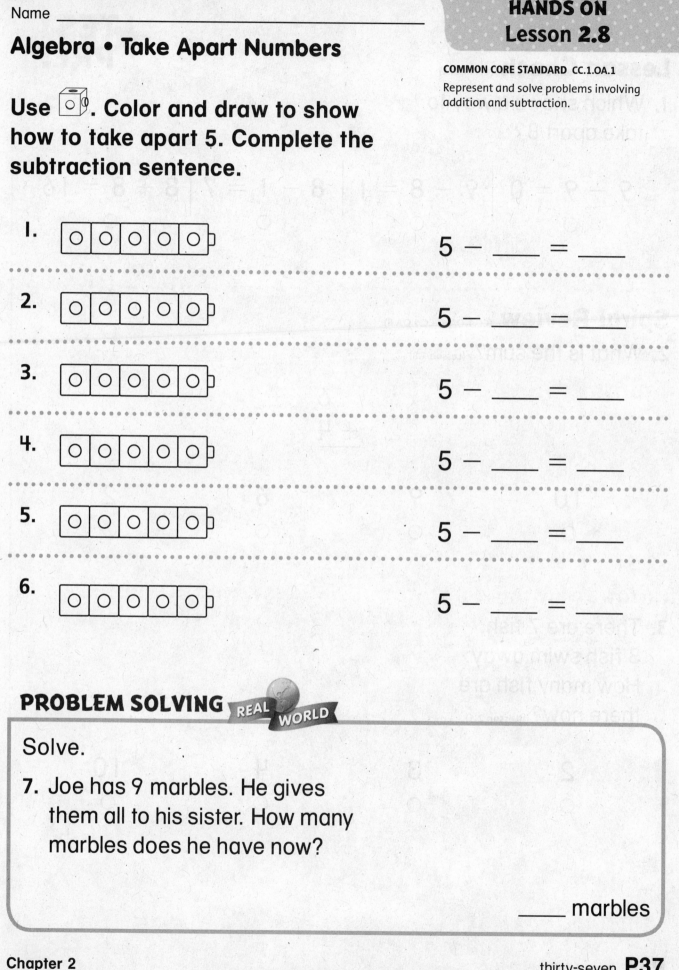. Color and draw to show how to take apart 5. Complete the subtraction sentence.

1.
    5 − ___ = ___

2.
    5 − ___ = ___

3.
    5 − ___ = ___

4.
    5 − ___ = ___

5.
    5 − ___ = ___

6.
    5 − ___ = ___

PROBLEM SOLVING REAL WORLD

Solve.

7. Joe has 9 marbles. He gives them all to his sister. How many marbles does he have now?

_____ marbles

Lesson Check (CC.1.OA.1)

1. Which shows a way to take apart 8?

$$9 - 9 = 0 \quad | \quad 9 - 8 = 1 \quad | \quad 8 - 1 = 7 \quad | \quad 8 + 8 = 16$$

○　　　　　　○　　　　　　○　　　　　　○

Spiral Review (CC.1.OA.1, CC.1.OA.6)

2. What is the sum? (Lesson 1.8)

$$\begin{array}{r} 6 \\ + 4 \\ \hline \end{array}$$

10　　　　　9　　　　　6　　　　　2

○　　　　　○　　　　　○　　　　　○

3. There are 7 fish.
   3 fish swim away.
   How many fish are
   there now? (Lesson 2.1)

2　　　　　3　　　　　4　　　　　10

○　　　　　○　　　　　○　　　　　○

Subtraction from 10 or Less

COMMON CORE STANDARD CC.1.OA.6
Add and subtract within 20.

Write the difference.

1. $\begin{array}{r} 5 \\ -1 \\ \hline \end{array}$

2. $\begin{array}{r} 3 \\ -2 \\ \hline \end{array}$

3. $\begin{array}{r} 8 \\ -3 \\ \hline \end{array}$

4. $\begin{array}{r} 6 \\ -4 \\ \hline \end{array}$

5. $\begin{array}{r} 7 \\ -0 \\ \hline \end{array}$

6. $\begin{array}{r} 5 \\ -3 \\ \hline \end{array}$

7. $\begin{array}{r} 4 \\ -4 \\ \hline \end{array}$

8. $\begin{array}{r} 8 \\ -1 \\ \hline \end{array}$

9. $\begin{array}{r} 8 \\ -7 \\ \hline \end{array}$

10. $\begin{array}{r} 6 \\ -3 \\ \hline \end{array}$

11. $\begin{array}{r} 5 \\ -5 \\ \hline \end{array}$

12. $\begin{array}{r} 7 \\ -6 \\ \hline \end{array}$

PROBLEM SOLVING REAL WORLD

Solve.

13. 6 birds are in the tree.
    None of the birds fly away.
    How many birds are left?

    ___ − ___ = ___

Lesson Check (CC.1.OA.6)

1. What is the difference?

$$
\begin{array}{r}
4 \\
- \; 0 \\
\hline
\end{array}
$$

10   9   4   0

○   ○   ○   ○

Spiral Review (CC.1.OA.1, CC.1.OA.3)

2. Which number sentence solves
   the problem?
   There are 8 pens. 3 pens
   are blue. The rest are red.
   How many pens are red? (Lesson 2.3)

$8 + 3 = 11$ | $3 - 1 = 2$ | $8 + 1 = 9$ | $8 - 3 = 5$

○   ○   ○   ○

3. Which shows the same
   addends in a different order? (Lesson 1.6)

$$5 + 4 = 9$$

$4 + 5 = 9$ | $4 + 4 = 8$ | $5 + 3 = 8$ | $9 - 4 = 5$

○   ○   ○   ○

==COMMON CORE STANDARDS CC.1.OA.1, CC.1.OA.6, CC.1.OA.8

Chapter 2 Extra Practice

Lessons 2.1 - 2.2 (pp. 53 - 60) . . . .

Use to show taking from. Draw the .
Circle the part you take from the group.
Then cross it out. Write the difference.

1. 5 whales   3 whales swim away.

$$5 - 3 = \underline{\quad}$$

Lesson 2.3 (pp. 61 - 64) . . . .

Use ● to solve. Draw to show your work.
Write the number sentence and how many.

1. There are 7 snails. 2 snails
are big. The rest are small.
How many snails are small?

____ small snails   ___ ◯ ___ ◯ ___

Lessons 2.5 - 2.6 (pp. 69 - 75) . . . .

Read the problem. Use the bar model
to solve. Write the number sentence.
Then write how many.

1. Tony has 9 buckets. Gina has 5 buckets.
How many fewer buckets does Gina
have than Tony?

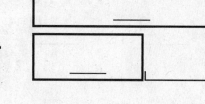

____ fewer buckets   ___ ◯ ___ ◯ ___

© Houghton Mifflin Harcourt Publishing Company

Lesson 2.7 (pp. 77 – 80)

Complete the subtraction sentence.

1. $5 - 0 =$ _____

2. $4 -$ _____ $= 0$

3. _____ $= 8 - 8$

4. $9 - 0 =$ _____

Lesson 2.8 (pp. 81 – 84)

Use 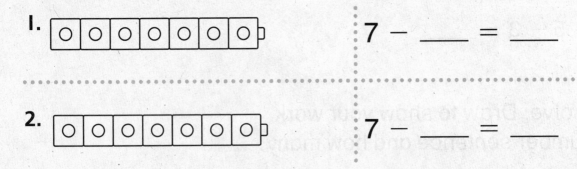. Color and draw to show how to take
apart 7. Complete the subtraction sentence.

1. ⬜⬜⬜⬜⬜⬜⬜ $7 -$ _____ $=$ _____

2. ⬜⬜⬜⬜⬜⬜ $7 -$ _____ $=$ _____

Lesson 2.9 (pp. 85 – 88)

Write the difference.

1. $\begin{array}{r} 8 \\ -8 \\ \hline \end{array}$	2. $\begin{array}{r} 5 \\ -4 \\ \hline \end{array}$	3. $\begin{array}{r} 10 \\ -0 \\ \hline \end{array}$	4. $\begin{array}{r} 9 \\ -4 \\ \hline \end{array}$	5. $\begin{array}{r} 7 \\ -6 \\ \hline \end{array}$
6. $\begin{array}{r} 9 \\ -2 \\ \hline \end{array}$	7. $\begin{array}{r} 10 \\ -4 \\ \hline \end{array}$	8. $\begin{array}{r} 5 \\ -2 \\ \hline \end{array}$	9. $\begin{array}{r} 6 \\ -1 \\ \hline \end{array}$	10. $\begin{array}{r} 8 \\ -6 \\ \hline \end{array}$

School-Home Letter

Dear Family,

My class started Chapter 3 this week. In this chapter, I will learn about addition strategies such as counting on, adding doubles, and adding in any order.

Love, _____

Vocabulary

doubles Two equal groups make a doubles fact.

$2 + 2 = 4$

doubles plus one $2 + 2 = 4$, so $2 + 3$ is 1 more, or 5.

$2 + 3 = 5$

Home Activity

Have your child find objects that show doubles facts. For example, he or she may find a pair of shoes to show $1 + 1$, a carton of eggs to show $6 + 6$, or a six-pack of juice cans to show $3 + 3$. Ask your child to say those doubles facts.

Add another item to one of the groups, and have your child name the doubles plus one fact.

Literature

Look for these books in a library. Point out examples of doubles and counting on facts in the pictures.

12 Ways to Get to 11 by Eve Merriam. Aladdin, 1996.

Two of Everything: A Chinese Folktale by Lily Toy Hong. Albert Whitman and Company, 1993.

Carta para la casa

Querida familia:

Mi clase comenzó el Capítulo 3 esta semana. En este capítulo, aprenderé estrategias de suma como contar hacia adelante, sumar dobles y sumar en cualquier orden.

Con cariño, _____

Vocabulario

dobles Dos grupos iguales forman una operación de dobles.

$2 + 2 = 4$

dobles más uno $2 + 2 = 4$, por lo tanto $2 + 3$ es 1 más o 5.

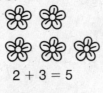

$2 + 3 = 5$

Actividad para la casa

Pida a su hijo que encuentre objetos que muestren operaciones de dobles. Por ejemplo, puede hallar un par de zapatos para mostrar $1 + 1$, una caja de huevos para mostrar $6 + 6$ o una caja de 6 latas de jugo para mostrar $3 + 3$. Pídale a su hijo que le diga cuáles son las operaciones de dobles.

Agregue otro artículo a uno de los grupos y pida a su hijo que nombre la operación de dobles más uno.

Literatura

Busque estos libros en una biblioteca. Señale ejemplos de operaciones de dobles y de contar uno hacia delante en las imágenes.

12 Ways to Get to 11 por Eve Merriam. Aladdin, 1996.

Two of Everything: A Chinese Folktale por Lily Toy Hong. Albert Whitman and Company, 1993.

Algebra • Add in Any Order

COMMON CORE STANDARD CC.1.OA.3
Understand and apply properties of operations and the relationship between addition and subtraction.

Add. Change the order of the addends. Add again.

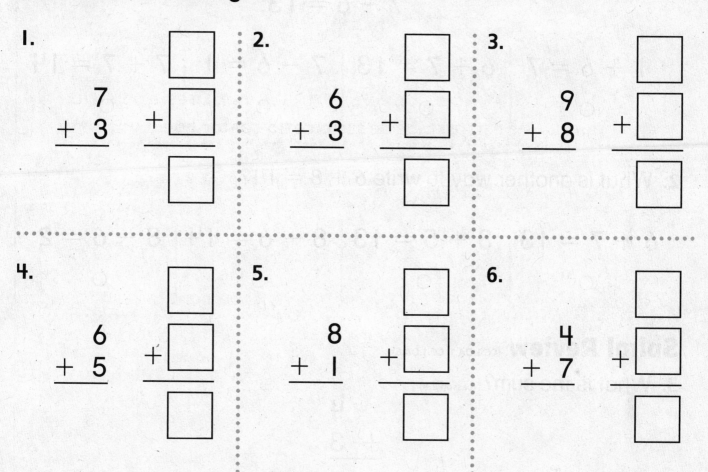

1.
$$\begin{array}{r} 7 \\ +\ 3 \\ \hline \end{array}$$
☐ + ☐ = ☐

2.
$$\begin{array}{r} 6 \\ +\ 3 \\ \hline \end{array}$$
☐ + ☐ = ☐

3.
$$\begin{array}{r} 9 \\ +\ 8 \\ \hline \end{array}$$
☐ + ☐ = ☐

4.
$$\begin{array}{r} 6 \\ +\ 5 \\ \hline \end{array}$$
☐ + ☐ = ☐

5.
$$\begin{array}{r} 8 \\ +\ 1 \\ \hline \end{array}$$
☐ + ☐ = ☐

6.
$$\begin{array}{r} 4 \\ +\ 7 \\ \hline \end{array}$$
☐ + ☐ = ☐

PROBLEM SOLVING REAL WORLD

Write two addition sentences you can use to solve the problem.

7. Camila has 5 pennies.
Then she finds 4 more pennies.
How many pennies does she have now?

___ + ___ = ___

___ + ___ = ___

Lesson Check (CC.1.OA.3)

1. Which shows the same addends in a different order?

$$7 + 6 = 13$$

$1 + 6 = 7$	$6 + 7 = 13$	$7 - 6 = 1$	$7 + 7 = 14$
○	○	○	○

2. What is another way to write $6 + 8 = 14$?

$6 + 7 = 13$	$8 + 5 = 13$	$8 + 6 = 14$	$8 - 6 = 2$
○	○	○	○

Spiral Review (CC.1.OA.1, CC.1.OA.6)

3. What is the sum? (Lesson 1.8)

$$\begin{array}{r} 4 \\ + 3 \\ \hline \end{array}$$

1	6	7	8
○	○	○	○

4. How many nests are there? (Lesson 1.1)

2 nests　　and　　1 more nest　　_____ nests

2	3	4	5
○	○	○	○

Count On

Circle the greater addend.
Count on to find the sum.

1.   8
   $+\ 2$

2.   1
   $+\ 7$

3.   3
   $+\ 9$

4.   5
   $+\ 3$

5.   7
   $+\ 3$

6.   3
   $+\ 4$

7.   6
   $+\ 2$

8.   1
   $+\ 8$

PROBLEM SOLVING REAL WORLD

Draw to solve.
Write the addition sentence.

9. Jon eats 6 crackers.
   Then he eats 3 more crackers.
   How many crackers does he eat?

_____ + _____ = _____ crackers

Lesson Check (CC.1.OA.5)

1. Count on to solve $5 + 2$.

   2   3   5   7
   ○   ○   ○   ○

2. Count on to solve $1 + 9$.

   10   8   5   4
   ○   ○   ○   ○

Spiral Review (CC.1.OA.1)

3. Which shows a way to make 6? (Lesson 1.7)

   ○   ○   ○   ○

4. 4 ducks swim in the pond.
   2 more ducks join them.
   How many ducks are in
   the pond now? (Lesson 1.4)

   2   4   6   7
   ○   ○   ○   ○

Add Doubles

HANDS ON
Lesson 3.3

COMMON CORE STANDARD CC.1.OA.6
Add and subtract within 20.

Use ⬛. Draw ⬛ to show your work.
Write the sum.

1.
$$\begin{array}{r} 4 \\ + \ 4 \\ \hline \end{array}$$

2.
$$\begin{array}{r} 6 \\ + \ 6 \\ \hline \end{array}$$

3.
$$\begin{array}{r} 3 \\ + \ 3 \\ \hline \end{array}$$

4.
$$\begin{array}{r} 8 \\ + \ 8 \\ \hline \end{array}$$

5.
$$\begin{array}{r} 5 \\ + \ 5 \\ \hline \end{array}$$

6.
$$\begin{array}{r} 7 \\ + \ 7 \\ \hline \end{array}$$

PROBLEM SOLVING REAL WORLD

Write a doubles fact to solve.

7. There are 16 crayons in the box.
Some are green and some are red.
The number of green crayons is the
same as the number of red crayons.

____ = ____ + ____

Lesson Check (CC.1.OA.6)

1. Which is a doubles fact?

$8 + 3 = 11$
○

$1 + 5 = 6$
○

$9 + 9 = 18$
○

$5 + 7 = 12$
○

2. Which is a doubles fact?

$6 + 3 = 9$
○

$6 + 4 = 10$
○

$6 + 6 = 12$
○

$6 + 7 = 13$
○

Spiral Review (CC.1.OA.1, CC.1.OA.3)

3. What is the sum of 3 and 2? (Lesson 1.2)

7   6   5   1
○   ○   ○   ○

4. What is the sum for $4 + 0$? (Lesson 1.5)

5   4   3   0
○   ○   ○   ○

Use Doubles to Add

COMMON CORE STANDARD CC.1.OA.6
Add and subtract within 20.

Use 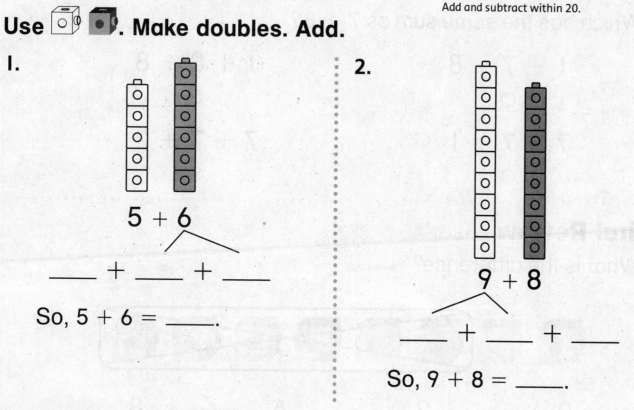 . Make doubles. Add.

1.

$5 + 6$

___ + ___ + ___

So, $5 + 6 =$ ___.

2.

$9 + 8$

___ + ___ + ___

So, $9 + 8 =$ ___.

Use doubles to help you add.

3. $8 + 7 =$ ___

4. $6 + 5 =$ ___

5. $7 + 6 =$ ___

6. $4 + 5 =$ ___

7. $7 + 8 =$ ___

8. $8 + 9 =$ ___

PROBLEM SOLVING REAL WORLD

Solve. Draw or write to explain.

9. Bo has 6 toys. Mia has 7 toys.
How many toys do they have?

_____ toys

Lesson Check (CC.1.OA.6)

1. Which has the same sum as 7 + 8?

1 + 7 + 8
○

1 + 8 + 8
○

7 + 7 + 1
○

7 + 7 + 2
○

Spiral Review (CC.1.OA.1)

2. What is the difference? (Lesson 2.2)

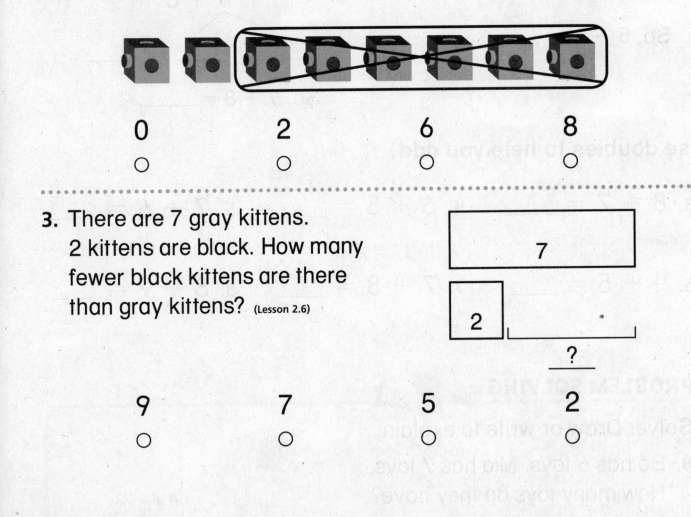

0
○

2
○

6
○

8
○

3. There are 7 gray kittens.
2 kittens are black. How many
fewer black kittens are there
than gray kittens? (Lesson 2.6)

7

2

?

9
○

7
○

5
○

2
○

Name _____

Doubles Plus I and Doubles Minus I

COMMON CORE STANDARD CC.1.OA.6
Add and subtract within 20.

Add. Write the doubles fact you used to solve the problem.

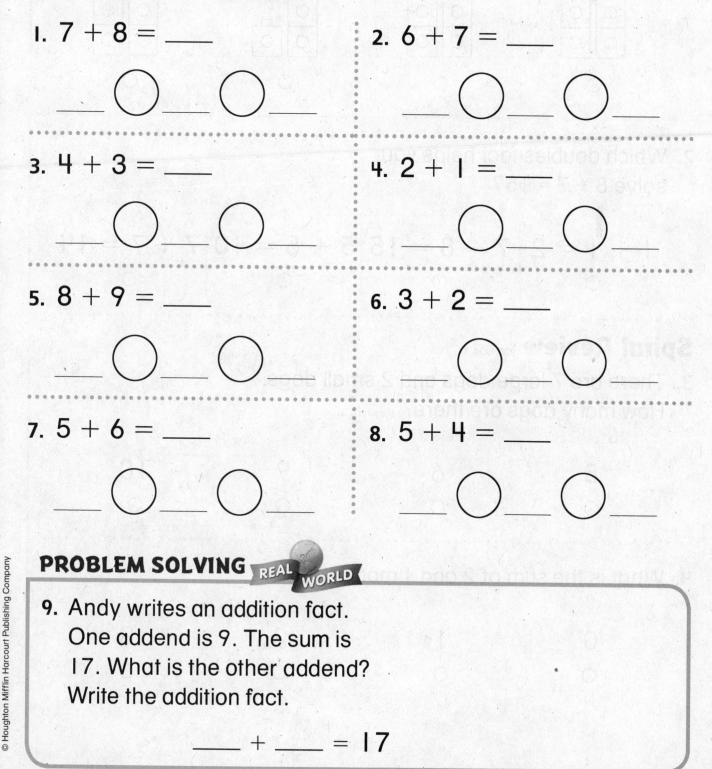

1. 7 + 8 = ___

___ ◯ ___ ◯ ___

2. 6 + 7 = ___

___ ◯ ___ ◯ ___

3. 4 + 3 = ___

___ ◯ ___ ◯ ___

4. 2 + 1 = ___

___ ◯ ___ ◯ ___

5. 8 + 9 = ___

___ ◯ ___ ◯ ___

6. 3 + 2 = ___

___ ◯ ___ ◯ ___

7. 5 + 6 = ___

___ ◯ ___ ◯ ___

8. 5 + 4 = ___

___ ◯ ___ ◯ ___

PROBLEM SOLVING REAL WORLD

9. Andy writes an addition fact.
One addend is 9. The sum is
17. What is the other addend?
Write the addition fact.

___ + ___ = 17

Lesson Check (CC.1.OA.6)

1. Which picture shows doubles plus one?

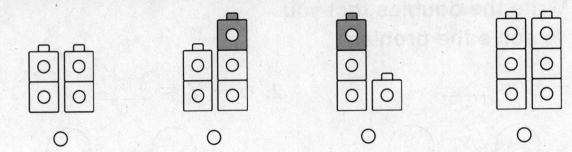

    ○   ○   ○   ○

2. Which doubles fact helps you
solve $8 + 7 = 15$?

$1 + 1 = 2$ $7 + 8 = 15$ $5 + 5 = 10$ $7 + 7 = 14$

    ○   ○   ○   ○

Spiral Review (CC.1.OA.1)

3. There are 7 large dogs and 2 small dogs.
How many dogs are there? (Lesson 1.3)

    5   6   9   10

    ○   ○   ○   ○

4. What is the sum of 2 and 1 more? (Lesson 1.2)

    0   1   2   3

    ○   ○   ○   ○

Practice the Strategies

COMMON CORE STANDARD CC.1.OA.6
Add and subtract within 20.

Add. Color doubles facts 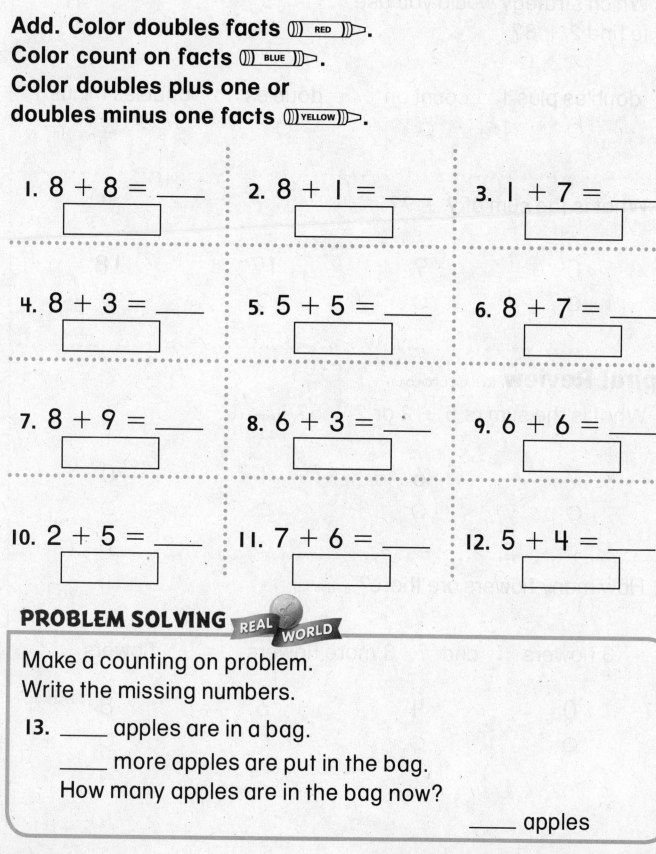 RED .
Color count on facts BLUE .
Color doubles plus one or
doubles minus one facts YELLOW .

1. 8 + 8 = ___

2. 8 + 1 = ___

3. 1 + 7 = ___

4. 8 + 3 = ___

5. 5 + 5 = ___

6. 8 + 7 = ___

7. 8 + 9 = ___

8. 6 + 3 = ___

9. 6 + 6 = ___

10. 2 + 5 = ___

11. 7 + 6 = ___

12. 5 + 4 = ___

PROBLEM SOLVING REAL WORLD

Make a counting on problem.
Write the missing numbers.

13. ___ apples are in a bag.

___ more apples are put in the bag.
How many apples are in the bag now?

___ apples

Lesson Check (CC.1.OA.6)

1. Which strategy would you use
   to find 2 + 8?

   doubles plus 1   count on   doubles   doubles minus 1
        ○   ○   ○   ○

2. What is the sum of 9 + 9?

        0   9   17   18
        ○   ○   ○   ○

Spiral Review (CC.1.OA.1, CC.1.OA.3)

3. What is the sum of 5 + 2 or 2 + 5? (Lesson 1.6)

        7   6   1   0
        ○   ○   ○   ○

4. How many flowers are there? (Lesson 1.1)

   3 flowers   and   3 more flowers   ___ flowers

        0   4   6   8
        ○   ○   ○   ○

Name _____

Add 10 and More

COMMON CORE STANDARD CC.1.OA.6
Add and subtract within 20.

Draw red ◯ to show 10. Draw
yellow ◯ to show the other addend.
Write the sum.

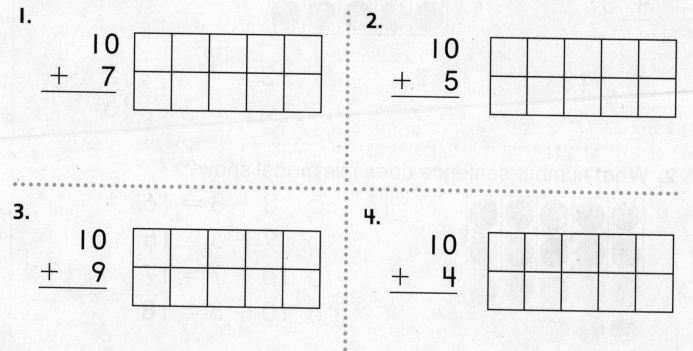

1.
$$10$$
$$+\ \ 7$$

2.
$$10$$
$$+\ \ 5$$

3.
$$10$$
$$+\ \ 9$$

4.
$$10$$
$$+\ \ 4$$

PROBLEM SOLVING REAL WORLD

Draw red and yellow ◯ to solve.
Write the addition sentence.

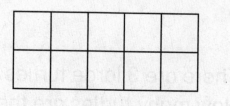

5. Linda has 10 toy cars.
She gets 6 more cars.
How many toy cars
does she have now?

_____ + _____ = _____ toy cars

Lesson Check (CC.1.OA.6)

1. How many ⬤ would you need to show the addition fact?

    10
    + 3
    ———

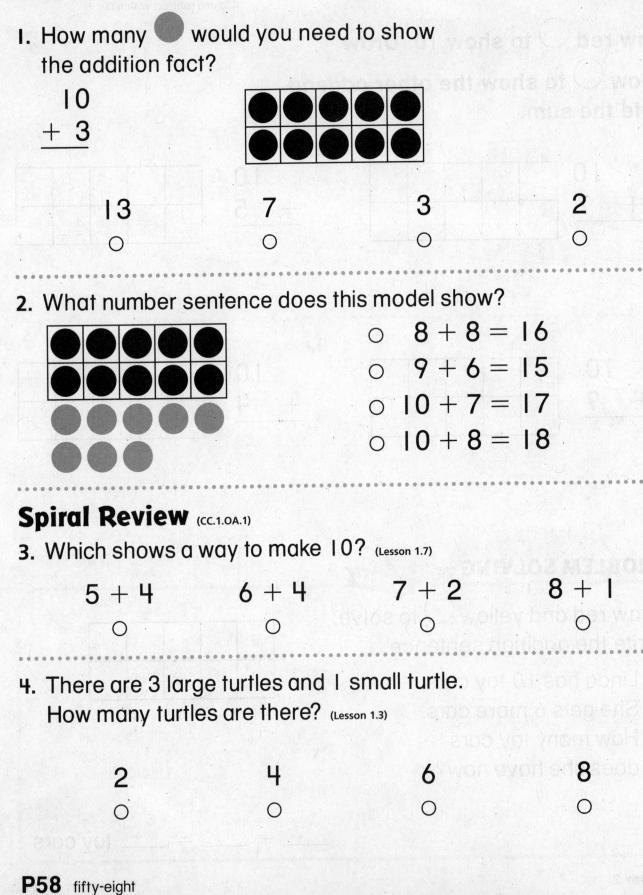

   13   7   3   2
   ○   ○   ○   ○

2. What number sentence does this model show?

   ○ 8 + 8 = 16
   ○ 9 + 6 = 15
   ○ 10 + 7 = 17
   ○ 10 + 8 = 18

Spiral Review (CC.1.OA.1)

3. Which shows a way to make 10? (Lesson 1.7)

   5 + 4   6 + 4   7 + 2   8 + 1
   ○   ○   ○   ○

4. There are 3 large turtles and 1 small turtle. How many turtles are there? (Lesson 1.3)

   2   4   6   8
   ○   ○   ○   ○

Name _____

Make a 10 to Add

COMMON CORE STANDARD CC.1.OA.6
Add and subtract within 20.

Use red and yellow ◯ and a ten frame.
Show both addends. Draw to make
a ten. Then write the new fact.
Add.

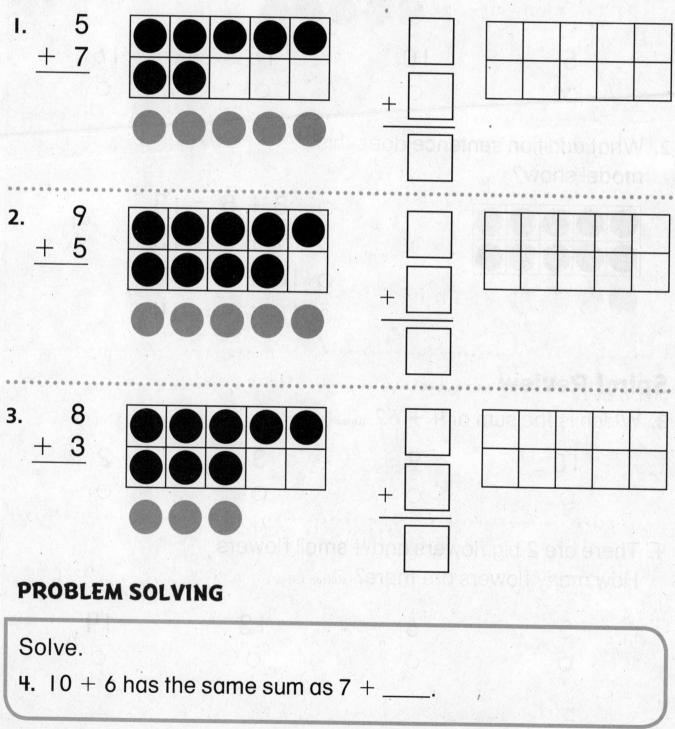

1. 5
  + 7

2. 9
  + 5

3. 8
  + 3

PROBLEM SOLVING

Solve.

4. 10 + 6 has the same sum as 7 + ____.

Lesson Check (CC.1.OA.6)

1. What sum does this model show?

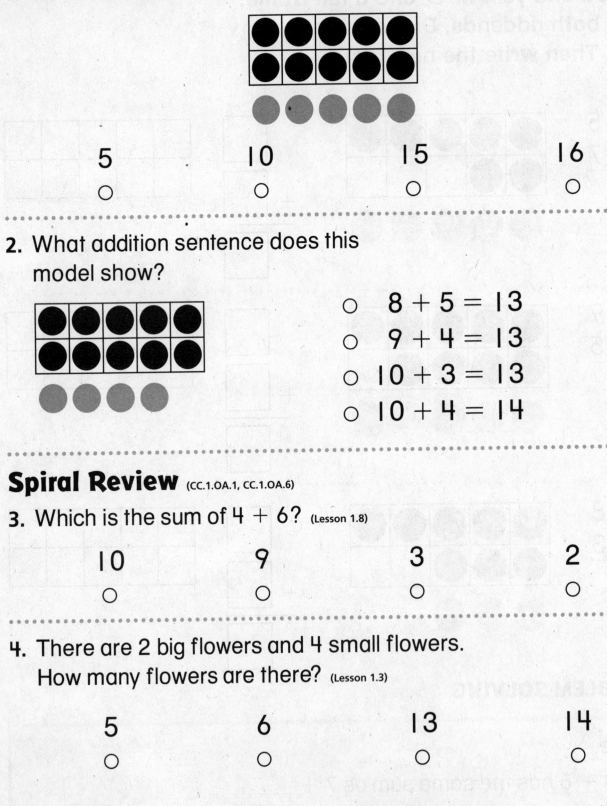

5	10	15	16
○	○	○	○

2. What addition sentence does this model show?

- ○ $8 + 5 = 13$
- ○ $9 + 4 = 13$
- ○ $10 + 3 = 13$
- ○ $10 + 4 = 14$

Spiral Review (CC.1.OA.1, CC.1.OA.6)

3. Which is the sum of $4 + 6$? (Lesson 1.8)

10	9	3	2
○	○	○	○

4. There are 2 big flowers and 4 small flowers. How many flowers are there? (Lesson 1.3)

5	6	13	14
○	○	○	○

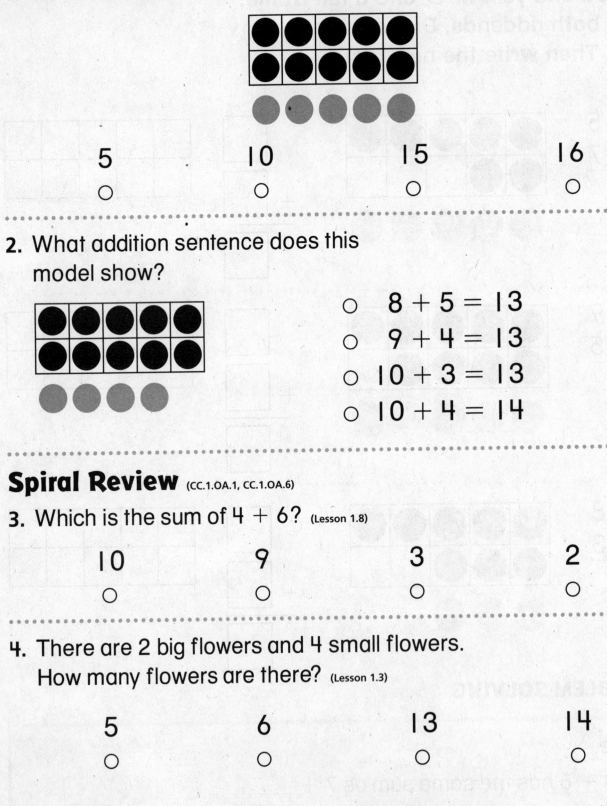

Use Make a 10 to Add

COMMON CORE STANDARD CC.1.OA.6
Add and subtract within 20.

**Write to show how you make a ten.
Then add.**

1. What is $9 + 7$?

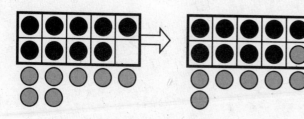

___ + ___ + ___

___ + ___ = ___

So, $9 + 7 =$ ___.

2. What is $5 + 8$?

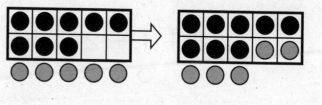

___ + ___ + ___

___ + ___ = ___

So, $5 + 8 =$ ___.

PROBLEM SOLVING REAL WORLD

Use the clues to solve.
Draw lines to match.

3. Ann and Gia are eating grapes.
   Ann eats 10 green grapes and
   6 red grapes. Gia eats the same
   number of grapes as Ann. Match
   each person to her grapes.

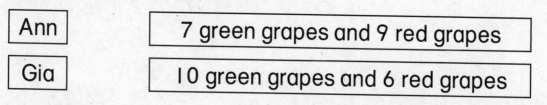

| Ann | 7 green grapes and 9 red grapes |
| Gia | 10 green grapes and 6 red grapes |

Lesson Check (CC.1.OA.6)

1. Which shows how to make a ten to find 8 + 4?

8 + 2 + 3
○

8 + 2 + 2
○

8 + 1 + 2
○

5 + 3 + 2
○

Spiral Review (CC.1.OA.6, CC.1.OA.8)

2. What is the difference? (Lesson 2.7)

$$9 - 9 = \underline{\hspace{1cm}}$$

0
○

1
○

9
○

18
○

3. What is the difference? (Lesson 2.9)

$$\begin{array}{r} 8 \\ -2 \\ \hline \end{array}$$

10
○

6
○

5
○

4
○

Algebra • Add 3 Numbers

COMMON CORE STANDARD CC.1.OA.3
Understand and apply properties of operations and the relationship between addition and subtraction.

Look at the 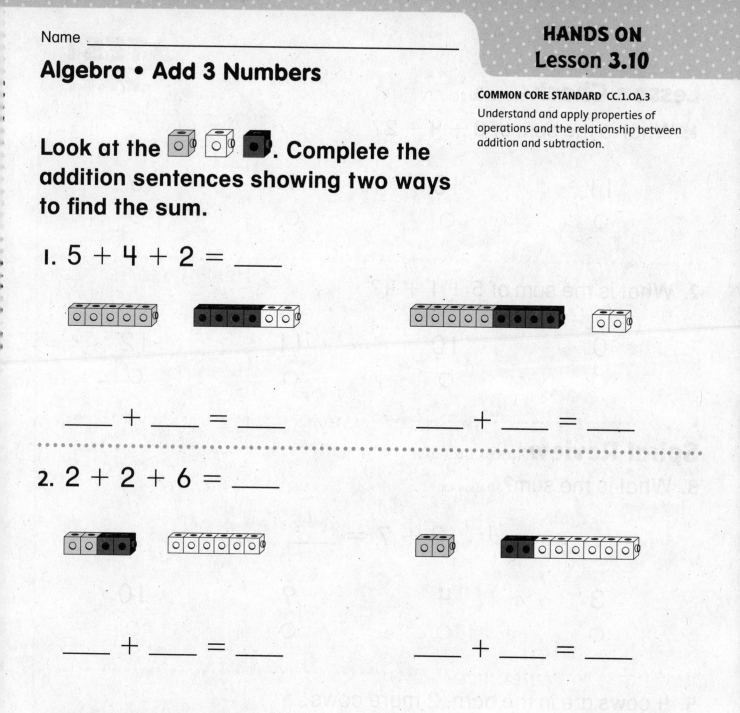 **. Complete the addition sentences showing two ways to find the sum.**

1. $5 + 4 + 2 =$ _____

___ + ___ = ___   ___ + ___ = ___

2. $2 + 2 + 6 =$ _____

___ + ___ = ___   ___ + ___ = ___

PROBLEM SOLVING

3. Choose three numbers from 1 to 6.
   Write the numbers in an addition sentence.
   Show two ways to find the sum.

Lesson Check (CC.1.OA.3)

1. What is the sum of 3 + 4 + 2?

11 ○   10 ○   9 ○   6 ○

2. What is the sum of 5 + 1 + 4?

0 ○   10 ○   11 ○   12 ○

Spiral Review (CC.1.OA.1, CC.1.OA.6)

3. What is the sum? (Lesson 1.8)

$$3 + 7 = \underline{}$$

3 ○   4 ○   9 ○   10 ○

4. 4 cows are in the barn. 2 more cows join them. How many cows are in the barn now? (Lesson 1.4)

2 ○   6 ○   7 ○   8 ○

Algebra • Add 3 Numbers

COMMON CORE STANDARD CC.1.OA.3
Understand and apply properties of operations and the relationship between addition and subtraction.

Choose a strategy.
Circle two addends to add first.
Write the sum.

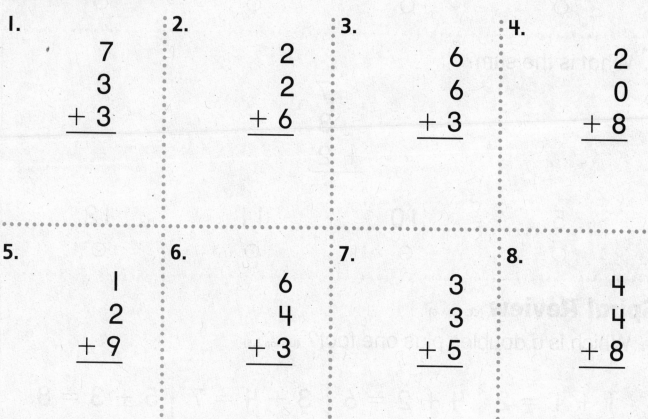

1.
```
  7
  3
+ 3
```

2.
```
  2
  2
+ 6
```

3.
```
  6
  6
+ 3
```

4.
```
  2
  0
+ 8
```

5.
```
  1
  2
+ 9
```

6.
```
  6
  4
+ 3
```

7.
```
  3
  3
+ 5
```

8.
```
  4
  4
+ 8
```

PROBLEM SOLVING REAL WORLD

Draw a picture. Write the number sentence.

9. Don has 4 black dogs.
   Tim has 3 small dogs.
   Sue has 3 big dogs.
   How many dogs do they have?

   ____ + ____ + ____ = ____ dogs

Lesson Check (CC.1.OA.3)

1. What is the sum of 4 + 4 + 2?

4 ○

8 ○

10 ○

14 ○

2. What is the sum?

$$\begin{array}{r} 7 \\ 3 \\ +\ 2 \\ \hline \end{array}$$

5 ○

10 ○

11 ○

12 ○

Spiral Review (CC.1.OA.6)

3. Which is a doubles plus one fact? (Lesson 3.5)

| 1 + 1 = 2 | 4 + 2 = 6 | 3 + 4 = 7 | 5 + 3 = 8 |
| ○ | ○ | ○ | ○ |

4. What number sentence does this model show? (Lesson 3.8)

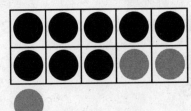

| 10 + 3 = 13 | 10 + 1 = 11 | 6 + 5 = 11 | 10 + 4 = 14 |
| ○ | ○ | ○ | ○ |

Problem Solving • Use Addition Strategies

COMMON CORE STANDARD CC.1.OA.2
Represent and solve problems involving
addition and subtraction.

Draw a picture to solve.

1. Franco has 5 crayons. He gets 8 more crayons. Then he gets 2 more crayons. How many crayons does he have now?

___ ◯ ___ ___ ◯ ___ ___ ◯ ___ _____ crayons

2. Jackson has 6 blocks. He gets 5 more blocks. Then he gets 3 more blocks. How many blocks does he have now?

___ ◯ ___ ◯ ___ ◯ ___ _____ blocks

3. Avni has 7 gifts. Then he gets 2 more gifts. Then he gets 3 more gifts. How many gifts does Avni have now?

___ ◯ ___ ◯ ___ ◯ ___ _____ gifts

4. Meeka has 4 rings. She gets 2 more rings. Then she gets 1 more ring. How many rings does she have now?

___ ◯ ___ ◯ ___ ◯ ___ _____ rings

Lesson Check (CC.1.OA.2)

1. Lila has 3 gray stones.
   She has 4 black stones.
   She also has 7 white stones.
   How many stones does she have?

   7   10   13   14
   ○   ○   ○   ○

2. Patrick has 3 red stickers, 6 pink
   stickers, and 8 green stickers. How
   many stickers does Patrick have?

   18   17   16   14
   ○   ○   ○   ○

Spiral Review (CC.1.OA.1, CC.1.OA.3)

3. What is the sum of $2 + 4$ or $4 + 2$? (Lesson 1.6)

   6   5   4   3
   ○   ○   ○   ○

4. There are 6 black pens.
   There are 3 blue pens.
   How many pens are there? (Lesson 1.3)

   2   5   8   9
   ○   ○   ○   ○

COMMON CORE STANDARDS CC.1.OA.2, CC.1.OA.3, CC.1.OA.5, CC.1.OA.6

Chapter 3 Extra Practice

Lesson 3.1
Add. Change the order of the addends. Add again.

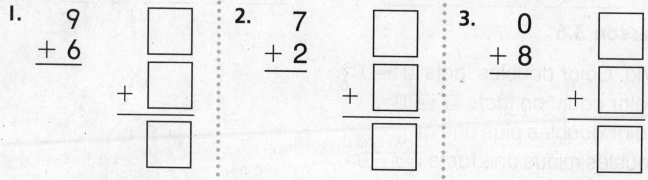

1.   9
   + 6

2.   7
   + 2

3.   0
   + 8

Lesson 3.2
Circle the greater addend.
Count on to find the sum.

1. $7 + 2 = $ _____

2. $3 + 5 = $ _____

3. $4 + 3 = $ _____

Lesson 3.4
Use 🎲 🎲. Make doubles. Add.

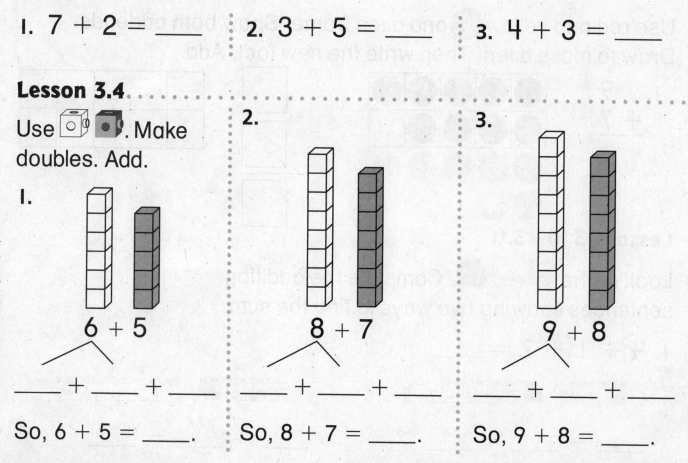

2.

3.

1.

6 + 5

8 + 7

9 + 8

___ + ___ + ___

___ + ___ + ___

___ + ___ + ___

So, $6 + 5 = $ _____.

So, $8 + 7 = $ _____.

So, $9 + 8 = $ _____.

Lesson 3.5

Add. Write the doubles fact
you used to solve the problem.

1. $6 + 7 =$ _____

_____ ◯ _____ ◯ _____

2. $5 + 6 =$ _____

_____ ◯ _____ ◯ _____

Lesson 3.6

Add. Color doubles facts 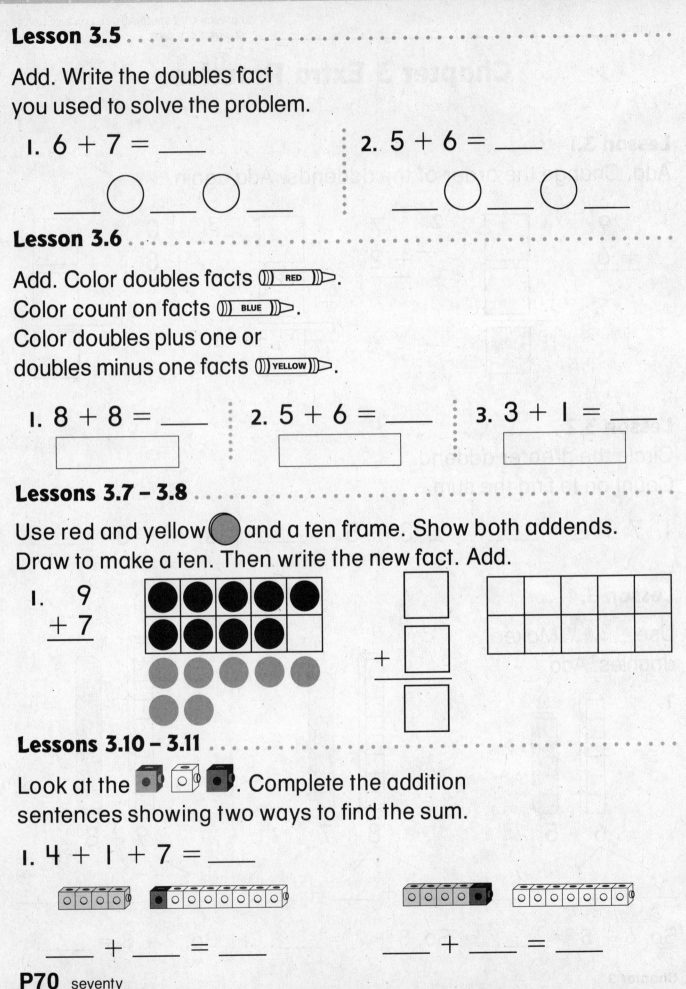 RED .
Color count on facts BLUE .
Color doubles plus one or
doubles minus one facts YELLOW .

1. $8 + 8 =$ _____

2. $5 + 6 =$ _____

3. $3 + 1 =$ _____

Lessons 3.7 – 3.8

Use red and yellow ◯ and a ten frame. Show both addends.
Draw to make a ten. Then write the new fact. Add.

1. $\begin{array}{r} 9 \\ +\ 7 \\ \hline \end{array}$

Lessons 3.10 – 3.11

Look at the 🎲 🎲 🎲 . Complete the addition
sentences showing two ways to find the sum.

1. $4 + 1 + 7 =$ _____

_____ $+$ _____ $=$ _____   _____ $+$ _____ $=$ _____

School-Home
Letter

Dear Family,

My class started Chapter 4 this week. In this chapter, I will learn about subtraction strategies and how to solve subtraction word problems.

Love, _____

Vocabulary

count back a way to subtract by counting back from the larger number

$$8 - 1 = 7$$

Start at 8.
Count back 1.
You are on 7.

Home Activity

Have your child practice counting from 1 to 8 and then from 8 to 1. Display numbers 1–8 on a piece of poster board or notebook paper. Each day, work with your child to solve simple subtraction problems by counting back 1, 2, or 3 using the list of numbers.

1 2 3 4 5 6 7 8

$$8 - 2 = 6$$

Literature

Look for these books in a library. Reading them together will reinforce your child's learning.

Monster Musical Chairs by Stuart J. Murphy. HarperCollins Children's Books, 2000.

Ten Little Ladybugs by Melanie Gerth. Piggy Toes Press, 2001.

Capítulo 4

Carta para la casa

Querida familia:

Mi clase comenzó hoy el Capítulo 4. En este capítulo, aprenderé estrategias de resta y a resolver problemas de resta en palabras.

Con cariño, _____

Vocabulario

contar hacia atrás un modo de restar contando hacia atrás de un número mayor

$$8 - 1 = 7$$

Comienza en 8.
Cuenta hacia atrás 1.
Quedas en 7.

Actividad para la casa

Pida a su hijo que cuente de 1 a 8 y de 8 a 1. Muestre los números de 1 a 8 en una cartulina o una hoja de cuaderno. Cada día, practique con su hijo resolver problemas simples de resta contando hacia atrás 1, 2 ó 3, en la lista de los números anotados.

1 2 3 4 5 6 7 8

$$8 - 2 = 6$$

Literatura

Busquen estos libros en la biblioteca. Si los lee con su hijo, ayudará a reforzar su aprendizaje.

Monster Musical Chairs
Stuart J. Murphy. HarperCollins Children's Books, 2000.

Ten Little Ladybugs
Melanie Gerth. Piggy Toes Press, 2001.

Count Back

COMMON CORE STANDARD CC.1.OA.5
Add and subtract within 20.

Count back 1, 2, or 3. Write the difference.

1. ___ = 7 − 3   2. 8 − 3 = ___   3. 4 − 3 = ___

4. ___ = 9 − 1   5. ___ = 7 − 1   6. ___ = 6 − 2

7. 6 − 1 = ___   8. 5 − 3 = ___   9. ___ = 11 − 3

10. 5 − 2 = ___   11. 10 − 2 = ___   12. ___ = 10 − 3

13. ___ = 9 − 3   14. 4 − 2 = ___   15. ___ = 7 − 2

16. ___ = 12 − 3   17. 8 − 1 = ___   18. 11 − 2 = ___

19. ___ = 9 − 2   20. 3 − 1 = ___   21. ___ = 4 − 1

PROBLEM SOLVING REAL WORLD

Write a subtraction sentence to solve.

22. Tina has 12 pencils.
She gives away 3 pencils.
How many pencils are left?

___ − ___ = ___

____ pencils

Lesson Check (CC.1.OA.5)

1. Count back 3. What is the difference?

$$\underline{\quad\quad} = 10 - 3$$

13	10	7	3
○	○	○	○

2. Count back 2. What is the difference?

$$7 - 2 = \underline{\quad\quad}$$

2	3	4	5
○	○	○	○

Spiral Review (CC.1.OA.1, CC.1.OA.6)

3. What is the sum of $4 + 4$? (Lesson 3.3)

7	8	9	10
○	○	○	○

4. There are 4 big dogs and 3 small dogs. How many dogs are there? (Lesson 1.3)

1	3	4	7
○	○	○	○

Think Addition to Subtract

COMMON CORE STANDARD CC.1.OA.4
Understand and apply properties of operations and the relationship between addition and subtraction.

Use 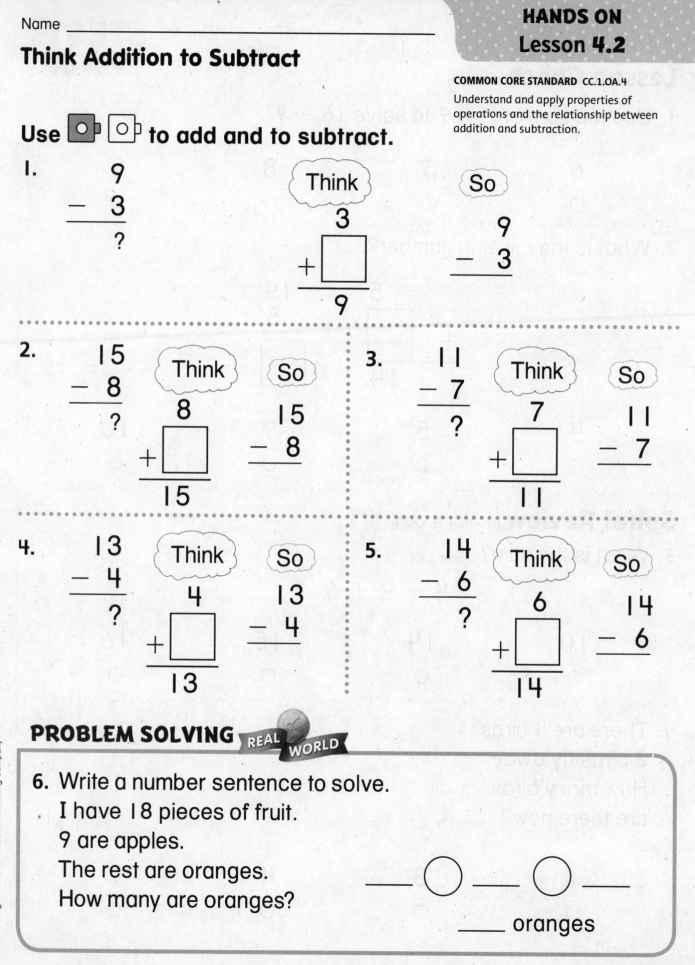 to add and to subtract.

1.
```
    9
  − 3
    ?
```
Think
```
    3
+ ☐
  ───
    9
```
So
```
    9
  − 3
  ───
```

2.
```
   1 5
  −  8
     ?
```
Think
```
    8
+ ☐
  ───
  1 5
```
So
```
  1 5
  −  8
  ───
```

3.
```
   1 1
  −  7
     ?
```
Think
```
    7
+ ☐
  ───
  1 1
```
So
```
  1 1
  −  7
  ───
```

4.
```
   1 3
  −  4
     ?
```
Think
```
    4
+ ☐
  ───
  1 3
```
So
```
  1 3
  −  4
  ───
```

5.
```
   1 4
  −  6
     ?
```
Think
```
    6
+ ☐
  ───
  1 4
```
So
```
  1 4
  −  6
  ───
```

PROBLEM SOLVING REAL WORLD

6. Write a number sentence to solve.
   I have 18 pieces of fruit.
   9 are apples.
   The rest are oranges.
   How many are oranges?

   ____ ◯ ____ ◯ ____

   ____ oranges

Lesson Check (CC.1.OA.4)

1. Use the sum of $7 + 9$ to solve $16 - 9$.

6	7	8	9
○	○	○	○

2. What is the missing number?

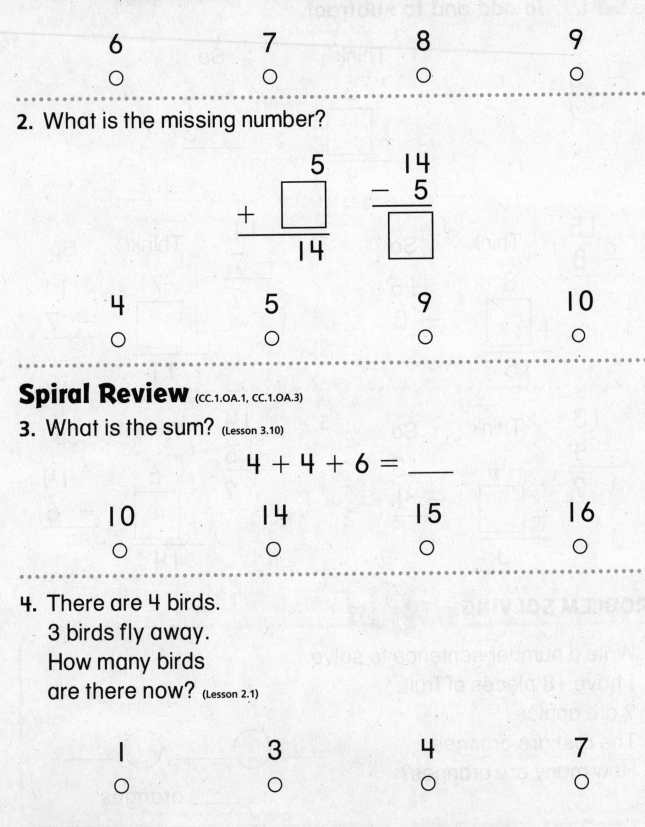

$$+ \quad \boxed{} \quad \begin{array}{r} 5 \\ \hline 14 \end{array}$$

4	5	9	10
○	○	○	○

Spiral Review (CC.1.OA.1, CC.1.OA.3)

3. What is the sum? (Lesson 3.10)

$$4 + 4 + 6 = \underline{}$$

10	14	15	16
○	○	○	○

4. There are 4 birds.
3 birds fly away.
How many birds
are there now? (Lesson 2.1)

1	3	4	7
○	○	○	○

Use Think Addition to Subtract

COMMON CORE STANDARD CC.1.OA.4
Understand and apply properties of
operations and the relationship between
addition and subtraction.

Think of an addition fact to help you subtract.

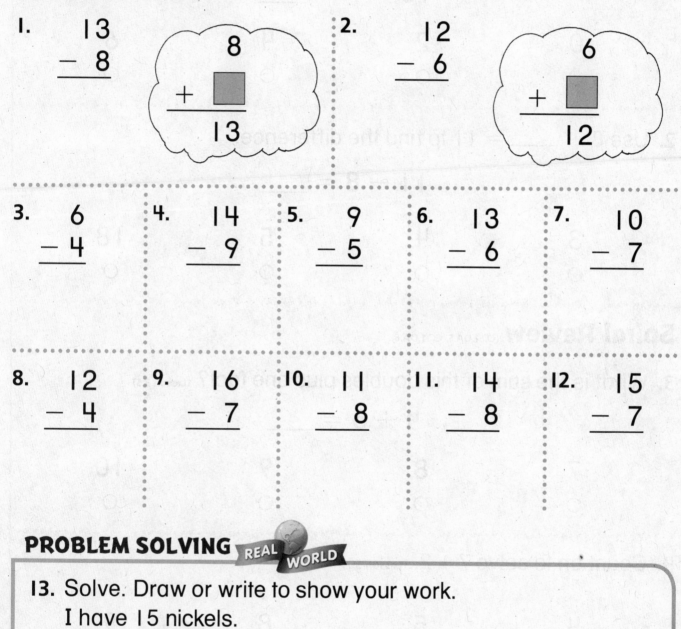

1. 13
    − 8

    8
    + ☐
    ___
    13

2. 12
    − 6

    6
    + ☐
    ___
    12

3. 6
    − 4

4. 14
    − 9

5. 9
    − 5

6. 13
    − 6

7. 10
    − 7

8. 12
    − 4

9. 16
    − 7

10. 11
    − 8

11. 14
    − 8

12. 15
    − 7

PROBLEM SOLVING REAL WORLD

13. Solve. Draw or write to show your work.
    I have 15 nickels.
    Some are old. 6 are new.
    How many nickels are old?

    _____ nickels

Lesson Check (CC.1.OA.4)

I. Use 9 + ____ = 13 to find the difference.

$$13 - 9 = \underline{\quad}$$

0	2	4	6
○	○	○	○

2. Use 8 + ____ = 11 to find the difference.

$$11 - 8 = \underline{\quad}$$

3	4	5	18
○	○	○	○

Spiral Review (CC.1.OA.5, CC.1.OA.6)

3. What is the sum of this doubles plus one fact? (Lesson 3.5)

$$4 + 5 = \underline{\quad}$$

7	8	9	10
○	○	○	○

4. Count on to solve 7 + 2. (Lesson 3.2)

4	5	8	9
○	○	○	○

Use 10 to Subtract

HANDS ON
Lesson 4.4

COMMON CORE STANDARD CC.1.OA.6
Add and subtract within 20.

**Use 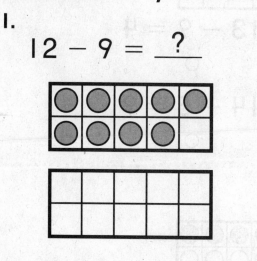 and ten frames. Make a
ten to subtract.
Draw to show your work.**

1.

$12 - 9 = \underline{\quad?\quad}$

$12 - 9 = \underline{\quad}$

2.

$12 - 8 = \underline{\quad?\quad}$

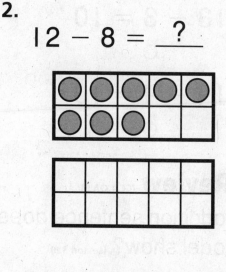

$12 - 8 = \underline{\quad}$

PROBLEM SOLVING REAL WORLD

Solve. Use the ten frames to
make a ten to help you subtract.

3. Marta has 15 stickers.
   8 are blue and the rest are red.
   How many stickers are red?

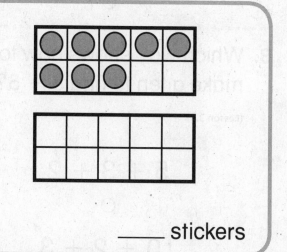

_____ stickers

Lesson Check (CC.1.OA.6)

1. Which subtraction sentence do the ten frames show?

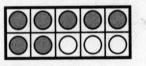

$13 - 3 = 10$
○

$13 - 9 = 4$
○

$14 - 4 = 10$
○

$14 - 5 = 9$
○

Spiral Review (CC.1.OA.6)

2. What addition sentence does this model show? (Lesson 3.8)

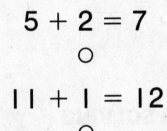
○

$3 + 2 = 5$
○

$5 + 2 = 7$
○

$10 + 1 = 11$
○

$11 + 1 = 12$
○

3. Which way shows how to make a ten to find $8 + 5$?

(Lesson 3.9)

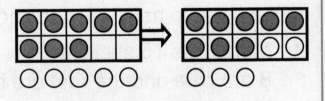

$5 + 3 + 2$
○

$8 + 2 + 3$
○

$10 + 2 + 3$
○

$10 + 3 + 2$
○

Break Apart to Subtract

COMMON CORE STANDARD CC.1.OA.6
Add and subtract within 20.

Subtract.

1. What is 13 − 5?

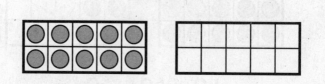

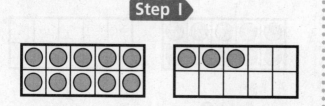

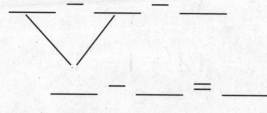

___ − ___ = ___

So, 13 − 5 = ___.

PROBLEM SOLVING 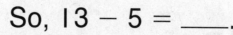 REAL WORLD

Use the ten frames. Write a number sentence.

2. There are 17 goats in the barn. 8 goats go outside.
How many goats are still in the barn?

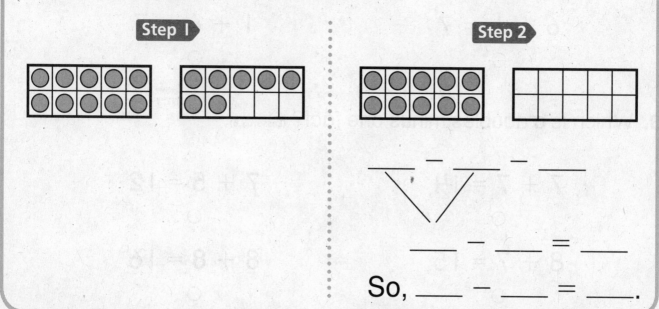

___ − ___ = ___

So, ___ − ___ = ___.

Lesson Check (CC.1.OA.6)

1. Which way shows how to make a ten to find $12 - 4$?

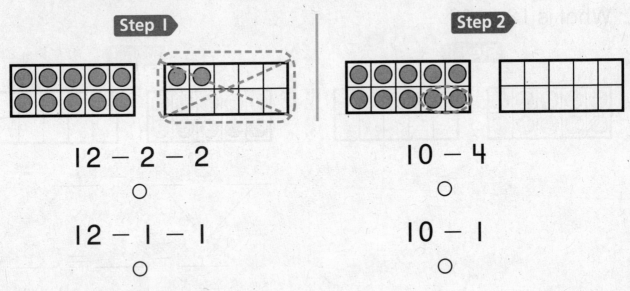

Step 1   Step 2

$12 - 2 - 2$
○

$10 - 4$
○

$12 - 1 - 1$
○

$10 - 1$
○

Spiral Review (CC.1.OA.1, CC.1.OA.6)

2. Which shows a way to take apart 7? (Lesson 2.8)

$8 - 7 = 1$
○

$7 - 1 = 6$
○

$6 + 1 = 7$
○

$1 + 6 = 7$
○

3. Which is a doubles minus one fact? (Lesson 3.6)

$7 + 7 = 14$
○

$7 + 5 = 12$
○

$8 + 7 = 15$
○

$8 + 8 = 16$
○

Name _____

Problem Solving • Use Subtraction Strategies

COMMON CORE STANDARD CC.1.OA.1
Represent and solve problems involving addition and subtraction.

**Act it out to solve.
Draw to show your work.**

1. There are 13 monkeys.
   6 are small. The rest are big.
   How many monkeys are big?

   $13 - 6 =$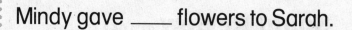

   _____ monkeys are big.

2. Mindy had 13 flowers. She gave some to Sarah. She has 9 left. How many flowers did she give to Sarah?

   $13 - $ ▢ $= 9$

   Mindy gave _____ flowers to Sarah.

3. There are 5 more horses in the barn than outside. 12 horses are in the barn. How many horses are outside?

   $12 - 5 =$ ▢

   _____ horses are outside.

4. Kim has 15 pennies.
   John has 6 pennies.
   How many fewer pennies does John have than Kim?

   $15 - 6 =$ ▢

   John has _____ fewer pennies.

Lesson Check (CC.1.OA.1)

1. Jack has 14 oranges.
He gives some away.
He has 6 left.
How many oranges did he give away?

3 ○   4 ○   7 ○   8 ○

2. 13 pears are in a basket.
Some are yellow and some
are green. 5 pears are green.
How many pears are yellow?

6 ○   7 ○   8 ○   9 ○

Spiral Review (CC.1.OA.2, CC.1.OA.6)

3. Rita has 4 plants.
She gets 9 more plants.
Then Rita gets 1 more plant.
How many plants does she have now? (Lesson 3.12)

14 ○   13 ○   10 ○   5 ○

4. What is the sum of 10 + 5? (Lesson 3.7)

15 ○   10 ○   5 ○   4 ○

COMMON CORE STANDARDS CC.1.OA.1,
CC.1.OA.4, CC.1.OA.5, CC.1.OA.6

Chapter 4 Extra Practice

Lesson 4.1 (pp. 153–156)

Count back 1, 2, or 3.
Write the difference.

1.
$$10 - 3 = \underline{\hspace{1cm}}$$

2.
$$\underline{\hspace{1cm}} = 11 - 3$$

3.
$$9 - 2 = \underline{\hspace{1cm}}$$

4.
$$\underline{\hspace{1cm}} = 6 - 1$$

5.
$$\underline{\hspace{1cm}} = 4 - 2$$

6.
$$8 - 3 = \underline{\hspace{1cm}}$$

Lesson 4.2 - 4.3 (pp. 157-163)

Think of an addition fact
to help you subtract.

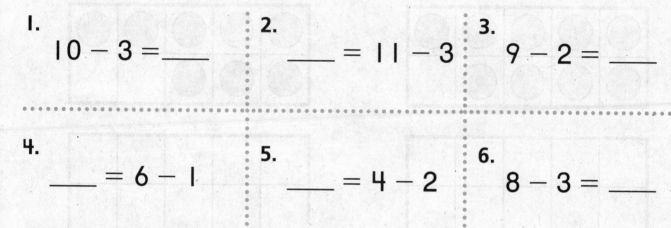

1.
$$\begin{array}{r} 13 \\ -\ 9 \\ \hline \end{array}$$

$$\begin{array}{r} 9 \\ +\ \blacksquare \\ \hline 13 \end{array}$$

2.
$$\begin{array}{r} 14 \\ -\ 7 \\ \hline \end{array}$$

$$\begin{array}{r} 7 \\ +\ \blacksquare \\ \hline 14 \end{array}$$

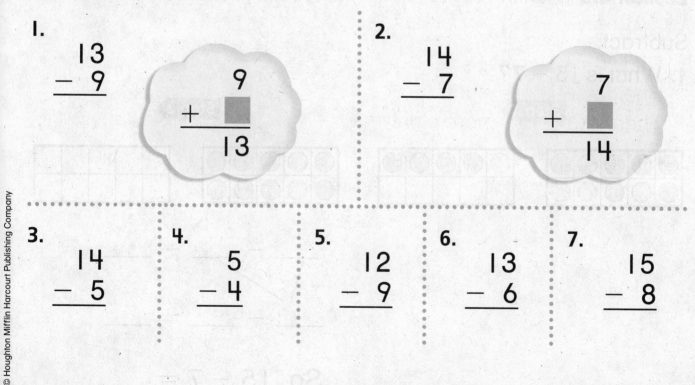

3.
$$\begin{array}{r} 14 \\ -\ 5 \\ \hline \end{array}$$

4.
$$\begin{array}{r} 5 \\ -\ 4 \\ \hline \end{array}$$

5.
$$\begin{array}{r} 12 \\ -\ 9 \\ \hline \end{array}$$

6.
$$\begin{array}{r} 13 \\ -\ 6 \\ \hline \end{array}$$

7.
$$\begin{array}{r} 15 \\ -\ 8 \\ \hline \end{array}$$

Lesson 4.4 (pp.165–168)

Use ⬤ and ten frames.
Make a ten to subtract.
Draw to show your work.

1.
$16 - 9 = $?

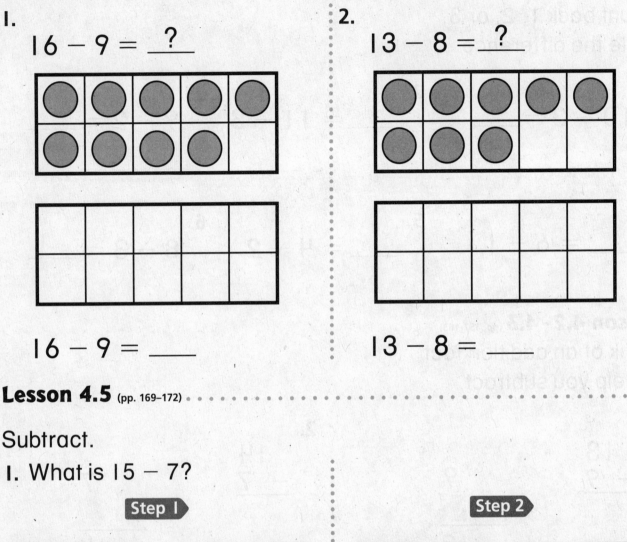

$16 - 9 = $ ___

2.
$13 - 8 = $?

$13 - 8 = $ ___

Lesson 4.5 (pp. 169–172)

Subtract.

1. What is $15 - 7$?

Step 1

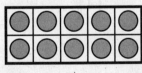

Step 2

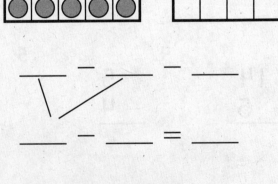

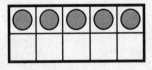

So, $15 - 7 = $ ___.

School-Home
Letter

Dear Family,

My class started Chapter 5 this week. In this chapter, I will learn how addition and subtraction are related. I will also learn how to identify and use related facts.

Love, _____

Vocabulary

related facts Related facts are facts that have the same parts and whole.

$$5 + 7 = 12$$
$$12 - 7 = 5$$

Home Activity

Make a poster with your child like the one below. Each day, write a different related fact. As you progress, leave spaces blank for your child to find missing numbers.

__ + 3 = 5	5 − 2 = 3
3 + __ = 5	5 − 3 = 2

Literature

Look for these books in a library. Read them together to reinforce learning.

Elevator Magic
by Stuart J. Murphy.
HarperCollins, 1997.

Animals on Board
by Stuart J. Murphy.
HarperCollins, 1998.

Carta
para la casa

Querida familia:

Mi clase comenzó el Capítulo 5 esta semana. En este capítulo, aprenderé cómo se relacionan la suma y la resta. También aprenderé cómo identificar las operaciones relacionadas.

Con cariño, _____

Vocabulario

Operaciones relacionadas Las operaciones relacionadas son operaciones que usan los mismos números.

$$5 + 7 = 12$$
$$12 - 7 = 5$$

Actividad para la casa

Haga un cartel con su hijo como el que está abajo. Cada día, escriba una operación relacionada distinta. A medida que avanzan, deje espacios en blanco para que su hijo complete los números que faltan.

__ + 3 = 5	5 − 2 = 3
3 + __ = 5	5 − 3 = 2

Literatura

Busque estos libros en una biblioteca. Léanlos juntos para reforzar el aprendizaje.

Elevator Magic
por Stuart J. Murphy.
Harper Collins, 1997.

Animals on Board
Por Stuart J. Murphy.
Harper Collins, 1998.

Add or Subtract

COMMON CORE STANDARD CC.1.OA.1
Represent and solve problems involving
addition and subtraction.

Make a model to solve.

1. Stan has 12 pennies.

Some pennies are new.

4 pennies are old.

How many pennies are new?

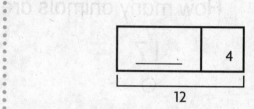

_____ new pennies

2. Liz has 9 toy bears.

Then she buys some more.

Now she has 15 toy bears.

How many toy bears did she buy?

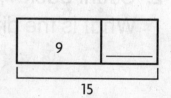

_____ toy bears

3. Eric buys 6 books.

Now he has 16 books.

How many books did he have to start?

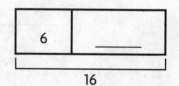

_____ books

4. Cho has 10 rings.

Some rings are silver.

4 rings are gold.

How many rings are silver?

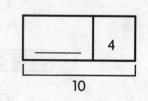

_____ silver rings

Lesson Check (CC.1.OA.1)

1. Arlo has 17 bean bag animals.
Some are fuzzy.
9 bean bag animals are not fuzzy.
How many animals are fuzzy?

17
○

9
○

8
○

7
○

Spiral Review (CC.1.OA.1, CC.1.OA.5)

2. Count back 1, 2, or 3.
What is the difference? (Lesson 4.1)

$$\underline{\quad} = 11 - 3$$

9
○

8
○

7
○

6
○

3. Which shows a way to make 10? (Lesson 1.7)

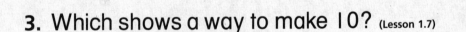

○

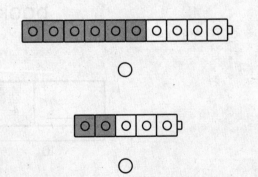

○

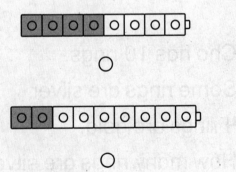

○

Name _____

Record Related Facts

HANDS ON
Lesson 5.2

COMMON CORE STANDARD CC.1.OA.6
Add and subtract within 20.

Use 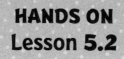. Add or subtract. Complete the related facts.

1. $4 + \boxed{} = 12$ $\boxed{} - 8 = 4$

$8 + 4 = \boxed{}$ $\boxed{} - \boxed{} = \boxed{}$

2. $\boxed{} + 4 = 9$ $9 - 4 = \boxed{}$

$\boxed{} + 5 = 9$ $\boxed{} - \boxed{} = \boxed{}$

3. $9 + 7 = \boxed{}$ $16 - 7 = \boxed{}$

$7 + \boxed{} = 16$ $\boxed{} - \boxed{} = \boxed{}$

4. $\boxed{} + 6 = 14$ $14 - \boxed{} = 8$

$6 + 8 = \boxed{}$ $\boxed{} - \boxed{} = \boxed{}$

PROBLEM SOLVING REAL WORLD

Choose a way to solve.
Write or draw to explain.

5. There are 16 apples on the tree. No apples fall off. How many apples are still on the tree?

_____ apples

Lesson Check (CC.1.OA.6)

1. Which fact is a related fact?

$$7 + 4 = 11$$
$$4 + 7 = 11$$
$$11 - 7 = 4$$

$7 - 4 = 3$ ○ $11 - 4 = 7$ ○

$11 - 7 = 4$ ○ $7 + 5 = 12$ ○

Spiral Review (CC.1.OA.4, CC.1.OA.8)

2. What is $6 - 6$? (Lesson 2.7)

0 ○   5 ○   8 ○   12 ○

3. Which addition sentence helps you solve $15 - 9$? (Lesson 4.2)

$15 - 6 = 9$ ○ $9 + 6 = 15$ ○

$4 + 5 = 9$ ○ $9 + 3 = 12$ ○

Name _____

Identify Related Facts

COMMON CORE STANDARD CC.1.OA.6
Add and subtract within 20.

Add and subtract.
Circle the related facts.

1. $5 + 6 =$ ____
    $11 - 6 =$ ____

2. $4 + 9 =$ ____
    $9 - 4 =$ ____

3. $4 + 7 =$ ____
    $11 - 7 =$ ____

4. $9 + 8 =$ ____
    $17 - 8 =$ ____

5. $5 + 7 =$ ____
    $7 - 5 =$ ____

6. $6 + 8 =$ ____
    $14 - 8 =$ ____

7. $4 + 6 =$ ____
    $10 - 5 =$ ____

8. $9 + 5 =$ ____
    $14 - 5 =$ ____

PROBLEM SOLVING

9. Use the numbers to write related addition
   and subtraction sentences.

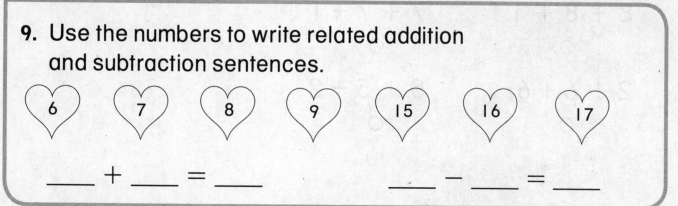

____ $+$ ____ $=$ ____   ____ $-$ ____ $=$ ____

Lesson Check (CC.1.OA.6)

1. Which is a related fact for $7 + 6 = 13$?

$6 + 6 = 12$ ○ $13 - 6 = 7$ ○

$7 + 3 = 10$ ○ $7 - 6 = 1$ ○

Spiral Review (CC.1.OA.6, CC.1.OA.8)

2. How many fewer 🪶 than 🐦 are there? (Lesson 2.5)

15 fewer 🪶 ○   2 fewer 🪶 ○   1 fewer 🪶 ○   0 fewer 🪶 ○

3. Which has the same sum as $7 + 8$? (Lesson 3.4)

$8 + 8 + 1$ ○ $7 + 7 + 1$ ○

$2 + 6 + 6$ ○ $5 + 5 + 2$ ○

Use Addition to Check Subtraction

COMMON CORE STANDARD CC.1.OA.6
Add and subtract within 20.

**Subtract. Then add to check
your answer.**

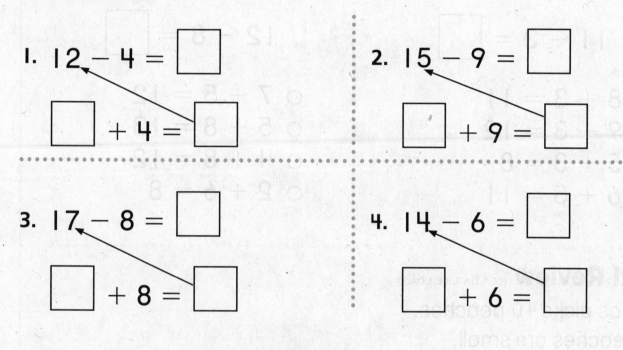

1. $12 - 4 = \boxed{}$

   $\boxed{} + 4 = \boxed{8}$

2. $15 - 9 = \boxed{}$

   $\boxed{} + 9 = \boxed{}$

3. $17 - 8 = \boxed{}$

   $\boxed{} + 8 = \boxed{}$

4. $14 - 6 = \boxed{}$

   $\boxed{} + 6 = \boxed{}$

PROBLEM SOLVING REAL WORLD

Subtract.
Then add to check your answer.

5. There are 13 grapes in a bowl.
   Justin ate some of them.
   Now there are only 7 grapes left.
   How many grapes did Justin eat?

   ___ − ___ = ___   ___ grapes.

   ___ + ___ = ___

Lesson Check (CC.1.OA.6)

1. Which addition sentence can you use to check the subtraction?

$$11 - 3 = \boxed{}$$

- ○ $8 + 3 = 11$
- ○ $9 + 3 = 12$
- ○ $5 + 3 = 8$
- ○ $6 + 5 = 11$

2. Which addition sentence can you use to check the subtraction?

$$12 - 8 = \boxed{}$$

- ○ $7 + 5 = 12$
- ○ $5 + 8 = 13$
- ○ $4 + 8 = 12$
- ○ $2 + 6 = 8$

Spiral Review (CC.1.OA.1, CC.1.OA.3)

3. Jonas picks 10 peaches.
   4 peaches are small.
   The rest are big.
   How many are big? (Lesson 5.1)

10	6	5	4
○	○	○	○

4. What is the sum of $3 + 3 + 4$? (Lesson 3.11)

8	9	10	11
○	○	○	○

Algebra • Missing Numbers

COMMON CORE STANDARD CC.1.OA.8
Work with addition and subtraction equations.

Write the missing numbers.
Use 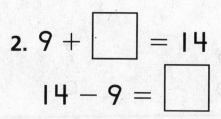 if you need to.

1. $6 + \boxed{} = 13$

   $13 - 6 = \boxed{}$

2. $9 + \boxed{} = 14$

   $14 - 9 = \boxed{}$

3. $\boxed{} + 7 = 15$

   $15 - 7 = \boxed{}$

4. $\boxed{} + 3 = 12$

   $12 - \boxed{} = 3$

5. $\boxed{} = 9 + 8$

   $8 = \boxed{} - 9$

6. $\boxed{} = 8 + 8$

   $8 = \boxed{} - 8$

PROBLEM SOLVING REAL WORLD

Use cubes or draw a picture to solve.

7. Sally has 9 toy trucks.
   She gets 3 more toy trucks.
   How many toy trucks does
   she have now?

   _____ toy trucks

Lesson Check

1. What is the missing number? (CC.1.OA.8)

$$9 + \boxed{} = 16$$

6	7	8	9
○	○	○	○

Spiral Review (CC.1.OA.3, CC.1.OA.6)

2. Which way shows how to
make a ten to solve $14 - 6$? (Lesson 4.5)

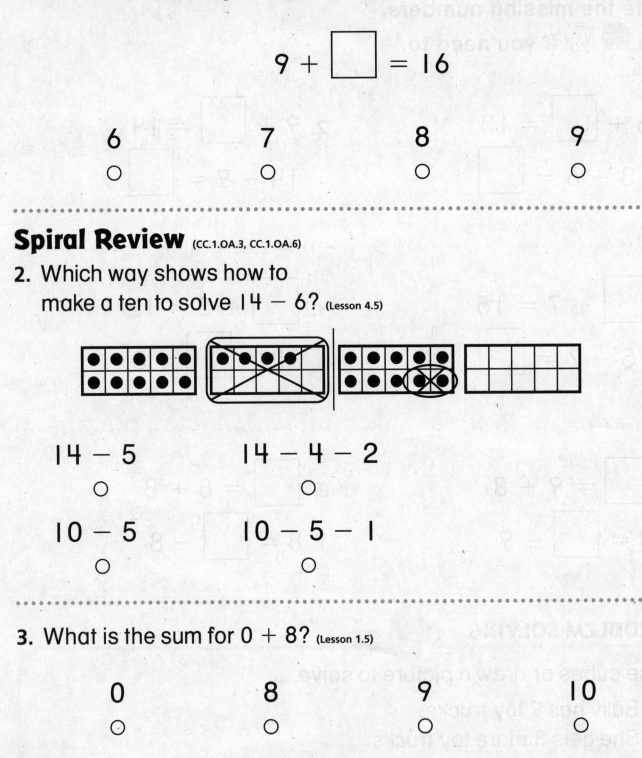

$14 - 5$	$14 - 4 - 2$
○	○
$10 - 5$	$10 - 5 - 1$
○	○

3. What is the sum for $0 + 8$? (Lesson 1.5)

0	8	9	10
○	○	○	○

Algebra • Use Related Facts

COMMON CORE STANDARD CC.1.OA.8
Work with addition and subtraction equations.

Write the missing numbers.

1. Find $16 - 9$.

$$9 + \boxed{} = 16$$

16

$16 - 9 = \boxed{}$

9

2. Find $12 - 7$.

$$7 + \boxed{} = 12$$

12

$12 - 7 = \boxed{}$

7

3. Find $15 - 6$.

$$6 + \boxed{} = 15$$

15

$15 - 6 = \boxed{}$

6

4. Find $18 - 9$.

$$9 + \boxed{} = 18$$

18

$18 - 9 = \boxed{}$

9

PROBLEM SOLVING

Look at the shapes in the addition sentence.
Draw a shape to show a related subtraction fact.

5.

⬕ + ⬯ = ◼   ◼ − _____ = ⬕

Lesson Check (CC.1.OA.8)

1. Which addition fact helps you solve $12 - 4$?

$4 + 6 = 10$
○

$8 + 4 = 12$
○

$7 + 4 = 11$
○

$9 + 3 = 12$
○

Spiral Review (CC.1.OA.5, CC.1.OA.6)

2. Count on to find $9 + 3$. (Lesson 3.2)

13   12   11   6
○   ○   ○   ○

3. Which doubles fact matches the picture? (Lesson 3.3)

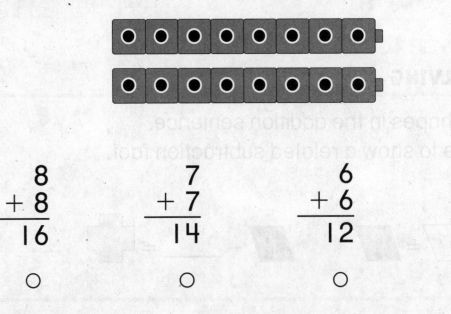

$$\begin{array}{r} 8 \\ + 8 \\ \hline 16 \end{array}$$
○

$$\begin{array}{r} 7 \\ + 7 \\ \hline 14 \end{array}$$
○

$$\begin{array}{r} 6 \\ + 6 \\ \hline 12 \end{array}$$
○

$$\begin{array}{r} 5 \\ + 5 \\ \hline 10 \end{array}$$
○

Choose an Operation

COMMON CORE STANDARD CC.1.OA.1
Represent and solve problems involving addition and subtraction.

Circle add or subtract.
Write a number sentence to solve.

1. Adam has a bag of 11 pretzels.
   He eats 2 of the pretzels.
   How many pretzels are left?

   _____

   add   subtract

   ____ pretzels

2. Greta makes 3 drawings.
   Kate makes 4 more drawings
   than Greta. How many
   drawings does Kate make?

   _____

   add   subtract

   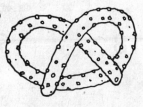

   ____ drawings

PROBLEM SOLVING REAL WORLD

Choose a way to solve.
Write or draw to explain.

3. Greg has 11 shirts.
   3 have long sleeves.
   The rest have short sleeves.
   How many short-sleeve
   shirts does Greg have?

   ____ short-sleeve shirts

© Houghton Mifflin Harcourt Publishing Company

Lesson Check (CC.1.OA.1)

1. There are 18 children on the bus. Then 9 children get off. Which number sentence shows how to find the number of children left on the bus?

$9 + 8 = 17$ ○ $18 - 9 = 9$ ○

$18 - 0 = 18$ ○ $9 - 9 = 0$ ○

Spiral Review (CC.1.OA.1, CC.1.OA.3)

2. Mike has 13 plants.
He gives some away.
He has 4 left.
How many plants
does he give away? (Lesson 4.6)

10 ○   9 ○   7 ○   4 ○

3. What is the sum for $3 + 2 + 8$? (Lesson 3.10)

13 ○   12 ○   11 ○   4 ○

Algebra • Ways to Make Numbers to 20

COMMON CORE STANDARD CC.1.OA.6
Add and subtract within 20.

Use 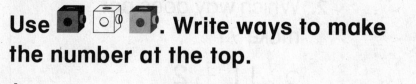. Write ways to make the number at the top.

1. 10

$$\underline{2} + \underline{7} + \underline{1}$$

$$\underline{5} + \underline{5}$$

$$\underline{10} - \underline{0}$$

$$\underline{9} \oplus \underline{1}$$

2. 13

$$\underline{} + \underline{} + \underline{}$$

$$\underline{} + \underline{}$$

$$\underline{} - \underline{}$$

$$\bigcirc \underline{}$$

3. 16

$$\underline{} + \underline{} + \underline{}$$

$$\underline{} + \underline{}$$

$$\underline{} - \underline{}$$

$$\bigcirc \underline{}$$

4. 12

$$\underline{} + \underline{} + \underline{}$$

$$\underline{} + \underline{}$$

$$\underline{} - \underline{}$$

$$\bigcirc \underline{}$$

PROBLEM SOLVING

Write numbers to make each line have the same sum.

5.

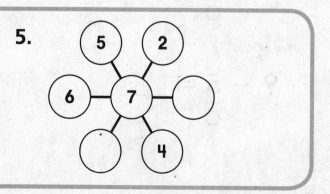

Lesson Check (CC.1.OA.6)

1. Which way makes 18?

   ○ 4 + 8
   ○ 9 + 0
   ○ 11 − 7
   ○ 8 + 10

2. Which way does **not** make 9?

   ○ 11 + 2
   ○ 11 − 2
   ○ 5 + 4
   ○ 3 + 6

Spiral Review (CC.1.OA.4, CC.1.OA.6)

3. Which is the doubles plus one fact for 7 + 7? (Lesson 3.5)

   ○ 7 + 7 = 14
   ○ 7 + 6 = 13
   ○ 7 + 8 = 15
   ○ 6 + 8 = 14

4. Which is the doubles minus one fact for 4 + 4? (Lesson 3.5)

   ○ 4 + 5 = 9
   ○ 4 + 3 = 7
   ○ 3 + 5 = 8
   ○ 4 + 4 = 8

5. Which subtraction sentence can you solve by using 9 + 5 = 14? (Lesson 4.3)

14 − 7 = ___
○

14 − 9 = ___
○

9 − 5 = ___
○

14 − 8 = ___
○

Algebra • Equal and Not Equal

COMMON CORE STANDARD CC.1.OA.7
Work with addition and subtraction equations.

Which are true? Circle your answers.
Which are false? Cross out your answers.

1. $6 + 4 = 5 + 5$

2. $10 = 6 - 4$

3. $8 + 8 = 16 - 8$

4. $14 = 1 + 4$

5. $8 - 0 = 12 - 4$

6. $17 = 9 + 8$

7. $8 + 3 = 8 - 3$

8. $15 - 6 = 6 + 9$

9. $12 = 5 + 5 + 2$

10. $7 + 6 = 6 + 7$

11. $5 - 4 = 4 + 5$

12. $0 + 9 = 9 - 0$

PROBLEM SOLVING REAL WORLD

13. Which are true? Use a ▱ to color.

$15 = 15$	$12 = 2$	$3 = 8 - 5$
$15 = 1 + 5$	$9 + 2 = 2 + 9$	$9 + 2 = 14$
$1 + 2 + 3 = 3 + 3$	$5 - 3 = 5 + 3$	$13 = 8 + 5$

Lesson Check (CC.1.OA.7)

1. Which is true?

$$4 + 3 = 9 - 2$$
○

$$4 + 3 = 9 + 2$$
○

$$4 + 3 = 4 - 3$$
○

$$4 + 3 = 7 - 3$$
○

Spiral Review (CC.1.OA.2, CC.1.OA.6)

2. Which subtraction fact is
related to $5 + 6 = 11$? (Lesson 5.3)

$$11 - 7 = 4$$
○

$$11 - 6 = 5$$
○

$$9 - 3 = 6$$
○

$$6 - 5 = 1$$
○

3. Leah has 4 green toys,
5 pink toys, and 2 blue toys.
How many toys does Leah have? (Lesson 3.12)

6
○

8
○

11
○

12
○

Basic Facts to 20

COMMON CORE STANDARD CC.1.OA.6
Add and subtract within 20.

Add or subtract.

1. $\begin{array}{r} 4 \\ + 9 \\ \hline \end{array}$

2. $\begin{array}{r} 13 \\ - 6 \\ \hline \end{array}$

3. $\begin{array}{r} 4 \\ + 5 \\ \hline \end{array}$

4. $\begin{array}{r} 8 \\ + 7 \\ \hline \end{array}$

5. $\begin{array}{r} 11 \\ - 6 \\ \hline \end{array}$

6. $\begin{array}{r} 17 \\ - 8 \\ \hline \end{array}$

7. $\begin{array}{r} 5 \\ + 7 \\ \hline \end{array}$

8. $\begin{array}{r} 13 \\ - 5 \\ \hline \end{array}$

9. $\begin{array}{r} 16 \\ - 9 \\ \hline \end{array}$

10. $\begin{array}{r} 3 \\ + 8 \\ \hline \end{array}$

11. $\begin{array}{r} 9 \\ - 8 \\ \hline \end{array}$

12. $\begin{array}{r} 7 \\ + 6 \\ \hline \end{array}$

13. $\begin{array}{r} 9 \\ - \square \\ \hline 7 \end{array}$

14. $\begin{array}{r} 6 \\ + \square \\ \hline 10 \end{array}$

15. $\begin{array}{r} 8 \\ - \square \\ \hline 3 \end{array}$

16. $\begin{array}{r} 6 \\ + \square \\ \hline 12 \end{array}$

17. $\begin{array}{r} 0 \\ + \square \\ \hline 9 \end{array}$

18. $\begin{array}{r} 15 \\ - \square \\ \hline 6 \end{array}$

PROBLEM SOLVING   REAL WORLD

Solve. Draw or write to explain.

19. Kara has 9 drawings.
    She gives 4 away. How many
    drawings does Kara have now?

    _____ drawings

Lesson Check (CC.1.OA.6)

I. What is $14 - 7$?

20	11	8	7
○	○	○	○

Spiral Review (CC.1.OA.3, CC.1.OA.8)

2. What is the missing number? (Lesson 5.5)

$$7 + \square = 12$$

5	6	7	8
○	○	○	○

3. Which shows the same addends in a different order? (Lesson 3.1)

$$7 + 4 = 11$$

$3 + 4 = 7$
○

$4 + 5 = 9$
○

$8 + 3 = 11$
○

$4 + 7 = 11$
○

Name _____

Chapter 5 Extra Practice

COMMON CORE STANDARDS CC.1.OA.1, CC.1.OA.6, CC.1.OA.7, CC.1.OA.8

Lessons 5.2 – 5.3 (pp. 189–196)

Add and subtract. Circle the related facts.

1.
$$5 + 8$$

$$13 - 5$$

2.
$$7 + 4$$

$$7 - 4$$

Lesson 5.4 (pp. 197–199)

Subtract. Then add to check your answer.

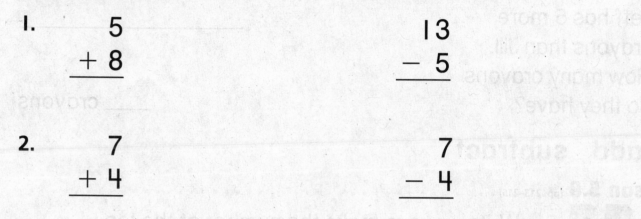

1. $15 - 8 = \boxed{}$

$\boxed{} + 8 = \boxed{}$

2. $12 - 8 = \boxed{}$

$4 + 8 = \boxed{}$

Lessons 5.5 – 5.6 (pp. 201–208)

Write the missing numbers.

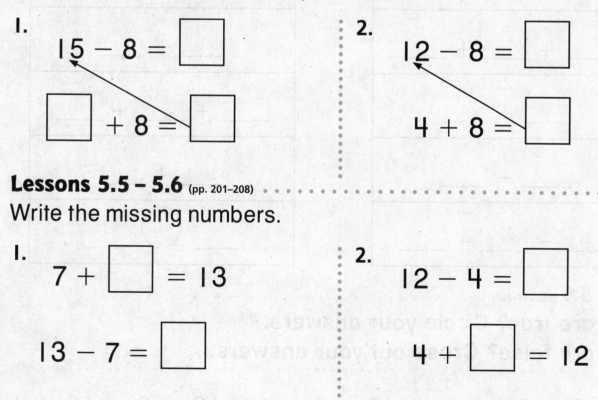

1. $7 + \boxed{} = 13$

$13 - 7 = \boxed{}$

2. $12 - 4 = \boxed{}$

$4 + \boxed{} = 12$

Lesson 5.7 (pp. 209–212)

Circle **add** or **subtract**.

Write a number sentence to solve.

1. Jill has 3 crayons.
   Jeff has 5 more
   crayons than Jill.
   How many crayons   _____
   do they have?

                                                           ____ crayons

   ## add   subtract

Lesson 5.8 (pp. 213–216)

Use 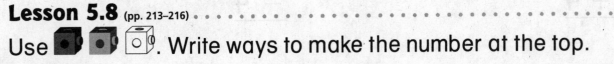. Write ways to make the number at the top.

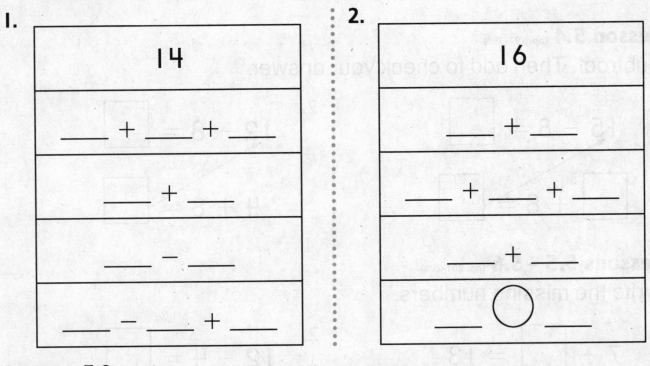

1. | 14 |
   | --- |
   | ___ + ___ + ___ |
   | ___ + ___ |
   | ___ – ___ |
   | ___ – ___ + ___ |

2. | 16 |
   | --- |
   | ___ + ___ |
   | ___ + ___ + ___ |
   | ___ + ___ |
   | ___ ◯ ___ |

Lesson 5.9 (pp. 217–220)

Which are true? Circle your answers.

Which are false? Cross out your answers.

1. $2 + 5 = 8 - 1$ $4 + 2 = 9 - 1$ $13 - 0 = 12 + 1$

School-Home Letter

Dear Family,

My class started Chapter 6 this week. In this chapter, I will count numbers to 120 and use tens and ones to make numbers.

Love, _____

Vocabulary

ones and **ten** You can group 10 📷 to make 1 ten.

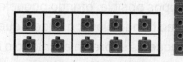

10 ones = 1 ten

hundred 10 tens is the same as 1 hundred.

10 tens = 100

Home Activity

Give your child a handful of craft sticks, chenille stems, or straws. Have your child make as many groups of 10 as possible, tying bundles of 10 with a rubber band. Have them place the bundles on a desk or table. Have your child put any leftover ones next to the bundles of 10. Then ask your child to write the number.

Literature

Reading math stories reinforces ideas. Look for these books in a library and read them with your child.

One Is a Snail, Ten Is a Crab by April Pulley Sayre. Candlewick, 2006.

The Counting Family by Jane Manners. Harcourt School Publishers, 2002.

Capítulo 6

Carta para la casa

Querida familia:

Mi clase comenzó el Capítulo 6 esta semana. En este capítulo, contaré números hasta el 120 y usaré decenas y unidades para formar números.

Con cariño, ______________________

Vocabulario

unidades y decenas puedes agrupar unidades para formar decenas

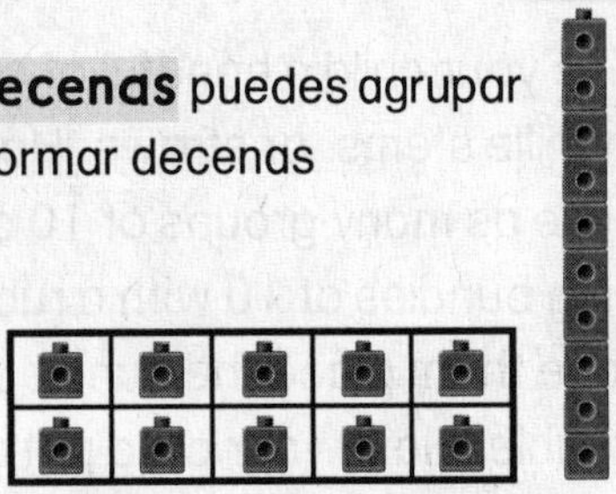

10 unidades = 1 decenas

centena 10 decenas es lo mismo que 1 centena

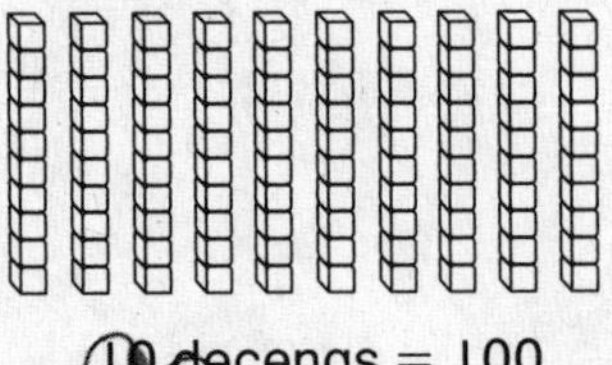

10 decenas = 100

Actividad para la casa

Entréguele a su hijo un puñado de palitos para manualidades, hilos de lana o pajitas. Pídale a su hijo que forme la mayor cantidad de grupos posible, atando paquetes de 10 con una banda elástica. Pídale que coloque los paquetes sobre un escritorio o mesa. Pídale que ponga las unidades sobrantes junto a los paquetes de 10. Luego, pídale a su hijo que escriba el número.

Literatura

Leer cuentos de matemáticas refuerza los conceptos. Busque estos libros en una biblioteca y léalos con su hijo.

One Is a Snail, Ten is a Crab
por April Pulley Sayre.
Candlewick, 2006.

The Counting Family
por Jane Manners.
Harcourt School Publishers, 2002.

© Houghton Mifflin Harcourt Publishing Company

Count by Ones to 120

COMMON CORE STANDARD CC.1.NBT.1
Extend the counting sequence.

Use a Counting Chart. Count forward. Write the numbers.

1. 40, _____, _____, _____, _____, _____, _____, _____, _____

2. 55, _____, _____, _____, _____, _____, _____, _____, _____

3. 37, _____, _____, _____, _____, _____, _____, _____, _____

4. 102, _____, _____, _____, _____, _____, _____, _____, _____

5. 96, _____, _____, _____, _____, _____, _____, _____, _____

PROBLEM SOLVING REAL WORLD

Use a Counting Chart. Draw and write numbers to solve.

6. The bag has 111 marbles. Draw more marbles so there are 117 marbles in all. Write the numbers as you count.

Lesson Check (CC.1.NBT.1)

1. Count forward. What number is missing?

110, 111, 112, _____, 114

105   109   113   115

○   ○   ○   ○

Spiral Review (CC.1.OA.1)

2. There are 6 bees. 2 bees fly away. How many bees are there now? (Lesson 2.1)

2   4   6   8

○   ○   ○   ○

3. There are 8 children. 6 children are boys. The rest are girls. How many children are girls? (Lesson 2.3)

2 girls | 3 girls | 6 girls | 8 girls

○   ○   ○   ○

Count by Tens to 120

COMMON CORE STANDARD CC.1.NBT.1
Extend the counting sequence.

Use a Counting Chart.
Count by tens.
Write the numbers.

1. 1, ____, ____, ____, ____, ____, ____, ____, ____, ____, ____

2. 14, ____, ____, ____, ____, ____, ____, ____, ____, ____, ____

3. 7, ____, ____, ____, ____, ____, ____, ____, ____, ____, ____

4. 29, ____, ____, ____, ____, ____, ____, ____, ____, ____, ____

5. 5, ____, ____, ____, ____, ____, ____, ____, ____, ____, ____

6. 12, ____, ____, ____, ____, ____, ____, ____, ____, ____, ____

7. 26, ____, ____, ____, ____, ____, ____, ____, ____, ____, ____

8. 3, ____, ____, ____, ____, ____, ____, ____, ____, ____, ____

9. 8, ____, ____, ____, ____, ____, ____, ____, ____, ____, ____

PROBLEM SOLVING REAL WORLD

Solve.

10. I am after 70.
I am before 90.
You say me when you count by tens.
What number am I?

_____

Lesson Check (CC.1.NBT.1)

1. Count by tens.
   What numbers are missing?

   44, 54, 64, ____, ____, 94

   34, 64   44, 45   73, 74   74, 84
   ○   ○   ○   ○

Spiral Review (CC.1.OA.6)

2. Which way shows how to
   make a ten to solve 8 + 5? (Lesson 3.9)

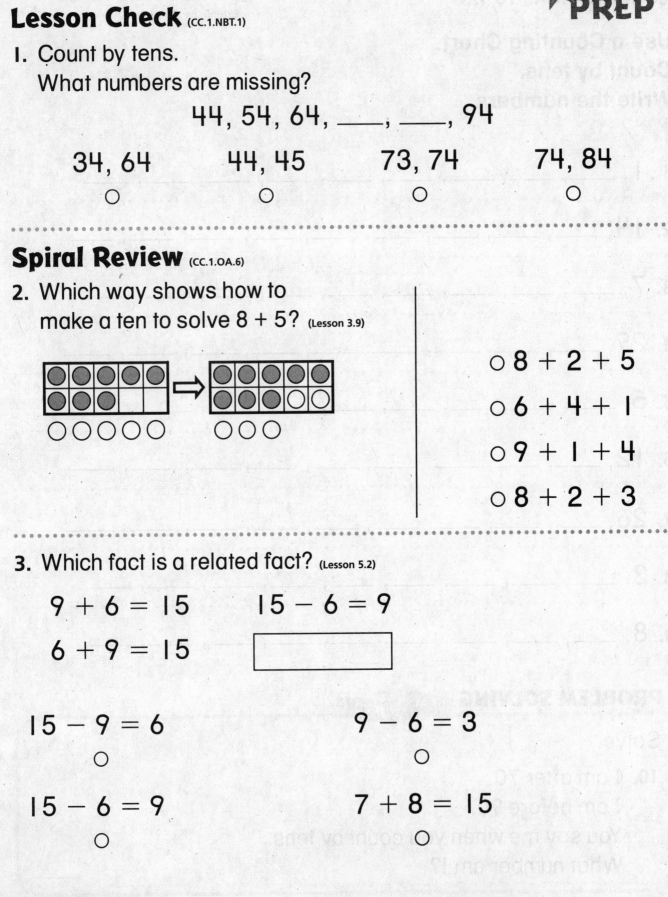

   ○ 8 + 2 + 5

   ○ 6 + 4 + 1

   ○ 9 + 1 + 4

   ○ 8 + 2 + 3

3. Which fact is a related fact? (Lesson 5.2)

   $9 + 6 = 15$ $15 - 6 = 9$

   $6 + 9 = 15$

   $15 - 9 = 6$ $9 - 6 = 3$
   ○   ○

   $15 - 6 = 9$ $7 + 8 = 15$
   ○   ○

Understand Ten and Ones

Use the model. Write the number three different ways.

1.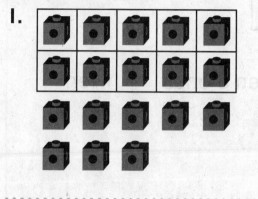

_____ ten _____ ones

_____ + _____

2.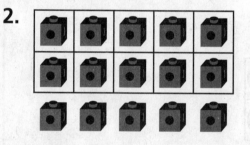

_____ ten _____ ones

_____ + _____

_____

PROBLEM SOLVING

Draw cubes to show the number.
Write the number different ways.

Rob has 7 ones. Nick has 5 ones. They put all their
ones together. What number did they make?

3.

_____ ten _____ ones

_____ + _____

_____

Lesson Check (CC.1.NBT.2b)

I. Which shows the same number?

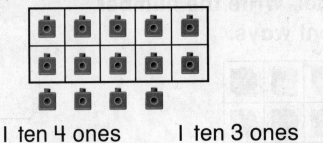

I ten 9 ones   I ten 4 ones   I ten 3 ones   I ten

○   ○   ○   ○

Spiral Review (CC.1.OA.6)

2. What number sentence does this model show? (Lesson 3.7)

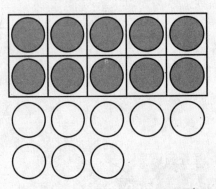

$10 - 8 = 2$ | $10 + 8 = 18$ | $5 + 8 = 13$ | $8 + 2 = 10$

○   ○   ○   ○

3. Which subtraction fact is related to $7 + 5 = 12$? (Lesson 5.3)

$12 - 6 = 6$ | $14 - 8 = 6$ | $12 - 5 = 7$ | $7 - 5 = 2$

○   ○   ○   ○

Make Ten and Ones

COMMON CORE STANDARD CC.1.NBT.2b
Understand place value.

Use ⬜. Make groups of ten
and ones. Draw your work.
Write how many.

1.

14
fourteen

_____ ten _____ ones

2.

12
twelve

_____ ten _____ ones

3.

15
fifteen

_____ ten _____ ones

4.

18
eighteen

_____ ten _____ ones

5.

11
eleven

_____ ten _____ one

PROBLEM SOLVING REAL WORLD

Solve.

6. Tina thinks of a number that has 3 ones and 1 ten.
   What is the number?

_____

Lesson Check (CC.1.NBT.2b)

1. How many tens and ones make this number?

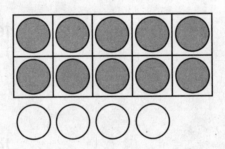

17
seventeen

1 ten 7 ones	1 ten 17 ones	10 tens 7 ones	17 tens
○	○	○	○

Spiral Review (CC.1.OA.1, CC.1.OA.6)

2. What number sentence does this model show? (Lesson 3.7)

$10 - 4 = 6$	$10 + 5 = 15$	$10 + 4 = 14$	$4 + 1 = 5$
○	○	○	○

3. Ben has 17 books. He gives some away. He has 8 left. How many books does he give away? (Lesson 4.6)

7	9	10	17
○	○	○	○

Tens

Use . Make groups of ten.
Write the tens and ones.

COMMON CORE STANDARDS CC.1.NBT.2a,
CC.1.NBT.2c
Understand place value.

I. 90 ones

____ tens = ____ ones

____ tens = ____
ninety

2. 50 ones

____ tens = ____ ones

____ tens = ____
fifty

3. 40 ones

____ tens = ____ ones

____ tens = ____
forty

4. 80 ones

____ tens = ____ ones

____ tens = ____
eighty

PROBLEM SOLVING REAL WORLD

Look at the model. Write the number.

5. What number does the model show?

____

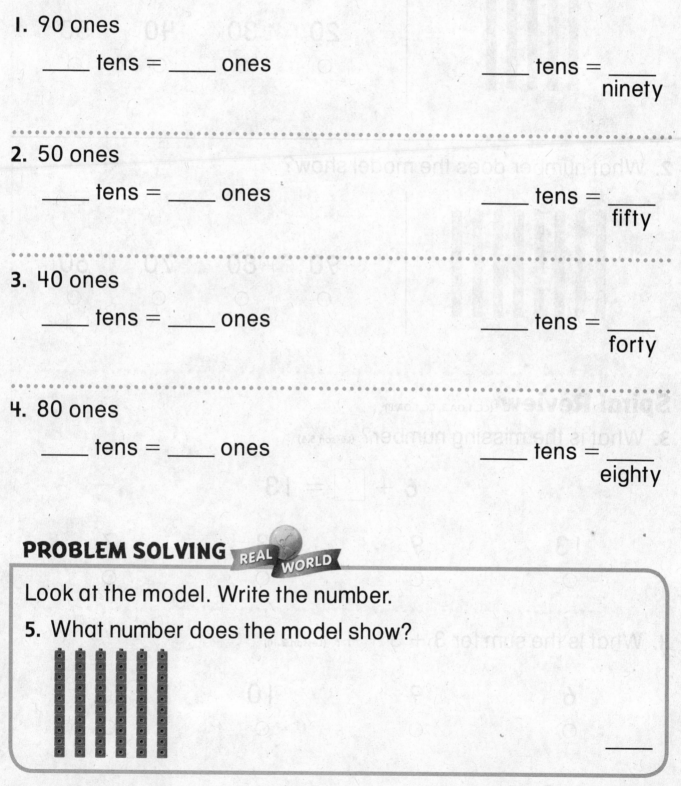

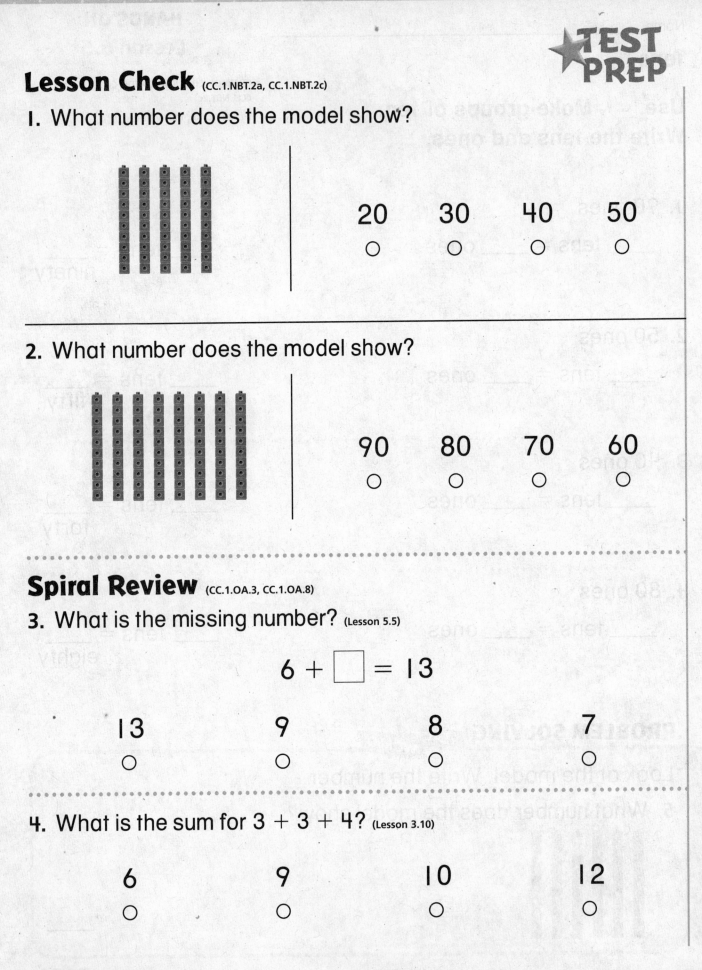

Lesson Check (CC.1.NBT.2a, CC.1.NBT.2c)

1. What number does the model show?

20   30   40   50
○   ○   ○   ○

2. What number does the model show?

90   80   70   60
○   ○   ○   ○

Spiral Review (CC.1.OA.3, CC.1.OA.8)

3. What is the missing number? (Lesson 5.5)

$$6 + \boxed{} = 13$$

13   9   8   7
○   ○   ○   ○

4. What is the sum for $3 + 3 + 4$? (Lesson 3.10)

6   9   10   12
○   ○   ○   ○

Name _____

Tens and Ones to 50

COMMON CORE STANDARD CC.1.NBT.2
Understand place value.

Write the numbers.

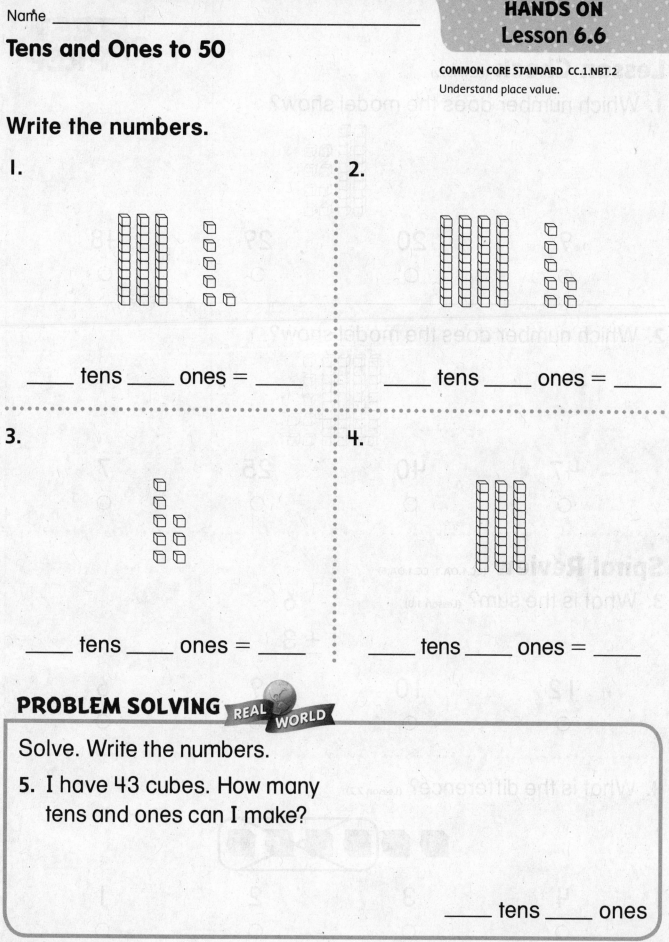

1.

_____ tens _____ ones = _____

2.

_____ tens _____ ones = _____

3.

_____ tens _____ ones = _____

4.

_____ tens _____ ones = _____

PROBLEM SOLVING REAL WORLD

Solve. Write the numbers.

5. I have 43 cubes. How many tens and ones can I make?

_____ tens _____ ones

Lesson Check (CC.1.NBT.2)

1. Which number does the model show?

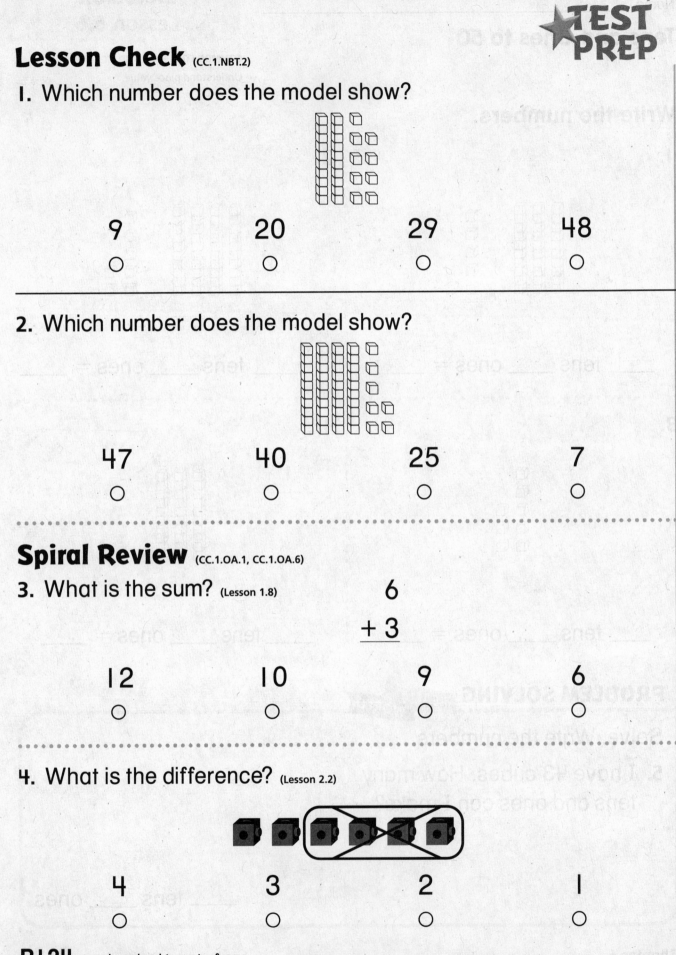

9	20	29	48
○	○	○	○

2. Which number does the model show?

47	40	25	7
○	○	○	○

Spiral Review (CC.1.OA.1, CC.1.OA.6)

3. What is the sum? (Lesson 1.8)

$$\begin{array}{r} 6 \\ +\ 3 \\ \hline \end{array}$$

12	10	9	6
○	○	○	○

4. What is the difference? (Lesson 2.2)

4	3	2	1
○	○	○	○

Name _____

Tens and Ones to 100

COMMON CORE STANDARD CC.1.NBT.2
Understand place value.

Write the numbers.

1.

_____ tens _____ ones = _____

2.

_____ tens _____ ones = _____

3.

_____ tens _____ ones = _____

4.

_____ tens _____ ones = _____

PROBLEM SOLVING

Draw a quick picture to show the number.
Write how many tens and ones there are.

5. Inez has 57 shells.

_____ tens _____ ones

Lesson Check (CC.1.NBT.2)

1. What number has 10 tens 0 ones?

10	20	50	100
○	○	○	○

2. What number does the model show?

11	47	74	77
○	○	○	○

Spiral Review (CC.1.OA.3, CC.1.OA.5)

3. Which shows the same addends in a different order? (Lesson 3.1)

$$6 + 5 = 11$$

$6 + 6 = 12$	$5 + 6 = 11$	$3 + 4 = 7$	$5 + 5 = 10$
○	○	○	○

4. Count on to solve $2 + 6$. (Lesson 3.2)

7	8	9	10
○	○	○	○

Name _____

Problem Solving • Show Numbers in Different Ways

COMMON CORE STANDARDS CC.1.NBT.2a, CC.1.NBT.3
Understand place value.

Use 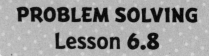 to show the number two different ways. Draw both ways.

1.   62

Tens	Ones

_____ ⃝ _____

2.   38

Tens	Ones

_____ ⃝ _____

3.   47

Tens	Ones

_____ ⃝ _____

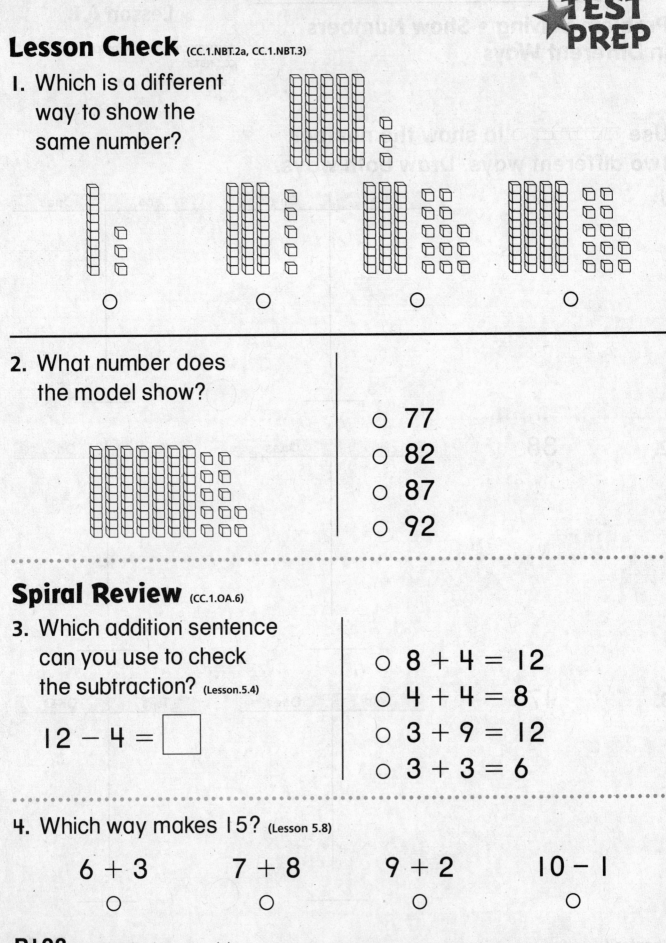

1. Which is a different way to show the same number?

   ○   ○   ○   ○

2. What number does the model show?

   ○ 77
   ○ 82
   ○ 87
   ○ 92

Spiral Review (CC.1.OA.6)

3. Which addition sentence can you use to check the subtraction? (Lesson.5.4)

   $12 - 4 = \boxed{}$

   ○ $8 + 4 = 12$
   ○ $4 + 4 = 8$
   ○ $3 + 9 = 12$
   ○ $3 + 3 = 6$

4. Which way makes 15? (Lesson 5.8)

   $6 + 3$ $7 + 8$ $9 + 2$ $10 - 1$
   ○   ○   ○   ○

Model, Read, and Write Numbers from 100 to 110

COMMON CORE STANDARD CC.1.NBT.1
Extend the counting sequence.

Use 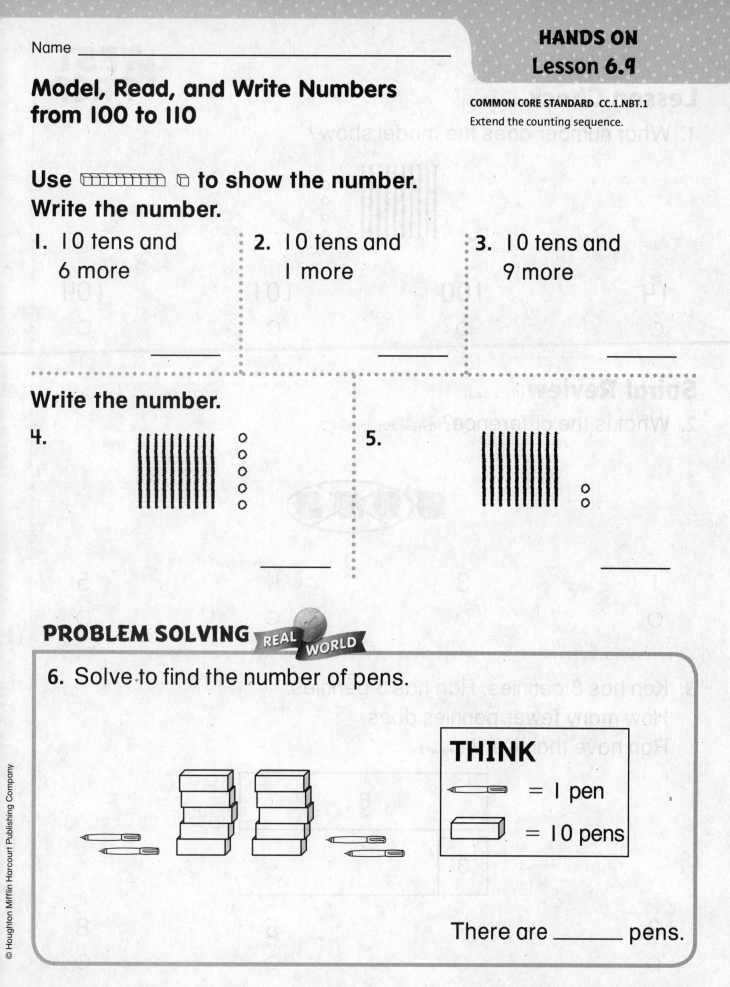 to show the number.
Write the number.

1. 10 tens and
6 more

_____

2. 10 tens and
1 more

_____

3. 10 tens and
9 more

_____

Write the number.

4.

_____

5.

_____

PROBLEM SOLVING REAL WORLD

6. Solve to find the number of pens.

THINK

= 1 pen

= 10 pens

There are _____ pens.

Lesson Check (CC.1.NBT.1)

1. What number does the model show?

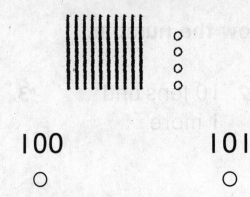

14   100   101   104

○   ○   ○   ○

Spiral Review (CC.1.OA.1)

2. What is the difference? (Lesson 2.2)

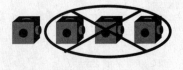

1   3   4   5

○   ○   ○   ○

3. Ken has 8 pennies. Ron has 3 pennies. How many fewer pennies does Ron have than Ken? (Lesson 2.6)

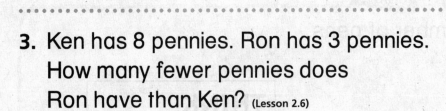

3   4   5   8

○   ○   ○   ○

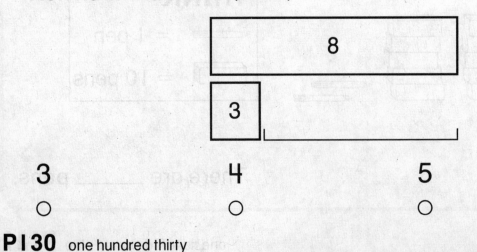

Name _____

Model, Read, and Write Numbers from 110 to 120

COMMON CORE STANDARD CC.1.NBT.1
Extend the counting sequence.

Use 🗆🗆🗆🗆🗆🗆🗆🗆🗆🗆 🗆 to model the number.
Write the number.

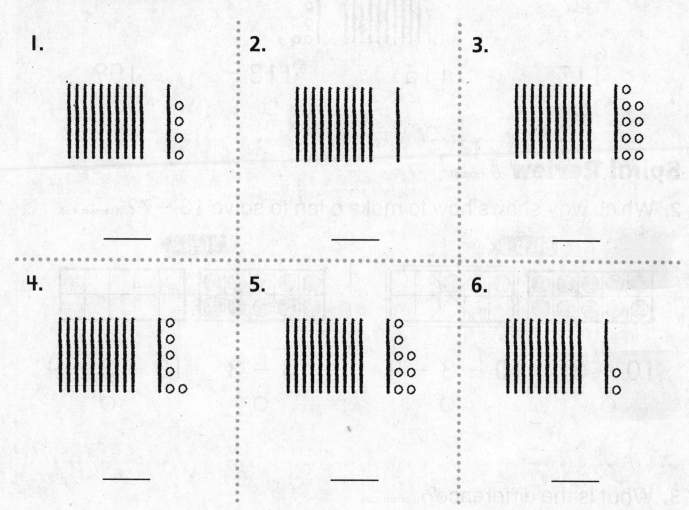

1. _____

2. _____

3. _____

4. _____

5. _____

6. _____

PROBLEM SOLVING REAL WORLD

Choose a way to solve. Draw or write to explain.

7. Dave collects rocks. He makes 12 groups of 10 rocks and has none left over. How many rocks does Dave have?

_____ rocks

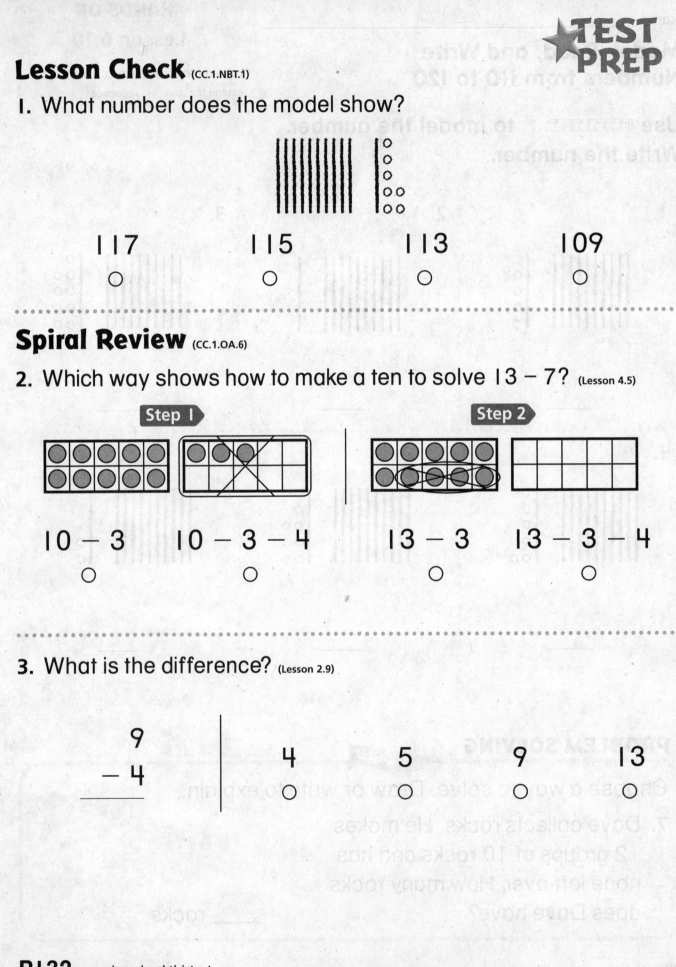

Lesson Check (CC.1.NBT.1)

1. What number does the model show?

117   115   113   109

○   ○   ○   ○

Spiral Review (CC.1.OA.6)

2. Which way shows how to make a ten to solve $13 - 7$? (Lesson 4.5)

Step 1   Step 2

$10 - 3$ $10 - 3 - 4$ $13 - 3$ $13 - 3 - 4$

○   ○   ○   ○

3. What is the difference? (Lesson 2.9)

$$\begin{array}{r} 9 \\ -\ 4 \\ \hline \end{array}$$

4   5   9   13

○   ○   ○   ○

Name _____

Chapter 6 Extra Practice

Lesson 6.1 (pp. 241–244)

Use a Counting Chart. Count forward.
Write the numbers.

1. 32, ____, ____, ____, ____, ____, ____, ____, ____

2. 94, ____, ____, ____, ____, ____, ____, ____, ____

Lesson 6.2 (pp. 245–248)

Use a Counting Chart. Count by tens.
Write the numbers.

1. 33, ____, ____, ____, ____, ____, ____, ____, ____

2. 11, ____, ____, ____, ____, ____, ____, ____, ____

Lesson 6.3 (pp. 249 – 252)

Use the model. Write the number
three different ways.

1.

____ ten ____ ones

____ + ____

____

Lessons 6.4 (pp. 253–256)

Use ⬜. Make groups of ten and ones.
Draw your work. Write how many.

17
seventeen

____ ten ____ ones

Lesson 6.5 (pp. 257–259)

Use 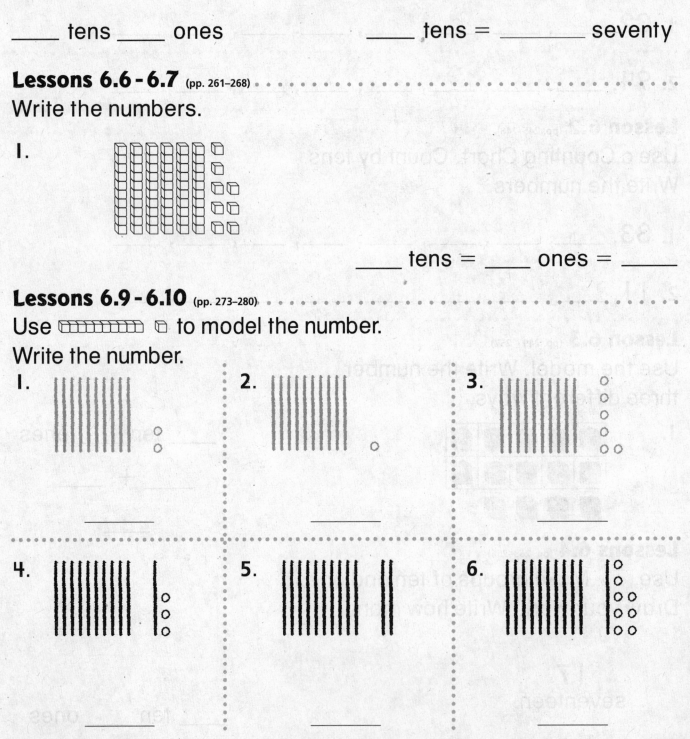. Make groups of ten.
Write the tens and ones.

I. 70 ones

_____ tens _____ ones   _____ tens = _____ seventy

Lessons 6.6 - 6.7 (pp. 261–268)

Write the numbers.

I.

_____ tens = _____ ones = _____

Lessons 6.9 - 6.10 (pp. 273–280)

Use ▭▭▭▭ ▯ to model the number.
Write the number.

1.	2.	3.
_____	_____	_____

4.	5.	6.
_____	_____	_____

School-Home Letter

Dear Family,

My class started Chapter 7 this week. In this chapter, I will compare numbers to show greater than or less than. I will also use <, >, and = to compare numbers.

Love, _____

Vocabulary

is greater than > a symbol used to show that a number is greater than another number

11 > 10
11 is greater than 10

is less than < a symbol used to show that a number is less than another number

10 < 11
10 is less than 11

Home Activity

Make flash cards for the greater than symbol >, and the less than symbol <. Each day, choose two numbers between 1 and 100. Use the flashcards with your child to compare the numbers.

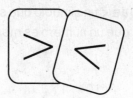

Literature

Look for these books in a library. Use < and > flashcards to compare the groups of objects.

Just Enough Carrots
by Stuart J. Murphy.
HarperTrophy, 1997.

More, Fewer, Less
by Tana Hoban.
Greenwillow, 1998.

Carta
para la casa

Querida familia:

Mi clase comenzó el Capítulo 7 esta semana. En este capítulo, compararé números para mostrar los conceptos de mayor que y menor que. También usaré los símbolos <, >, e = para comparar números.

Con cariño, _____

Vocabulario

es mayor que > un símbolo que se usa para mostrar que un número es mayor que otro número

$$11 > 10$$
11 es mayor que 10

es menor que < un símbolo que se usa para mostrar que un número es menor que otro número

$$10 < 11$$
10 es menor que 11

Actividad para la casa

Haga tarjetas nemotécnicas con el símbolo es mayor que > y el símbolo es menor que <. Cada día, elija dos números entre 1 y 100. Use las tarjetas nemotécnicas con su hijo para comparar los números.

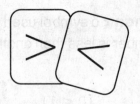

Literatura

Busque estos libros en una biblioteca. Use tarjetas nemotécnicas con < y > para comparar grupos de objetos.

Just Enough Carrots
por Stuart J. Murphy. Harper Collins, 1997.

More, Fewer, Less
por Tana Hoban. Greenwillow, 1998.

Algebra • Greater Than

COMMON CORE STANDARD CC.1.NBT.3
Understand place value.

Use ▭ ▫ if you need to.

Circle the greater number.	Did tens or ones help you decide?	Write the numbers.
1. 22 42	tens ones	____ is greater than ____. ____ > ____
2. 46 64	tens ones	____ is greater than ____. ____ > ____
3. 88 86	tens ones	____ is greater than ____. ____ > ____
4. 92 29	tens ones	____ is greater than ____. ____ > ____

PROBLEM SOLVING REAL WORLD

5. Color the blocks that show numbers greater than 47.

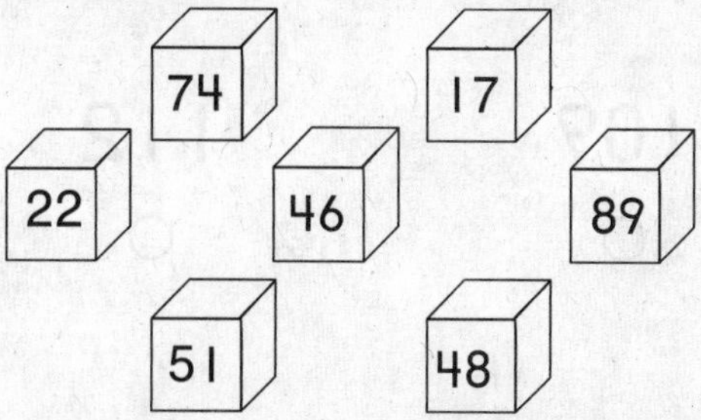

74
17
22
46
89
51
48

Lesson Check (CC.1.NBT.3)

1. Which number is greater than 65?

37 ○   49 ○   56 ○   66 ○

---

2. Which number is greater than 29?

19 ○   20 ○   28 ○   92 ○

- -

Spiral Review (CC.1.OA.6, CC.1.NBT.1)

3. What is 5 + 7? (Lesson 5.10)

8 ○   9 ○   11 ○   12 ○

- -

4. Count forward. What number is missing? (Lesson 6.1)

110, 111, ___, 113, 114

108 ○   109 ○   112 ○   115 ○

Algebra • Less Than

COMMON CORE STANDARD CC.1.NBT.3
Understand place value.

Use ▭▭▭▭▭▭ ▯ if you need to.

Circle the number that is less.	Did tens or ones help you decide?	Write the numbers.
1. 34 36	tens ones	____ is less than ____. ____ < ____
2. 75 57	tens ones	____ is less than ____. ____ < ____
3. 80 89	tens ones	____ is less than ____. ____ < ____
4. 13 31	tens ones	____ is less than ____. ____ < ____

PROBLEM SOLVING REAL WORLD

Write a number to solve.

5. Lori makes the number 74. Gabe makes
a number that is less than 74. What
could be a number Gabe makes?   ____

Lesson Check (CC.1.NBT.3)

1. Which number is less than 52?

25	52	64	88
○	○	○	○

2. Which number is less than 76?

100	81	77	59
○	○	○	○

Spiral Review (CC.1.NBT.1, CC.1.NBT.2)

3. Which number does the model show? (Lesson 6.6)

29	30	37	38
○	○	○	○

4. Count by tens.
What numbers are missing?

(Lesson 6.2)

8, 18, 28, ____, ____, 58

19, 29	27, 39	38, 48	46, 57
○	○	○	○

Algebra • Use Symbols to Compare

COMMON CORE STANDARD CC.1.NBT.3
Understand place value.

Write <, >, or =.
Draw a quick picture if you need to.

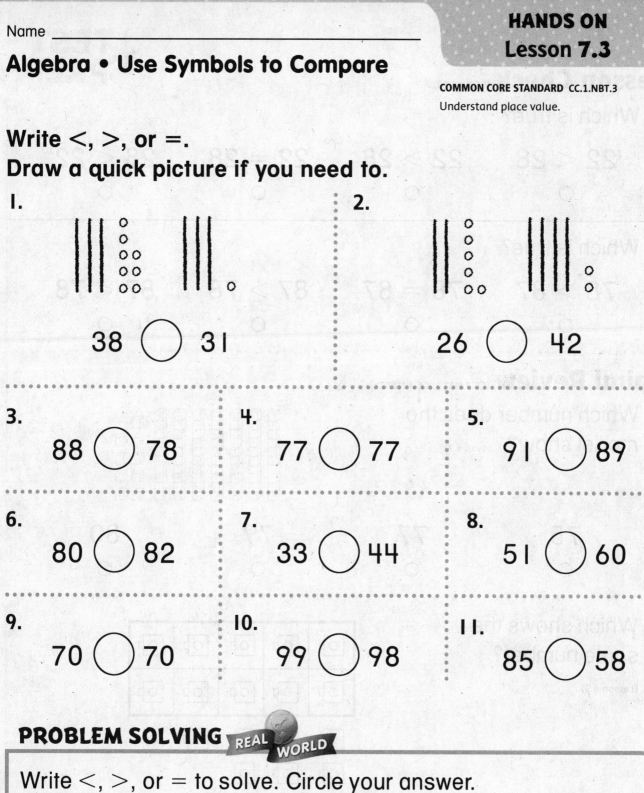

1.

38 ◯ 31

2.

26 ◯ 42

3. 88 ◯ 78

4. 77 ◯ 77

5. 91 ◯ 89

6. 80 ◯ 82

7. 33 ◯ 44

8. 51 ◯ 60

9. 70 ◯ 70

10. 99 ◯ 98

11. 85 ◯ 58

PROBLEM SOLVING REAL WORLD

Write <, >, or = to solve. Circle your answer.

12. Tracey has 26 pennies. Heba has 29 pennies. Who has a greater number of pennies?

Tracey   Heba

29 ◯ 26

Lesson Check (CC.1.NBT.3)

1. Which is true?

   22 < 28   22 > 28   22 = 28   28 < 22

    ○   ○   ○   ○

2. Which is true?

   78 > 87   78 = 87   87 > 78   87 < 78

    ○   ○   ○   ○

Spiral Review (CC.1.NBT.2, CC.1.NBT.2b)

3. Which number does the
model show? (Lesson 6.7)

   75   77   79   80

  ○   ○   ○   ○

4. Which shows the
same number?

(Lesson 6.3)

  1 ten 2 ones   1 ten 3 ones   1 ten 5 ones   1 ten 8 ones

     ○   ○   ○   ○

Problem Solving • Compare Numbers

COMMON CORE STANDARD CC.1.NBT.3
Understand place value.

Make a model to solve.

1. Ava has these number cards. She gives away cards with numbers less than 34 and greater than 38. Which number cards does Ava have now?

| 32 | 33 | 35 | 37 | 39 |

Ava has number cards _____ .

2. Ron has these number cards. He keeps the cards with numbers greater than 60 and less than 56. Circle the number cards Ron keeps.

Ron keeps number cards _____ .

3. Mia has these number cards. She keeps the cards with numbers less than 85 and greater than 88. Circle the cards Mia keeps.

Mia keeps number cards _____ .

Lesson Check (CC.1.NBT.3)

1. Juan crosses out the numbers that are less than 45 and greater than 50. Which numbers are left?

| 43 | 44 | 46 | 49 | 52 |

43 and 44   44 and 46   46 and 49   49 and 52
   ○   ○   ○   ○

Spiral Review (CC.1.OA.5, CC.1.OA.6)

2. Count back 1, 2, or 3.
What is the difference? (Lesson 4.1)

$$9 - 3 = \underline{}$$

5   6   7   9
○   ○   ○   ○

---

3. Which completes the related facts? (Lesson 5.2)

$$4 + 7 = 11 \qquad 11 - 4 = 7$$
$$7 + 4 = 11 \qquad \boxed{}$$

$7 + 7 = 14$ $11 - 7 = 4$ $6 + 5 = 11$ $11 - 5 = 6$
   ○   ○   ○   ○

10 Less, 10 More

COMMON CORE STANDARD CC.1.NBT.5
Use place value understanding and
properties of operations to add
and subtract.

Use mental math.
Complete the chart.

	10 Less		10 More
1.	_____	48	_____
2.	_____	25	_____
3.	_____	73	_____
4.	_____	89	_____
5.	8	_____	_____
6.	_____	_____	47

PROBLEM SOLVING REAL WORLD

Choose a way to solve. Draw or write to show your work.

7. Jim has 16 pennies. Doug
has 10 fewer pennies than
Jim. How many pennies
does Doug have?

_____ pennies

Lesson Check (CC.1.NBT.5)

1. Which number is 10 less than 67?

77 ○   68 ○   66 ○   57 ○

2. Which number is 10 more than 39?

49 ○   40 ○   38 ○   29 ○

Spiral Review (CC.1.NBT.2b, CC.1.NBT.2c)

3. How many tens and ones make this number? (Lesson 6.4)

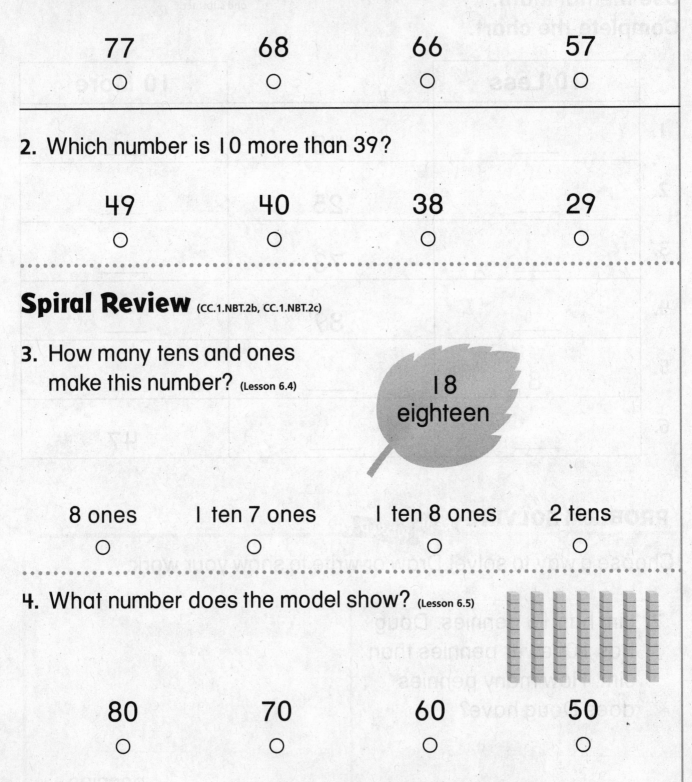

18
eighteen

8 ones ○   1 ten 7 ones ○   1 ten 8 ones ○   2 tens ○

4. What number does the model show? (Lesson 6.5)

80 ○   70 ○   60 ○   50 ○

Chapter 7 Extra Practice

Lesson 7.1 (pp. 289–292)

Use ▭▭▭▭▭▭ ▱ if you need to.

Circle the greater number.	Did tens or ones help you decide?	Write the numbers.
I. 46 34	tens ones	___ is greater than ___. ___ > ___
2. 77 79	tens ones	___ is greater than ___. ___ > ___

Lesson 7.2 (pp. 293 – 296)

Use ▭▭▭▭▭▭ ▱ if you need to.

Circle the number that is less.	Did tens or ones help you decide?	Write the numbers.
I. 23 29	tens ones	___ is less than ___. ___ < ___
2. 64 95	tens ones	___ is less than ___. ___ < ___

Lesson 7.3 (pp. 297–299)

Write <, >, or =.

Draw a quick picture if you need to.

1. 24 ◯ 42

2. 32 ◯ 22

3. 76 ◯ 76

4. 91 ◯ 81

5. 61 ◯ 63

6. 58 ◯ 58

Lesson 7.5 (pp. 305–308)

Use mental math.

Complete the chart.

	10 **Less**		10 **More**
1.	_____	26	_____
2.	_____	75	_____
3.	_____	44	_____

School-Home
Letter

Dear Family,

My class started Chapter 8 this week. In this chapter, I will learn how to add and subtract two-digit numbers.

Love, _____

Vocabulary

ones and tens You can group ones to make tens.

20 ones = 2 tens

Home Activity

Using a jar and pennies, work with your child to add and subtract two-digit numbers. Start with 11 pennies in the jar. Have your child add 13 pennies. Ask your child to explain a way to find the sum of 11 and 13. Then count with your child to find how many pennies in all. Repeat with different quantities each day. Work with your child to subtract numbers as well.

Literature

Reading math stories reinforces ideas. Look for these books in a library and read them with your child.

One Is a Snail, Ten Is a Crab by April Pulley Sayre. Candlewick, 2006.

Safari Park by Stuart J. Murphy. Steck-Vaughn, 2002.

© Houghton Mifflin Harcourt Publishing Company

Carta
para la casa

Querida familia:

Mi clase comenzó el Capítulo 8 esta semana. En este capítulo, aprenderé a sumar y restar números de dos dígitos.

Con cariño, _____

Vocabulario

unidades y decenas Puedes agrupar unidades para formar decenas.

20 unidades = 2 decenas

Actividad para la casa

Con un tarro y centavos, trabaje con su hijo para sumar y restar números de dos dígitos. Comience con 11 monedas de 1¢ en el tarro. Pídale que sume 13 monedas de 1¢. Pídale que explique cómo encontrar la suma de 11 y 13. Luego, cuente con su hijo para saber cuántos centavos hay en total. Repita con diferentes cantidades cada día. Trabaje con él para restar números también.

Literatura

Leer cuentos de matemáticas refuerza las ideas. Busque estos libros en la biblioteca y léalos con su hijo.

One Is a Snail, Ten Is a Crab
por April Pulley Sayre.
Candlewick, 2006.

Safari Park
por Stuart J. Murphy.
Steck-Vaughn, 2002.

Add and Subtract within 20

COMMON CORE STANDARD CC.1.OA.6
Add and subtract within 20.

Add or subtract.

1. 6
   +0

2. 11
   − 2

3. 4
   +5

4. 9
   +8

5. 4
   +10

6. 14
   − 9

7. 7
   +4

8. 8
   −5

9. 12
   − 3

10. 6
    +7

11. 18
    − 9

12. 15
    − 6

13. 6
    +5

14. 12
    − 6

15. 10
    −10

16. 13
    − 7

17. 2
    +7

18. 6
    +4

PROBLEM SOLVING REAL WORLD

Solve. Draw or write to explain.

19. Jesse has 4 shells. He finds some
    more. Now he has 12 shells. How
    many more shells did Jesse find?

_____ more shells

Lesson Check (CC.1.OA.6)

1. What is the sum?

$$8 + 5 = \underline{\hspace{1cm}}$$

3   12   13   16
○   ○   ○   ○

2. What is the difference?

$$11 - 4 = \underline{\hspace{1cm}}$$

6   7   9   15
○   ○   ○   ○

Spiral Review (CC.1.NBT.3)

3. Which number is greater than 43? (Lesson 7.1)

34   40   42   46
○   ○   ○   ○

4. Which number is less than 84? (Lesson 7.2)

94   93   85   69
○   ○   ○   ○

Add Tens

COMMON CORE STANDARD CC.1.NBT.4
Use place value understanding and
properties of operations to add and subtract.

Draw to show tens. Write the sum.
Write how many tens.

1. $10 + 30 =$ _____

_____ tens

2. $30 + 30 =$ _____

_____ tens

3. $60 + 10 =$ _____

_____ tens

4. $20 + 20 =$ _____

_____ tens

5. $30 + 20 =$ _____

_____ tens

6. $10 + 70 =$ _____

_____ tens

PROBLEM SOLVING   REAL WORLD

Draw tens to solve.

7. Drew makes 20 posters. Tia makes
   30 posters. How many posters do
   they make?

_____ posters

8. Regina read 40 pages. Alice
   read 50 pages. How many
   pages did they read?

_____ pages

Lesson Check (CC.1.NBT.4)

1. What is the sum?

$$20 + 30 = \underline{\qquad}$$

60   50   30   10
○   ○   ○   ○

2. What is the sum?

$$30 + 10 = \underline{\qquad}$$

20   30   40   50
○   ○   ○   ○

Spiral Review (CC.1.OA.6, CC.1.NBT.3)

3. Which doubles fact helps you solve $6 + 5 = 11$? (Lesson 3.5)

$3 + 3 = 6$ | $4 + 4 = 8$ | $5 + 5 = 10$ | $7 + 7 = 14$
○   ○   ○   ○

4. Which is **not** true? (Lesson 7.3)

$35 > 30$ $35 < 30$ $30 < 35$ $37 > 36$
○   ○   ○   ○

Name _____

Subtract Tens

COMMON CORE STANDARD CC.1.NBT.6
Use place value understanding and
properties of operations to add and subtract.

Draw to show tens. Write the difference. Write how many tens.

1. $40 - 10 = $ _____

_____ tens

2. $80 - 40 = $ _____

_____ tens

3. $50 - 30 = $ _____

_____ tens

4. $60 - 30 = $ _____

_____ tens

PROBLEM SOLVING REAL WORLD

Draw tens to solve.

5. Mario has 70 baseball cards.
He gives 30 to Lisa.
How many baseball cards
does Mario have left?

_____ baseball cards

Chapter 8

Lesson Check (CC.1.NBT.6)

1. What is the difference?

$$60 - 20 = \underline{\hspace{1cm}}$$

80 ○   50 ○   40 ○   20 ○

2. What is the difference?

$$70 - 30 = \underline{\hspace{1cm}}$$

30 ○   40 ○   50 ○   70 ○

Spiral Review (CC.1.OA.6, CC.1.NBT.3)

3. What is the sum?   (Lesson 3.8)

$$\begin{array}{r} 9 \\ +\,4 \\ \hline \end{array}$$

4 ○   5 ○   6 ○   13 ○

4. Bo crosses out the numbers that are less than 33 and greater than 38. What numbers are left?   (Lesson 7.4)

| 30 | 32 | 36 | 37 | 39 |

30 and 32   32 and 36   36 and 37   37 and 39
○   ○   ○   ○

Use a Hundred Chart to Add

COMMON CORE STANDARD CC.1.NBT.4
Use place value understanding and
properties of operations to add and subtract.

Use the hundred chart to add.
Count on by ones or tens.

1. $47 + 2 = $ _____

2. $26 + 50 = $ _____

3. $22 + 5 = $ _____

4. $40 + 41 = $ _____

5. $4 + 85 = $ _____

1	2	3	4	5	6	7	8	9	10
11	12	13	14	15	16	17	18	19	20
21	22	23	24	25	26	27	28	29	30
31	32	33	34	35	36	37	38	39	40
41	42	43	44	45	46	47	48	49	50
51	52	53	54	55	56	57	58	59	60
61	62	63	64	65	66	67	68	69	70
71	72	73	74	75	76	77	78	79	80
81	82	83	84	85	86	87	88	89	90
91	92	93	94	95	96	97	98	99	100

PROBLEM SOLVING REAL WORLD

Choose a way to solve. Draw or write to show your work.

6. 17 children are on the bus.
Then 20 more children get on
the bus. How many children
are on the bus now?

_____ children

Lesson Check (CC.1.NBT.4)

1. What is 42 + 50?

    47   82
    ○   ○

    92   97
    ○   ○

2. What is 11 + 8?

    19   81
    ○   ○

    91   99
    ○   ○

1	2	3	4	5	6	7	8	9	10
11	12	13	14	15	16	17	18	19	20
21	22	23	24	25	26	27	28	29	30
31	32	33	34	35	36	37	38	39	40
41	42	43	44	45	46	47	48	49	50
51	52	53	54	55	56	57	58	59	60
61	62	63	64	65	66	67	68	69	70
71	72	73	74	75	76	77	78	79	80
81	82	83	84	85	86	87	88	89	90
91	92	93	94	95	96	97	98	99	100

Spiral Review (CC.1.OA.8, CC.1.NBT.5)

3. What number is ten less than 52? (Lesson 7.5)

    50   48   42   41
    ○   ○   ○   ○

4. Which addition fact helps you solve 16 − 9? (Lesson 5.6)

    6 + 9 = 15   9 + 7 = 16
    ○   ○

    8 + 8 = 16   9 + 9 = 18
    ○   ○

Name _____

Use Models to Add

COMMON CORE STANDARD CC.1.NBT.4
Use place value understanding and
properties of operations to add and subtract.

Use  and your MathBoard.
Add the ones or tens. Write the sum.

1. $44 + 5 =$ ____

2. $16 + 70 =$ ____

3. $78 + 20 =$ ____

4. $52 + 7 =$ ____

5. $2 + 13 =$ ____

6. $73 + 4 =$ ____

7. $84 + 3 =$ ____

8. $20 + 25 =$ ____

9. $49 + 30 =$ ____

10. $81 + 8 =$ ____

PROBLEM SOLVING REAL WORLD

Solve. Draw or write to explain.

11. Maria has 21 marbles.
    She buys a bag of 20 marbles.
    How many marbles does
    Maria have now?

____ marbles

Lesson Check (CC.1.NBT.4)

1. What is the sum?

$$62 + 30 = \underline{}$$

11	32	59	92
○	○	○	○

2. What is the sum?

$$37 + 2 = \underline{}$$

49	47	39	25
○	○	○	○

Spiral Review (CC.1.OA.6, CC.1.NBT.1)

3. Which way makes 15? (Lesson 5.8)

$15 + 0$	$15 - 6$	$6 + 8$	$4 + 3 + 3$
○	○	○	○

4. What number does the model show? (Lesson 6.9)

104	103	102	101
○	○	○	○

Name _____

Make Ten to Add

COMMON CORE STANDARD CC.1.NBT.4
Use place value understanding and
properties of operations to add and subtract.

Use ⬜⬜⬜⬜⬜⬜ ⬜. Draw to show how you make a ten. Find the sum.

1. $26 + 5 =$ ___

2. $68 + 4 =$ ___

3. $35 + 8 =$ ___

PROBLEM SOLVING REAL WORLD

Choose a way to solve. Draw or write to show your work.

4. Debbie has 27 markers. Sal has 9 markers. How many markers do they have?

_____ markers

Lesson Check (CC.1.NBT.4)

1. What is 47 + 6?

53 ○   54 ○   56 ○   57 ○

2. What is 84 + 8?

91 ○   92 ○   94 ○   96 ○

Spiral Review (CC.1.OA.7, CC.1.NBT.1)

3. What number does the model show? (Lesson 6.10)

100 ○   104 ○   114 ○   140 ○

4. Which makes the sentence true? (Lesson 5.9)

$$5 + 4 = 10 - \underline{}$$

1 ○   3 ○   4 ○   5 ○

Use Place Value to Add

COMMON CORE STANDARD CC.1.NBT.4
Use place value understanding and
properties of operations to add and subtract.

Draw a quick picture. Use tens and ones to add.

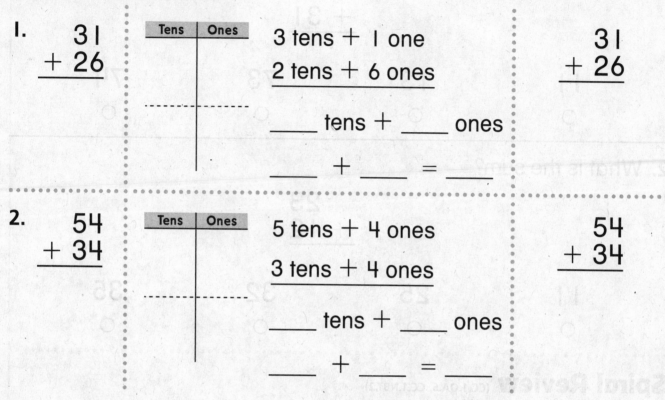

1.
$$\begin{array}{r} 31 \\ + 26 \\ \hline \end{array}$$

Tens	Ones

3 tens + 1 one
2 tens + 6 ones
_____
____ tens + ____ ones
____ + ____ = ____

$$\begin{array}{r} 31 \\ + 26 \\ \hline \end{array}$$

2.
$$\begin{array}{r} 54 \\ + 34 \\ \hline \end{array}$$

Tens	Ones

5 tens + 4 ones
3 tens + 4 ones
_____
____ tens + ____ ones
____ + ____ = ____

$$\begin{array}{r} 54 \\ + 34 \\ \hline \end{array}$$

PROBLEM SOLVING

3. Write two addition sentences you can use
to find the sum. Then solve.

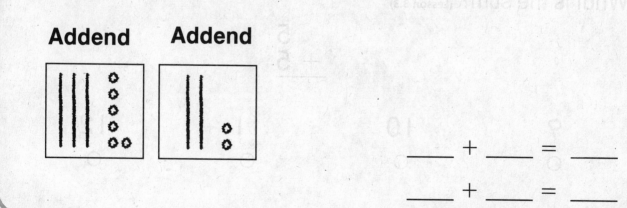

Addend   **Addend**

____ + ____ = ____

____ + ____ = ____

Lesson Check (CC.1.NBT.4)

1. What is the sum?

$$\begin{array}{r} 42 \\ + 31 \\ \hline \end{array}$$

11	13	73	74
○	○	○	○

2. What is the sum?

$$\begin{array}{r} 23 \\ + 12 \\ \hline \end{array}$$

11	25	32	35
○	○	○	○

Spiral Review (CC.1.OA.6, CC.1.NBT.2)

3. What number is the same as 2 tens 8 ones? (Lesson 6.6)

82	28	10	8
○	○	○	○

4. What is the sum? (Lesson 3.3)

$$\begin{array}{r} 5 \\ + 5 \\ \hline \end{array}$$

9	10	11	12
○	○	○	○

Name _____

Problem Solving • Addition Word Problems

COMMON CORE STANDARD CC.1.NBT.4
Use place value understanding and
properties of operations to add and subtract.

Draw and write to solve. Explain your reasoning.

1. Dale saved 19 pennies. Then he found 5 more pennies. How many pennies does Dale have now?

   _____

   _____

   _____

   _____ pennies

2. Jean has 10 fish. She gets 4 more fish. How many fish does she have now?

   _____

   _____

   _____

   _____ fish

3. Courtney buys 2 bags of apples. Each bag has 20 apples. How many apples does she buy?

   _____

   _____

   _____

   _____ apples

4. John bakes 18 blueberry muffins and 12 banana muffins for the bake sale. How many muffins does he bake?

   _____

   _____

   _____

   _____ muffins

Lesson Check (CC.1.NBT.4)

1. Amy has 9 books about dogs.
   She has 13 books about cats.
   How many books does she
   have about dogs and cats?

   20   22   23   25
   ○   ○   ○   ○

Spiral Review (CC.1.OA.3, CC.1.OA.6)

2. What is the sum for $4 + 2 + 4$? (Lesson 3.10)

   12   11   10   9
   ○   ○   ○   ○

3. Which shows a way
   to make a ten to subtract? (Lesson 4.4)

   $$14 - 8 = ?$$

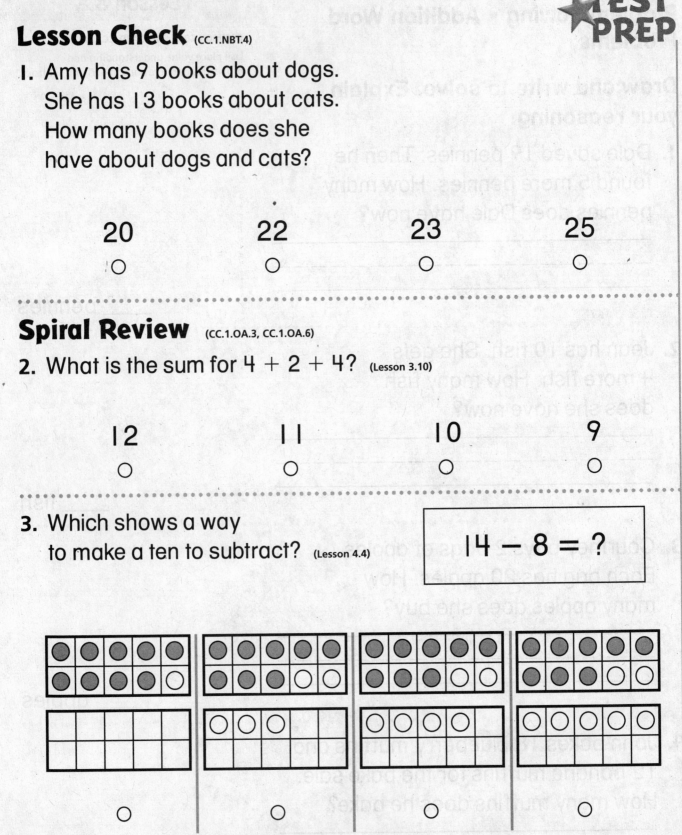

   ○   ○   ○   ○

Practice Addition and Subtraction

COMMON CORE STANDARDS CC.1.NBT.4, CC.1.NBT.6
Use place value understanding and properties of operations to add and subtract.

Add or subtract.

1. $\begin{array}{r} 20 \\ + 20 \\ \hline \end{array}$

2. $\begin{array}{r} 90 \\ - 30 \\ \hline \end{array}$

3. $\begin{array}{r} 52 \\ + 4 \\ \hline \end{array}$

4. $\begin{array}{r} 62 \\ + 21 \\ \hline \end{array}$

5. $\begin{array}{r} 39 \\ - 10 \\ \hline \end{array}$

6. $\begin{array}{r} 8 \\ + 2 \\ \hline \end{array}$

7. $\begin{array}{r} 47 \\ + 34 \\ \hline \end{array}$

8. $\begin{array}{r} 4 \\ - 0 \\ \hline \end{array}$

9. $\begin{array}{r} 49 \\ - 6 \\ \hline \end{array}$

10. $\begin{array}{r} 64 \\ + 30 \\ \hline \end{array}$

11. $\begin{array}{r} 63 \\ + 11 \\ \hline \end{array}$

12. $\begin{array}{r} 37 \\ - 6 \\ \hline \end{array}$

13. $\begin{array}{r} 85 \\ + 13 \\ \hline \end{array}$

14. $\begin{array}{r} 48 \\ + 11 \\ \hline \end{array}$

15. $\begin{array}{r} 76 \\ - 15 \\ \hline \end{array}$

PROBLEM SOLVING REAL WORLD

Solve. Write or draw to explain.

16. Andrew read 17 pages of his book before dinner. He read 9 more pages after dinner. How many pages did he read?

_____ pages

Lesson Check (CC.1.NBT.4)

1. Which is the sum of 20 + 18?

40	38	28	2
○	○	○	○

2. Which is the difference of 90 − 50?

60	50	40	30
○	○	○	○

Spiral Review (CC.1.OA.1, CC.1.OA.6)

3. What number sentence does this model show? (Lesson 3.7)

○ ○ ○

$10 - 3 = 7$
○

$10 + 3 = 13$
○

$5 + 3 = 8$
○

$3 + 1 = 4$
○

4. Mo had some toys. He gave 6 away. Now he has 6 toys. How many toys did Mo start with? (Lesson 4.6)

0	6	10	12
○	○	○	○

COMMON CORE STANDARDS CC.1.OA.6, CC.1.NBT.4, CC.1.NBT.6

Chapter 8 Extra Practice

Lesson 8.1 (pp. 317 – 320)
Add or subtract.

1. $10 + 3 = $ _____

2. $16 - 9 = $ _____

Lessons 8.2 - 8.3 (pp. 321 – 327)
Draw to show tens. Write the sum or difference. Write how many tens.

1. $30 + 60 = $ _____

2. $70 - 20 = $ _____

_____ tens

_____ tens

Lesson 8.4 (pp. 329 – 332)
Use the hundred chart to add. Count on by ones or tens.

1. $81 + 6 = $ _____

2. $75 + 20 = $ _____

3. $30 + 42 = $ _____

1	2	3	4	5	6	7	8	9	10
11	12	13	14	15	16	17	18	19	20
21	22	23	24	25	26	27	28	29	30
31	32	33	34	35	36	37	38	39	40
41	42	43	44	45	46	47	48	49	50
51	52	53	54	55	56	57	58	59	60
61	62	63	64	65	66	67	68	69	70
71	72	73	74	75	76	77	78	79	80
81	82	83	84	85	86	87	88	89	90
91	92	93	94	95	96	97	98	99	100

Lesson 8.5 (pp. 333 – 336)

Use ▱▱▱▱▱▱▱▱ ⬚ and your MathBoard.
Add the ones or tens.
Write the sum.

1. $35 + 30 = \underline{\hphantom{00}}$

2. $3 + 71 = \underline{\hphantom{00}}$

3. $44 + 5 = \underline{\hphantom{00}}$

4. $20 + 11 = \underline{\hphantom{00}}$

Lessons 8.6 - 8.7 (pp. 337 – 344)

Write the sum.

1. $56 + 8 = \underline{\hphantom{00}}$

2. $5 + 27 = \underline{\hphantom{00}}$

3. $13 + 7 = \underline{\hphantom{00}}$

4. $33 + 9 = \underline{\hphantom{00}}$

5. $6 + 64 = \underline{\hphantom{00}}$

6.
$$\begin{array}{r} 61 \\ + 29 \\ \hline \end{array}$$

7.
$$\begin{array}{r} 73 \\ + 18 \\ \hline \end{array}$$

Lesson 8.9 (pp. 349 – 352)

Add or subtract.

1. $16 - 8 = \underline{\hphantom{00}}$

2. $35 + 53 = \underline{\hphantom{00}}$

3.
$$\begin{array}{r} 48 \\ - 5 \\ \hline \end{array}$$

4.
$$\begin{array}{r} 10 \\ + 80 \\ \hline \end{array}$$

5.
$$\begin{array}{r} 79 \\ - 9 \\ \hline \end{array}$$

6.
$$\begin{array}{r} 3 \\ - 3 \\ \hline \end{array}$$

School-Home
Letter

Dear Family,

My class started Chapter 9 this week. In this chapter, I will learn about measurement. I will use length to compare, order, and measure objects. I will also use time to tell time to the hour and half hour.

Love, _____

Vocabulary

hour

half hour

Home Activity

Cut strips of paper in varying lengths and place them in random order on a table. Have children put the strips of paper in order from longest to shortest.

Literature

Look for these books in a library.

How Big Is a Foot?
Rolf Myller.
Dell Yearling, 1991.

Super Sand Castle Saturday
Stuart J. Murphy.
HarperTrophy, 1999.

Carta
para la casa

Querida familia:

Mi clase comenzó el Capítulo 9 esta semana. En este capítulo, aprenderé sobre medidas. Usaré la longitud para comparar, ordenar y medir objetos. También usaré el tiempo para decir la hora y la media hora.

Con cariño, _____

Vocabulario

hora

media hora

Actividad para la casa

Corte tiras de papel que tengan una longitud variada y colóquelas sobre una mesa en orden aleatorio. Pídales a los niños que pongan las tiras de papel en orden, de la más larga a la más corta.

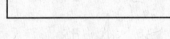

Literatura

Busque estos libros en una biblioteca.

How Big Is a Foot?
por Rolf Myller.
Dell Yearling, 1991.

Sábado de super castillos
por Stuart J. Murphy.
HarperTrophy, 1998.

Order Length

COMMON CORE STANDARD CC.1.MD.1
Measure lengths indirectly and by
iterating length units.

Draw three pencils in order from shortest to longest.

1. shortest

2.

3. longest

Draw three markers in order from longest to shortest.

4. longest

5.

6. shortest

PROBLEM SOLVING REAL WORLD

Solve.

7. Fred has the shortest
toothbrush in the bathroom.
Circle Fred's toothbrush.

Lesson Check (CC.1.MD.1)

1. Which line is the longest?

○
○
○
○

2. Which paintbrush is the shortest?

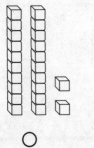

○
○
○
○

Spiral Review (CC.1.NBT.2a, CC.1.NBT.3)

3. Which is a different way
to show the same number? (Lesson 6.8)

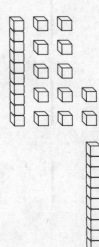

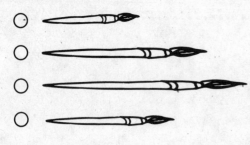

○   ○   ○   ○

Indirect Measurement

COMMON CORE STANDARD CC.1.MD.1
Measure lengths indirectly and by
iterating length units.

**Read the clues. Write shorter or
longer to complete the sentence.
Then draw to prove your answer.**

1. Clue 1: A yarn is longer than a ribbon.

Clue 2: The ribbon is longer than a crayon.

So, the yarn is _____ than the crayon.

yarn |

ribbon |

crayon |

PROBLEM SOLVING REAL WORLD

Solve. Draw or write to explain.

2. Megan's pencil is shorter
than Tasha's pencil.

Tasha's pencil is shorter
than Kim's pencil.

Is Megan's pencil shorter or
longer than Kim's pencil?

_____

Lesson Check (CC.1.MD.1)

1. A black line is longer than the gray line. The gray line is longer than a white line. Which is correct?

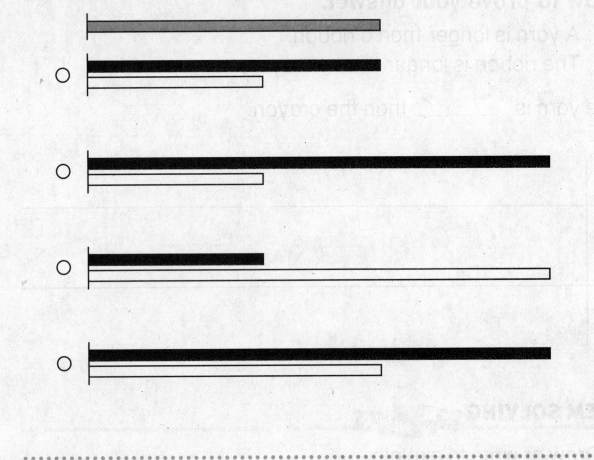

....

Spiral Review (CC.1.NBT.4)

2. What is the sum? (Lesson 8.4)

$$42 + 20 = \underline{\quad}$$

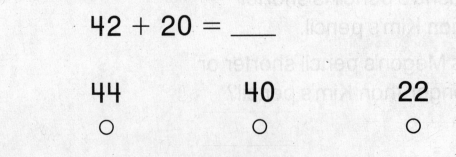

62	44	40	22
○	○	○	○

P176 one hundred seventy-six

Name _____

Use Nonstandard Units to Measure Length

COMMON CORE STANDARD CC.1.MD.2
Measure lengths indirectly and by iterating length units.

Use real objects. Use 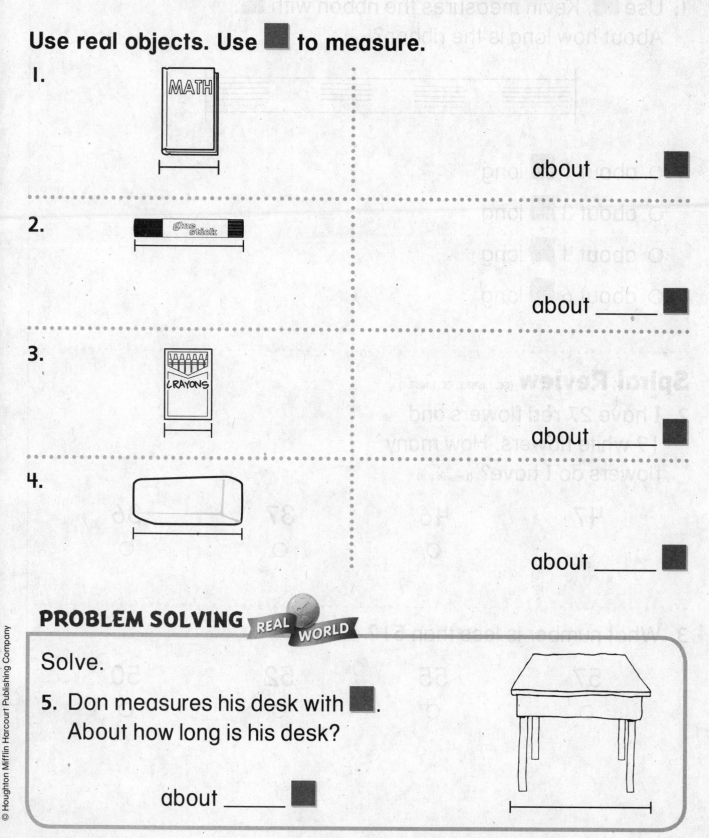 to measure.

1.

about _____ ▪

2.

about _____ ▪

3.

about _____ ▪

4.

about _____ ▪

PROBLEM SOLVING REAL WORLD

Solve.

5. Don measures his desk with ▪.
About how long is his desk?

about _____ ▪

Lesson Check (CC.1.MD.2)

1. Use ■. Kevin measures the ribbon with ■.
   About how long is the ribbon?

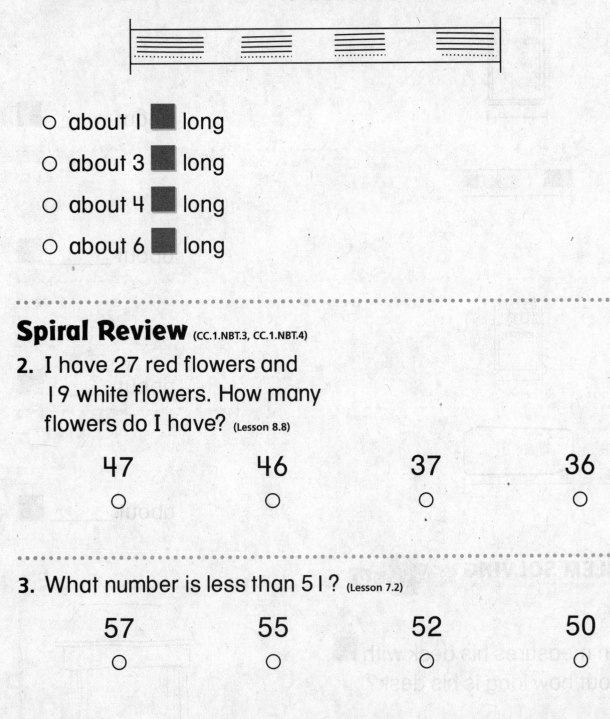

- ○ about 1 ■ long
- ○ about 3 ■ long
- ○ about 4 ■ long
- ○ about 6 ■ long

Spiral Review (CC.1.NBT.3, CC.1.NBT.4)

2. I have 27 red flowers and
   19 white flowers. How many
   flowers do I have? (Lesson 8.8)

   47   46   37   36
   ○   ○   ○   ○

3. What number is less than 51? (Lesson 7.2)

   57   55   52   50
   ○   ○   ○   ○

Make a Nonstandard Measuring Tool

COMMON CORE STANDARD CC.1.MD.2
Measure lengths indirectly and by
iterating length units.

Use the measuring tool you made.
Measure real objects.

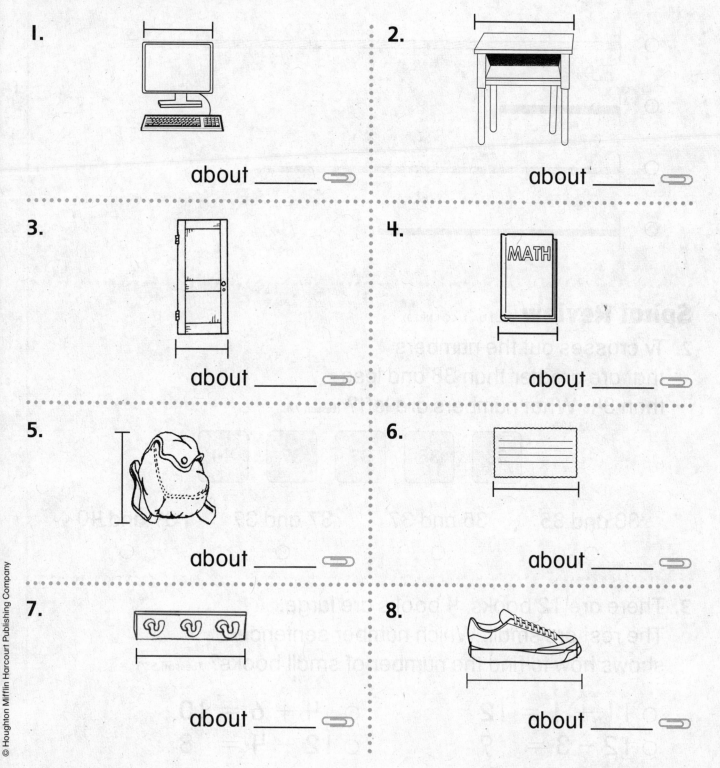

1.

about _____

2.

about _____

3.

about _____

4.

MATH

about _____

5.

about _____

6.

about _____

7.

about _____

8.

about _____

Lesson Check (CC.1.MD.2)

1. Use the ⬭ below. Which string is about 4 ⬭ long?

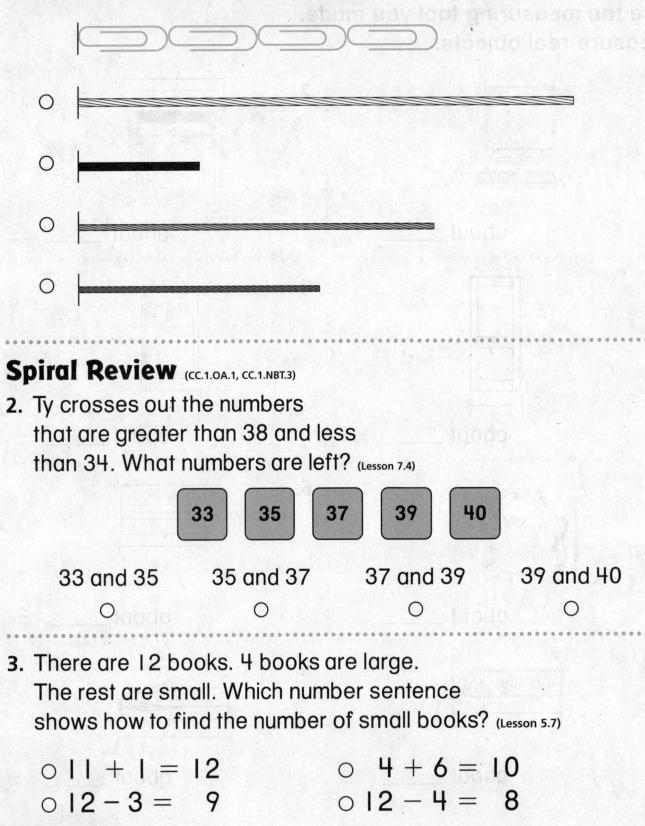

○

○

○

○

Spiral Review (CC.1.OA.1, CC.1.NBT.3)

2. Ty crosses out the numbers that are greater than 38 and less than 34. What numbers are left? (Lesson 7.4)

| 33 | 35 | 37 | 39 | 40 |

33 and 35   35 and 37   37 and 39   39 and 40
    ○   ○   ○   ○

3. There are 12 books. 4 books are large. The rest are small. Which number sentence shows how to find the number of small books? (Lesson 5.7)

○ 11 + 1 = 12   ○ 4 + 6 = 10
○ 12 − 3 = 9   ○ 12 − 4 = 8

Problem Solving • Measure and Compare

COMMON CORE STANDARD CC.1.MD.2
Measure lengths indirectly and by
iterating length units.

The blue string is about 3 ⚬ long.
The green string is 2 ⚬ longer than the blue
string. The red string is 1 ⚬ shorter than the
blue string. Measure and draw the strings in
order from **longest** to **shortest**.

1. |

about ____ ⚬

2. |

about ____ ⚬

3. |

about ____ ⚬

PROBLEM SOLVING REAL WORLD

4. Sandy has a ribbon about 4 ⚬ long.
   She cut a new ribbon 2 ⚬ longer.
   Measure and draw the two ribbons.

   |
   |

The new ribbon is about ____ ⚬ long.

Lesson Check (CC.1.MD.2)

1. Mia measures a stapler with her paper clip ruler. About how long is the stapler?

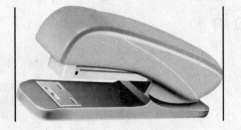

about 2 ⊂⊃   about 5 ⊂⊃   about 7 ⊂⊃   about 20 ⊂⊃

○   ○   ○   ○

Spiral Review (CC.1.OA.6, CC.1.NBT.1)

2. What is the missing number? (Lesson 8.1)

$$4 + 9 = \underline{\hspace{1cm}}$$

13   9   8   4

○   ○   ○   ○

3. Count by tens. What numbers are missing? (Lesson 6.2)

17, 27, ____, ____, 57, 67

77, 87   28, 29   37, 38   37, 47

○   ○   ○   ○

Time to the Hour

COMMON CORE STANDARD CC.1.MD.3
Tell and write time.

Look at where the hour hand points. Write the time.

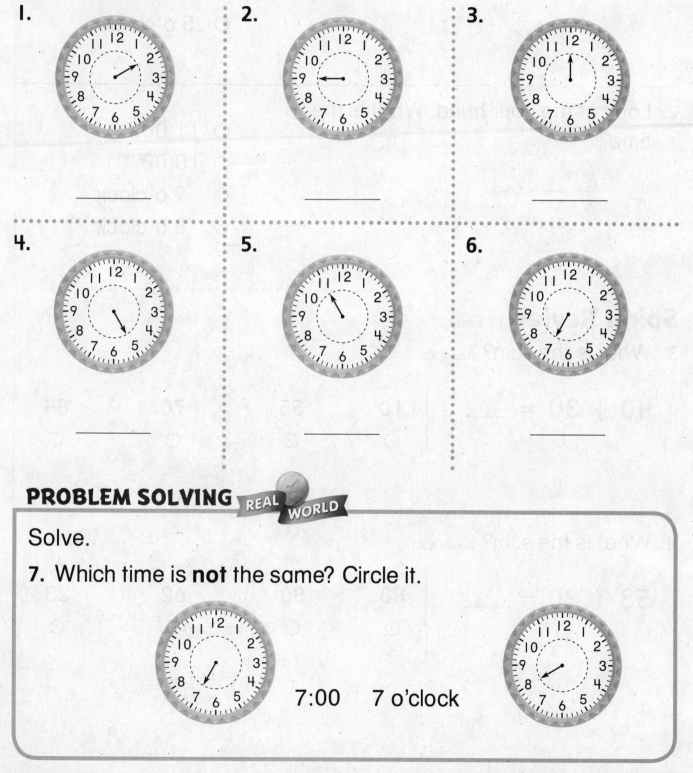

1.

_____

2.

_____

3.

_____

4.

_____

5.

_____

6.

_____

PROBLEM SOLVING REAL WORLD

Solve.

7. Which time is **not** the same? Circle it.

7:00   7 o'clock

Lesson Check (CC.1.MD.3)

1. Look at the hour hand. What is the time?

- ○ 2:00
- ○ 3:00
- ○ 4 o'clock
- ○ 5 o'clock

2. Look at the hour hand. What is the time?

- ○ 11:00
- ○ 10:00
- ○ 9 o'clock
- ○ 8 o'clock

Spiral Review (CC.1.NBT.4)

3. What is the sum? (Lesson 8.2)

$40 + 30 =$ ___

10	55	70	84
○	○	○	○

4. What is the sum? (Lesson 8.5)

$53 + 30 =$ ___

83	80	62	23
○	○	○	○

Time to the Half Hour

COMMON CORE STANDARD CC.1.MD.3
Tell and write time.

Look at where the hour hand points.
Write the time.

1.

_____

- - - - - - - - - - - - - -

2.

_____

- - - - - - - - - - - - - -

3.

_____

- - - - - - - - - - - - - -

4.

_____

- - - - - - - - - - - - - -

5.

_____

- - - - - - - - - - - - - -

6.

_____

- - - - - - - - - - - - - -

PROBLEM SOLVING REAL WORLD

Solve.

7. Greg rides his bike at half
   past 4:00. He eats dinner
   at half past 6:00. He reads
   a book at half past 8:00.

   Look at the clock.
   Write what Greg does.

   Greg _____.

   _____

   - - - - - - - - - - -

Lesson Check (CC.1.MD.3)

1. Look at the hour hand. What is the time?

- ○ 5:00
- ○ half past 5:00
- ○ 6:00
- ○ half past 6:00

2. Look at the hour hand. What is the time?

- ○ 10:00
- ○ half past 10:00
- ○ half past 9:00
- ○ 9:00

Spiral Review (CC.1.NBT.1, CC.1.NBT.2b)

3. What number does the model show? (Lesson 6.9)

102	103	107	113
○	○	○	○

4. How many tens and ones make this number? (Lesson 6.4)

14
fourteen

2 tens 4 ones	1 ten 5 ones	1 ten 4 ones	1 ten 2 ones
○	○	○	○

Tell Time to the Hour and Half Hour

COMMON CORE STANDARD CC.1.MD.3
Tell and write time.

Write the time.

1.

2.

3.

4.

5.

6.

PROBLEM SOLVING REAL WORLD

Solve.

7. Lulu walks her dog at
7 o'clock. Bill walks
his dog 30 minutes later.
Draw to show what time Bill
walks his dog.

Lesson Check (CC.1.MD.3)

1. What time is it?

- ○ 6:30
- ○ 7:00
- ○ 7:30
- ○ 8:30

2. What time is it?

- ○ 12:00
- ○ 2:00
- ○ 2:30
- ○ 3:30

Spiral Review (CC.1.NBT.4)

3. What is the sum? (Lesson 8.4)

$$48 + 20 = \underline{\quad}$$

- ○ 69
- ○ 68
- ○ 60
- ○ 28

4. How many tens and ones are in the sum? (Lesson 8.7)

$$\begin{array}{r} 67 \\ + 25 \\ \hline \end{array}$$

- ○ 9 tens 2 ones
- ○ 8 tens 7 ones
- ○ 8 tens 2 ones
- ○ 4 tens 2 ones

Practice Time to the Hour and Half Hour

COMMON CORE STANDARD CC.1.MD.3
Tell and write time.

**Use the hour hand to write the time.
Draw the minute hand.**

1.

2.

3.

4.

5.

6.

PROBLEM SOLVING REAL WORLD

Solve.

7. Billy played outside for a half hour.
Write how many minutes Billy
played outside.

_____ minutes

Lesson Check (CC.1.MD.3)

1. Which clock shows 11:00?

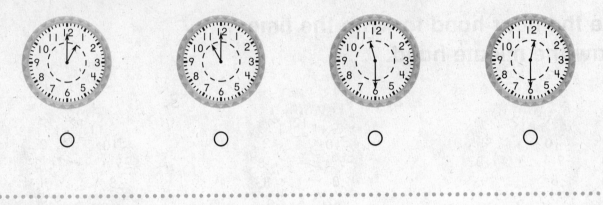

○   ○   ○   ○

Spiral Review (CC.1.NBT.6, CC.1.MD.2)

2. What is the difference? (Lesson 8.3)

$$80 - 30 = \underline{\quad}$$

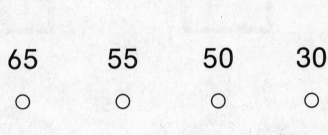

65	55	50	30
○	○	○	○

3. Use . Amy measures the eraser with ■.
About how long is the eraser? (Lesson 9.3)

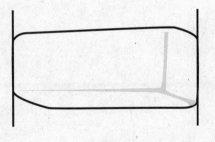

○ about 1 ■ long

○ about 2 ■ long

○ about 3 ■ long

○ about 4 ■ long

COMMON CORE STANDARDS CC.1.MD.1, CC.1.MD.2, CC.1.MD.3

Chapter 9 Extra Practice

Lesson 9.1 (pp. 369–372) ·

Draw three paint brushes in order
from **shortest** to **longest**.

I.   shortest

· ·

· ·

longest

Lesson 9.2 (pp. 373–376) ·

Read the clues. Write **shorter** or **longer**
to complete the sentence. Then draw to
prove your answer.

I. Clue I: A gray line is longer than a white line.
   Clue 2: A white line is longer than a black line.

So, the gray line is _____ than the black line.

black	
white	
gray	

Lesson 9.3 (pp. 377–380) ·

Use real objects. Use ■ to measure.

I.

about _____ ■

Lesson 9.4 (pp. 381–384)

Use the measuring tool you made.
Measure real objects.

I.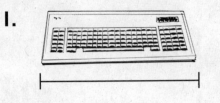

about _____ ⬭

Lessons 9.6 – 9.7 (pp. 389–396)

Look at where the hour hand points. Write the time.

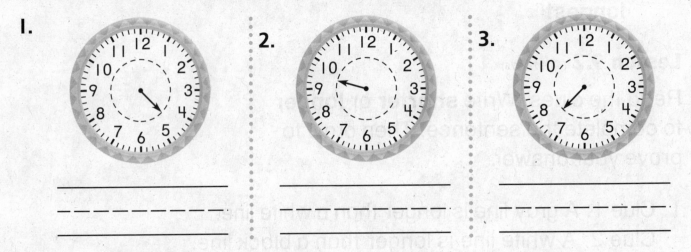

I.

2.

3.

_____

_ _ _ _ _ _ _ _ _ _

_____

Lessons 9.8 – 9.9 (pp. 397–404)

Write the time.

I.

2.

3.

School-Home Letter

Dear Family,

My class started Chapter 10 this week. In this chapter, I will show data with tally charts and graphs. I will also ask and answer questions about the charts and graphs.

Love, _____

Vocabulary

bar graph a graph that uses bars to show information

picture graph a graph that uses pictures to show information

tally chart a chart that uses tally marks to record information

tally mark a line that stands for one person or thing

Home Activity

Help your child keep track of the weather on a calendar for a week or longer. Then help your child use the data to make a picture graph. Use the graph to compare the number of days that were sunny, cloudy, and rainy.

Weather This Week						
sunny	○	○	○	○		
cloudy	○	○	○			
raniy	○					

Each ○ stands for 1 day.

Literature

Look for these books in a library. These books will reinforce your child's understanding of data and graphs.

The Great Graph Contest by Loreen Leedy. Holiday House, 2006.

Graphing Favorite Things by Jennifer Marrewa. Weekly Reader® Books, 2008.

Carta
para la casa

Querida familia:

Mi clase comenzó el Capítulo 10 esta semana. En este capítulo, mostraré datos con tablas de conteo y gráficas. También haré y responderé preguntas sobre tablas y gráficas.

Con cariño, _____

Vocabulario

gráfica de barras una gráfica que utiliza barras para mostrar información

pictografía una gráfica que utiliza dibujos para mostrar información

tabla de conteo una tabla que utiliza marcas para registrar información

marca de conteo una línea que representa una persona o una cosa

Actividad para la casa

Ayude a su hijo para que siga el clima usando un calendario durante una semana o más. Luego ayude a su hijo para que use los datos para hacer una pictografía. Usen la gráfica para comparar el número de días soleados, nublados y lluviosos.

Weather This Week						
sunny	○	○	○	○		
cloudy	○	○	○			
rainy	○					

Cada ○ representa 1 diá.

Literatura

Busque estos libros en una biblioteca. Estos libros reforzarán el aprendizaje de su hijo sobre datos y gráficas.

The Great Graph Contest por Loreen Leedy. Holiday House, 2006.

Graphing Favorite Things por Jennifer Marrewa. Weekly Reader® Books, 2008. Albert Whitman and Company, 1993.

Read Picture Graphs

COMMON CORE STANDARD CC.1.MD.4
Represent and interpret data.

Our Favorite Outdoor Activity

	biking	𝟃	𝟃	𝟃	𝟃	𝟃	𝟃	𝟃	𝟃
	skating	𝟃	𝟃						
	running	𝟃	𝟃	𝟃	𝟃				

Each 𝟃 stands for 1 child.

Use the picture graph to answer the question.

1. How many children chose 🚲?

   _____ children

2. How many children chose 🛹 and 🏃 altogether?

   _____ children

3. Which activity did the most children choose? Circle.

   🚲   🛹   🏃

PROBLEM SOLVING REAL WORLD

Write a number sentence to solve the problem.
Use the picture graph at the top of the page.

4. How many more children chose 🚲 than 🏃?

   _____ more children

   ___ ◯ ___ ◯ ___

Lesson Check (CC.1.MD.4)

Use the picture graph to answer the question.

Do you do chores at home?								
yes	☺	☺	☺	☺	☺	☺	☺	☺
no	☺	☺	☺	☺	☺	☺		

Each ☺ stands for 1 child.

1. How many children do chores at home?

   2 children   6 children   8 children   14 children
   ○   ○   ○   ○

2. How many more children answered yes
   than no?

   2 more   6 more   8 more   16 more
   ○   ○   ○   ○

Spiral Review (CC.1.NBT.1, CC.1.NBT.5)

3. What number is ten less than 82? (Lesson 7.5)

   92   83   81   72
   ○   ○   ○   ○

4. Count forward. What number is missing? (Lesson 6.1)

   110, 111, 112, _____, 114

   100   113   114   115
   ○   ○   ○   ○

Name _____

Make Picture Graphs

COMMON CORE STANDARD CC.1.MD.4
Represent and interpret data.

**Which dinosaur do the most children like best? Ask 10 friends.
Draw 1 circle for each child's answer.**

Our Favorite Dinosaur									
Tyrannosaurus									
Triceratops									
Apatosaurus									

Each ○ stands for 1 child.

Use the picture graph to answer the question.

1. How many children chose 🦖 ?

   _____ children

2. How many children chose 🦕 and 🦕 altogether?

   _____ children

3. Which dinosaur did the fewest children choose? Circle.

4. Which dinosaur did the most children choose? Circle.

PROBLEM SOLVING REAL WORLD

5. Write your own question about the graph.

_____

_____

_____

_____

Lesson Check (CC.1.MD.4)

Use the picture graph to answer the question.

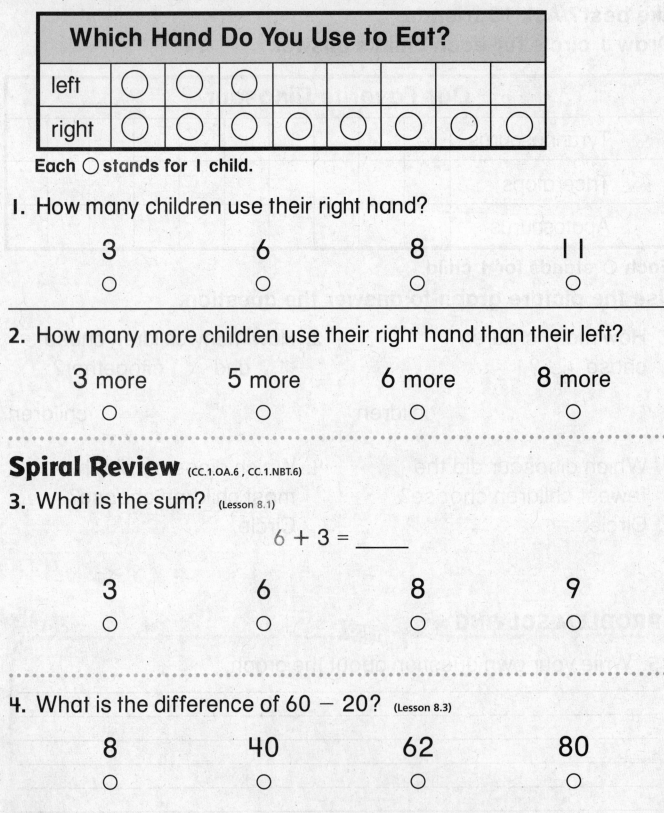

Which Hand Do You Use to Eat?								
left	○	○	○					
right	○	○	○	○	○	○	○	○

Each ○ stands for 1 child.

1. How many children use their right hand?

   3   6   8   11
   ○   ○   ○   ○

2. How many more children use their right hand than their left?

   3 more   5 more   6 more   8 more
   ○   ○   ○   ○

Spiral Review (CC.1.OA.6 , CC.1.NBT.6)

3. What is the sum? (Lesson 8.1)

   6 + 3 = ____

   3   6   8   9
   ○   ○   ○   ○

4. What is the difference of 60 − 20? (Lesson 8.3)

   8   40   62   80
   ○   ○   ○   ○

Read Bar Graphs

COMMON CORE STANDARD CC.1.MD.4
Represent and interpret data.

Use the bar graph to answer the question.

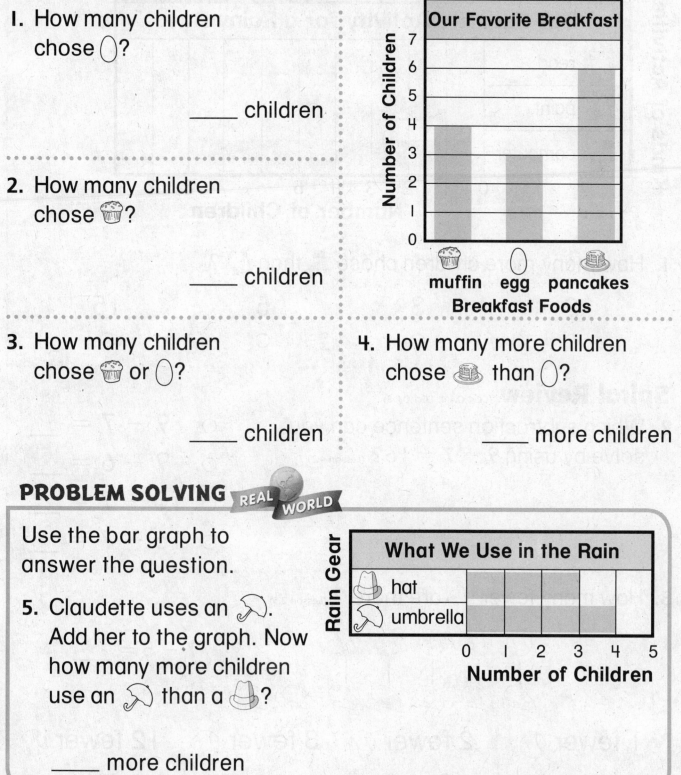

1. How many children chose ⬭?

   _____ children

2. How many children chose 🧁?

   _____ children

3. How many children chose 🧁 or ⬭?

   _____ children

4. How many more children chose 🥞 than ⬭?

   _____ more children

Our Favorite Breakfast

Breakfast Foods: muffin egg pancakes

PROBLEM SOLVING REAL WORLD

Use the bar graph to answer the question.

5. Claudette uses an ☂. Add her to the graph. Now how many more children use an ☂ than a 🎩?

   _____ more children

What We Use in the Rain

Rain Gear: hat, umbrella

Number of Children

Lesson Check (CC.1.MD.4)

Use the bar graph to answer the question.

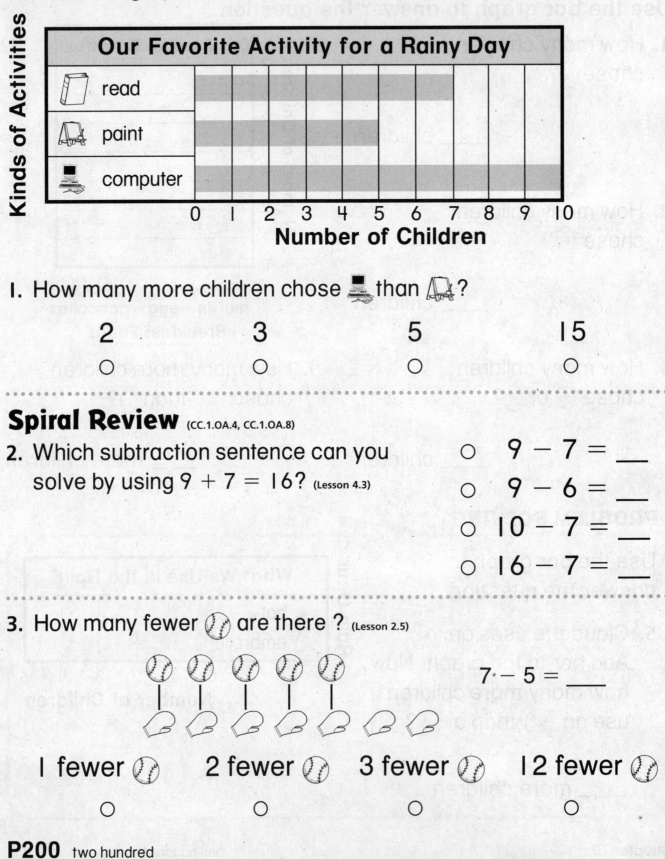

1. How many more children chose 🖥 than 📖?

   2   3   5   15

   ○   ○   ○   ○

Spiral Review (CC.1.OA.4, CC.1.OA.8)

2. Which subtraction sentence can you solve by using 9 + 7 = 16? (Lesson 4.3)

   ○ 9 − 7 = ___

   ○ 9 − 6 = ___

   ○ 10 − 7 = ___

   ○ 16 − 7 = ___

3. How many fewer ⚾ are there ? (Lesson 2.5)

   7 − 5 = ___

   1 fewer ⚾   2 fewer ⚾   3 fewer ⚾   12 fewer ⚾

   ○   ○   ○   ○

Make Bar Graphs

COMMON CORE STANDARD CC.1.MD.4
Represent and interpret data.

Which is your favorite meal?

1. Ask 10 friends which meal they like best.
Make a bar graph.

2. How many children chose
breakfast?

_____ children

3. Which meal was chosen by
the most children?

_____

PROBLEM SOLVING REAL WORLD

4. What if 10 children chose breakfast?
How many children could choose lunch or dinner?

_____ children

Lesson Check (CC.1.MD.4)

Use the bar graph to answer the question.

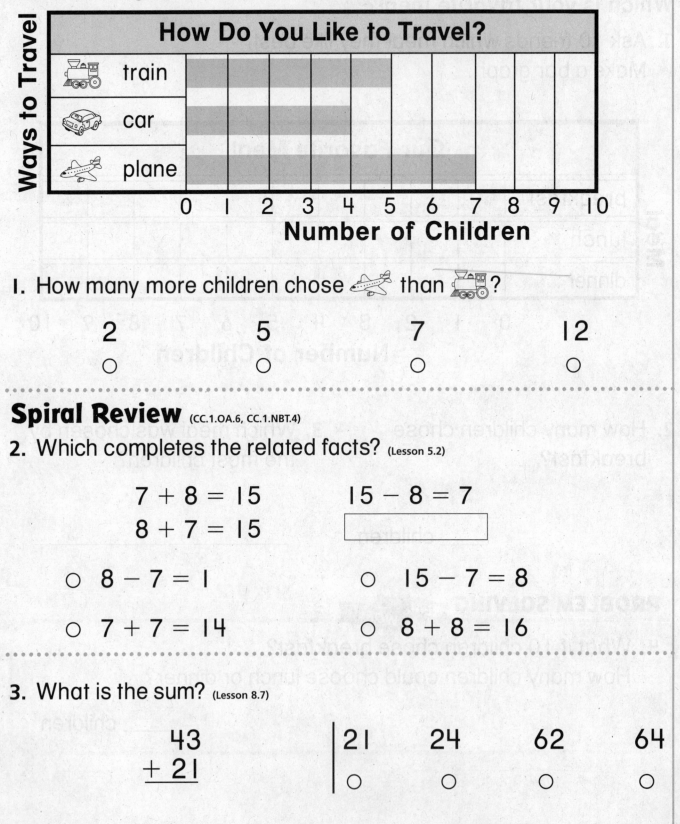

1. How many more children chose ✈ than 🚂?

   2   5   7   12
   ○   ○   ○   ○

···

Spiral Review (CC.1.OA.6, CC.1.NBT.4)

2. Which completes the related facts? (Lesson 5.2)

$$7 + 8 = 15 \qquad\quad 15 - 8 = 7$$
$$8 + 7 = 15 \qquad\quad \boxed{}$$

   ○ $8 - 7 = 1$ ○ $15 - 7 = 8$

   ○ $7 + 7 = 14$ ○ $8 + 8 = 16$

···

3. What is the sum? (Lesson 8.7)

$$\begin{array}{r} 43 \\ + 21 \\ \hline \end{array}$$

   21   24   62   64
   ○   ○   ○   ○

Read Tally Charts

COMMON CORE STANDARD CC.1.MD.4
Represent and interpret data.

Complete the tally chart.

Our Favorite Vegetable		Total
beans	IIII	
corn	IIIII III	
carrots	IIIII	

Use the tally chart to answer each question.

1. How many children chose 🥕 ? _____ children

2. How many children chose 🫘 ? _____ children

3. How many more children chose 🌽 than 🥕 ? _____ more children

4. Which vegetable did the most children choose? Circle.

PROBLEM SOLVING REAL WORLD

Complete each sentence about the tally chart.
Write **greater than**, **less than**, or **equal to**.

5. The number of children who chose 🫘 is _____ the number who chose 🥕 .

6. The number of children who chose 🌽 is _____ the number who chose 🫘 .

Lesson Check (CC.1.MD.4)

Use the tally chart to answer each question.

Our Favorite Pet	
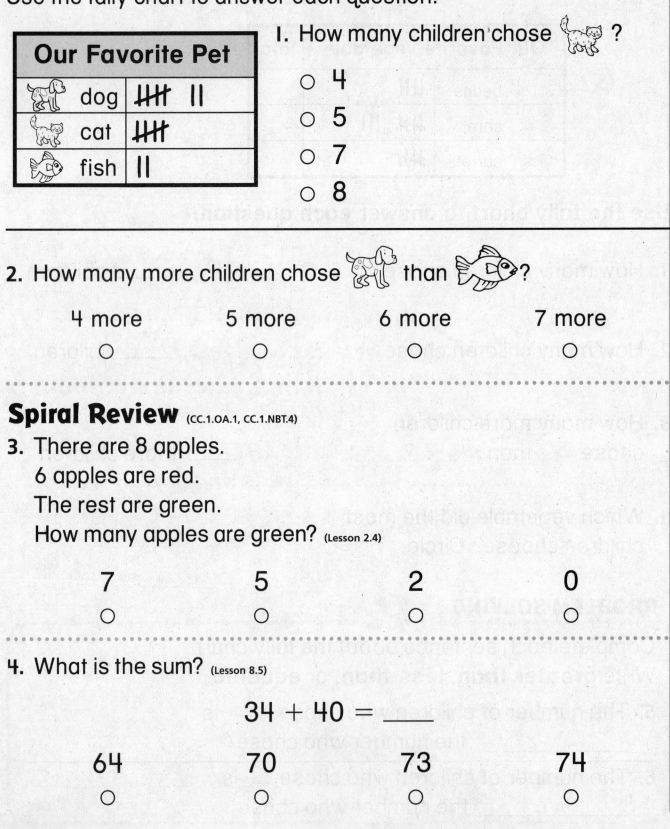 dog	IIII II
cat	IIII
fish	II

1. How many children chose 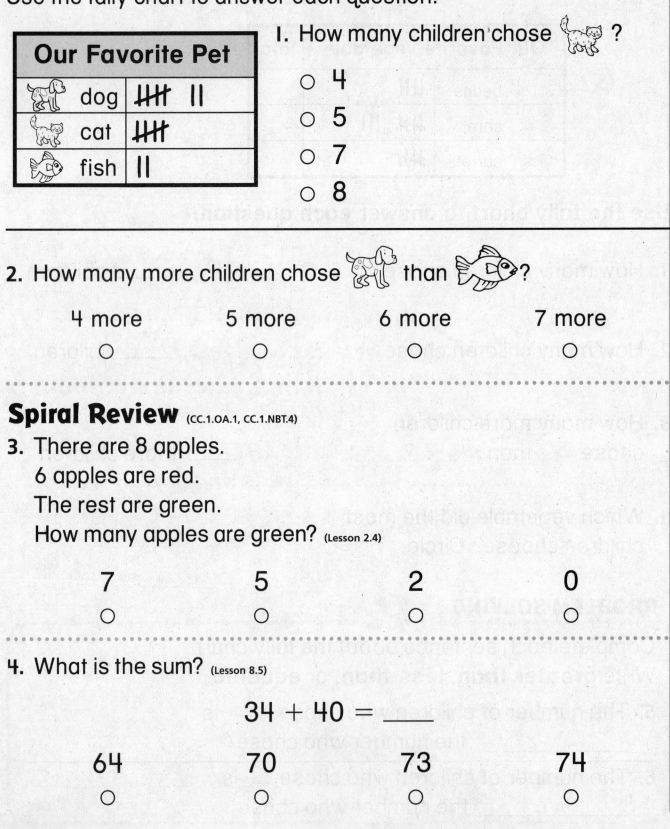 ?

   ○ 4
   ○ 5
   ○ 7
   ○ 8

2. How many more children chose 🐕 than 🐟 ?

   4 more   5 more   6 more   7 more
   ○   ○   ○   ○

Spiral Review (CC.1.OA.1, CC.1.NBT.4)

3. There are 8 apples.
   6 apples are red.
   The rest are green.
   How many apples are green? (Lesson 2.4)

   7   5   2   0
   ○   ○   ○   ○

4. What is the sum? (Lesson 8.5)

   $$34 + 40 = \underline{\hspace{1cm}}$$

   64   70   73   74
   ○   ○   ○   ○

Make Tally Charts

COMMON CORE STANDARD CC.1.MD.4
Represent and interpret data.

Which color do most children like best? Ask 10 friends. Make 1 tally mark for each child's answer.

Favorite Color		Total
red		
blue		

1. How many children chose red?

    _____ children

2. How many children chose blue?

    _____ children

3. Circle the color that was chosen by fewer children.

    red   blue

PROBLEM SOLVING 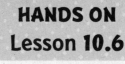 REAL WORLD

Jason asked 10 friends to choose their favorite game. He will ask 10 more children.

Our Favorite Game	
tag	I
kickball	⊞II
hopscotch	II

4. Predict. Which game will children most likely choose?

    _____

5. Predict. Which game will children least likely choose?

    _____

Lesson Check (CC.1.MD.4)

1. Which insect did the most children choose?

Our Favorite Insect		Total
ladybug	III	3
bee	I	I
butterfly	HHH II	7

○   ○   ○   ○

Spiral Review (CC.1.NBT.2b, CC.1.NBT.3)

2. Which number is greater than 54? (Lesson 7.1)

45   50   54   57

○   ○   ○   ○

3. Which shows the same number? (Lesson 6.3)

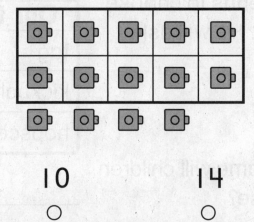

4   10   14   41

○   ○   ○   ○

Problem Solving • Represent Data

PROBLEM SOLVING
Lesson 10.7

COMMON CORE STANDARD CC.1.MD.4
Represent and interpret data.

Bella made a tally chart to show the favorite sport of 10 friends.

Our Favorite Sport	
Soccer	ⅢⅠ I
Basketball	III
Baseball	I

Use the tally chart to make a bar graph.

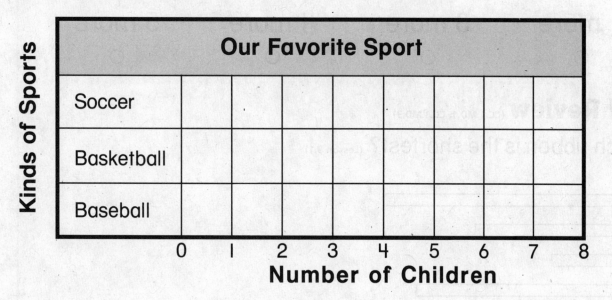

Kinds of Sports

Our Favorite Sport								
Soccer								
Basketball								
Baseball								

0 1 2 3 4 5 6 7 8
Number of Children

Use the graph to solve.

1. How many friends chose soccer?

_____ friends

2. How many friends chose soccer or basketball?

_____ friends

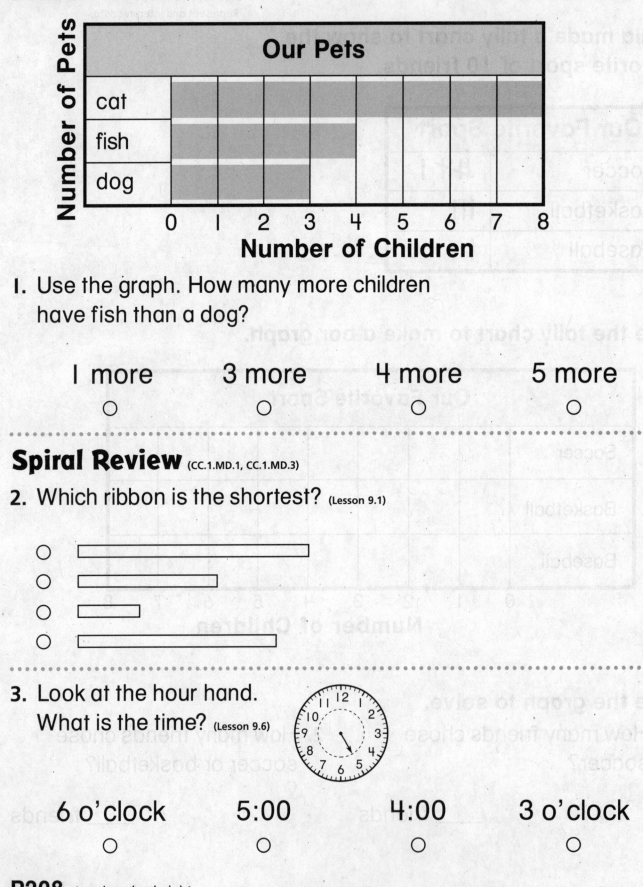

Our Pets

Number of Pets

cat

fish

dog

0 1 2 3 4 5 6 7 8

Number of Children

1. Use the graph. How many more children have fish than a dog?

1 more	3 more	4 more	5 more
○	○	○	○

Spiral Review (CC.1.MD.1, CC.1.MD.3)

2. Which ribbon is the shortest? (Lesson 9.1)

○ ▭

○ ▭

○ ▭

○ ▭

3. Look at the hour hand. What is the time? (Lesson 9.6)

6 o'clock	5:00	4:00	3 o'clock
○	○	○	○

Name _____

Chapter 10 Extra Practice

Lessons 10.1 – 10.2 (pp. 413–420)

Use the picture graph to answer the question.

What We Read Last Night							
picture book	☺	☺	☺	☺	☺		
chapter book	☺	☺	☺	☺			
comic book	☺	☺	☺	☺	☺	☺	☺

Each ☺ stands for 1 child.

1. How many children read 📖 last night? _____ children

2. Which book did the most children read? Circle. 📖 📖 📖

Lesson 10.3 (pp. 421–424)

Use the bar graph to answer the question.

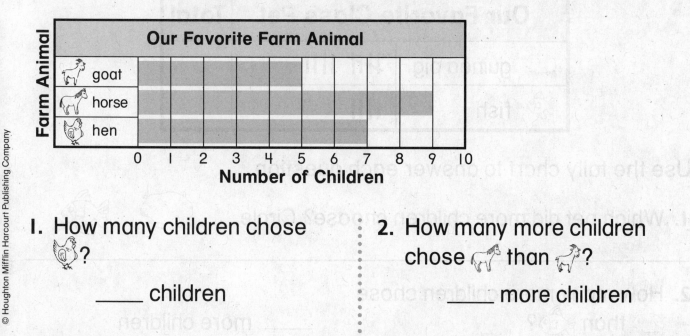

1. How many children chose 🐔?

_____ children

2. How many more children chose 🐴 than 🐐?

_____ more children

Lesson 10.4 (pp. 425–427) . . . .

Ask 10 friends which toy they like best.

1. Make a bar graph.

Our Favorite Toy											
🐰 toy rabbit											
🧩 puzzle											
⚾ baseball											

Toy

0 1 2 3 4 5 6 7 8 9 10
Number of Children

2. Which toy did the most children choose? Circle.

3. How many children chose 🐰? _____ children

Lessons 10.5 – 10.6 (pp. 429–436) . . . .

Complete the tally chart.

Our Favorite Class Pet		Total
🐹 guinea pig	~~IIII~~ IIII	
🐟 fish	IIII	

Use the tally chart to answer each question.

1. Which pet did more children choose? Circle. 🐹 🐟

_____

2. How many more children chose
🐹 than 🐟? _____ more children

P210 two hundred ten

School-Home Letter

Dear Family,

My class started Chapter 11 this week. In this chapter, I will learn about three-dimensional shapes. I will learn how to make objects and larger shapes from other shapes.

Love, _____

Vocabulary Builder

flat surface

curved surface

Home Activity

Use a paper towel roll (cylinder), a tennis ball (sphere), a cube-shaped box or building block (cube), and a book (rectangular prism). Build objects using these or other household items of the same shapes. Have children name each shape used in the objects you make.

Literature

Look for these books in a library. Point out shapes and how they can be found in everyday objects.

The Greedy Triangle
Marilyn Burns. Scholastic, 2008.

Captain Invincible and the Space Shapes
Stuart J. Murphy. HarperCollins Publishers, 2001.

Carta para la casa

Querida familia:

Mi clase comenzó el Capítulo 11 esta semana. En este capítulo, aprenderé sobre las guras tridimensionales. Aprenderé a hacer objetos y guras más grandes tomando como base otras guras.

Con cariño, _____

Vocabulario

superficie plana

superficie curva

Actividad para la casa

Use un rollo de papel (cilindro), una pelota de tenis (esfera), una caja con forma de cubo o un bloque de construcción (cubo) y un libro (prisma rectangular). Construya objetos usando estas u otras cosas con formas similares que encuentre en la casa. Pídale a su hijo que nombre cada figura usada en los objetos que usted haga.

Literatura

Busque estos libros en una biblioteca. Señale las figuras y muestre a su hijo cómo las puede encontrar en los objetos que ve a diario.

The Greedy Triangle
por Marilyn Burns. Scholastic, 2008.

Captain Invincible and the Space Shapes
por Stuart J. Murphy. HarperCollins Publishers, 2001.

Three-Dimensional Shapes

COMMON CORE STANDARD CC.1.G.1
Reason with shapes and their attributes.

Use three-dimensional shapes.
Write the number of flat surfaces for each shape.

1. A cylinder has ___ flat surfaces.

2. A rectangular prism has ___ flat surfaces.

3. A cone has ___ flat surface.

4. A cube has ___ flat surfaces.

PROBLEM SOLVING REAL WORLD

5. Circle the object that matches the clue.
   Mike finds an object that has only a curved surface.

Lesson Check (CC.1.G.1)

1. Which shape has both flat and curved surfaces?

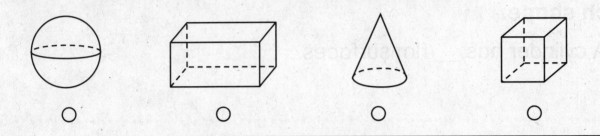

○   ○   ○   ○

2. Which shape has only a curved surface?

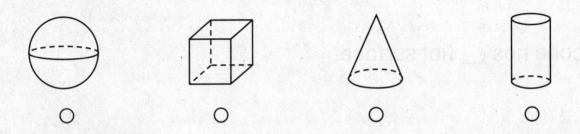

○   ○   ○   ○

Spiral Review (CC.1.OA.1, CC.1.NBT.1)

3. Count forward. What number is missing? (Lesson 6.1)

109, 110, 111, ____, 113

107   108   112   117

○   ○   ○   ○

4. What is the sum of 2 and 3? (Lesson 1.2)

1   4   5   6

○   ○   ○   ○

Combine Three-Dimensional Shapes

COMMON CORE STANDARD CC.1.G.2
Reason with shapes and their attributes.

Use three-dimensional shapes.

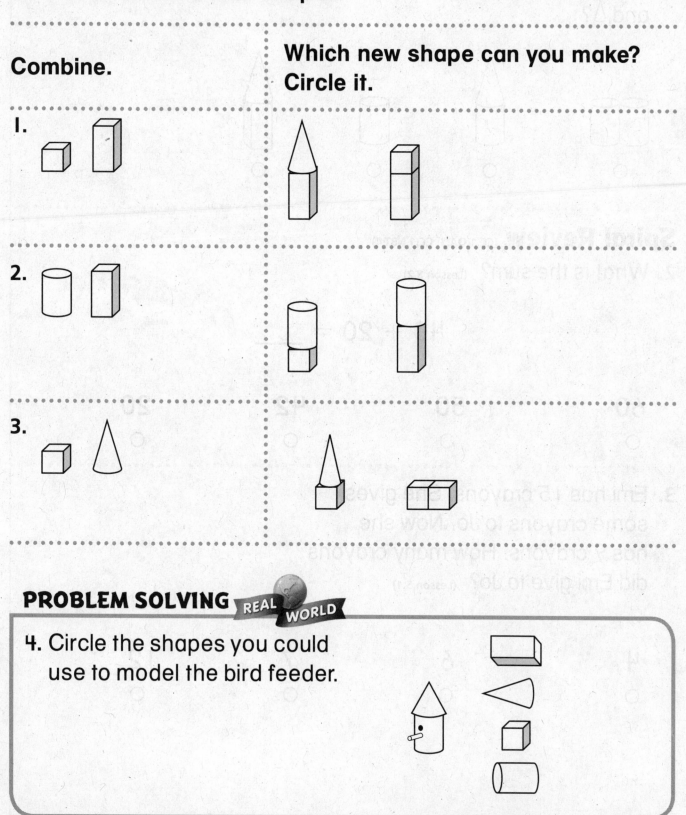

Combine.

**Which new shape can you make?
Circle it.**

1.

2.

3.

PROBLEM SOLVING REAL WORLD

4. Circle the shapes you could
   use to model the bird feeder.

Lesson Check (CC.1.G.2)

1. Which shape combines ▯ and △?

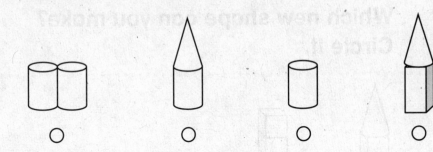

○   ○   ○   ○

. . . .

Spiral Review (CC.1.OA.1, CC.1.NBT.4)

2. What is the sum? (Lesson 8.2)

$$40 + 20 = \underline{\quad}$$

60   50   42   20
○   ○   ○   ○

. . . .

3. Emi has 15 crayons. She gives some crayons to Jo. Now she has 9 crayons. How many crayons did Emi give to Jo? (Lesson 5.1)

4   6   7   12
○   ○   ○   ○

Make New Three-Dimensional Shapes

COMMON CORE STANDARD CC.1.G.2
Reason with shapes and their attributes.

Use three-dimensional shapes.

Build and Repeat.	**Combine. Which new shape can you make? Circle it.**
1. 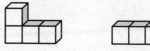	
2.	
3.	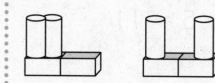

PROBLEM SOLVING REAL WORLD

4. Dave builds this shape.
   Then he repeats and combines.
   Draw a shape he can make.

Lesson Check (CC.1.G.2)

1. Which new shape can you make?

Combine 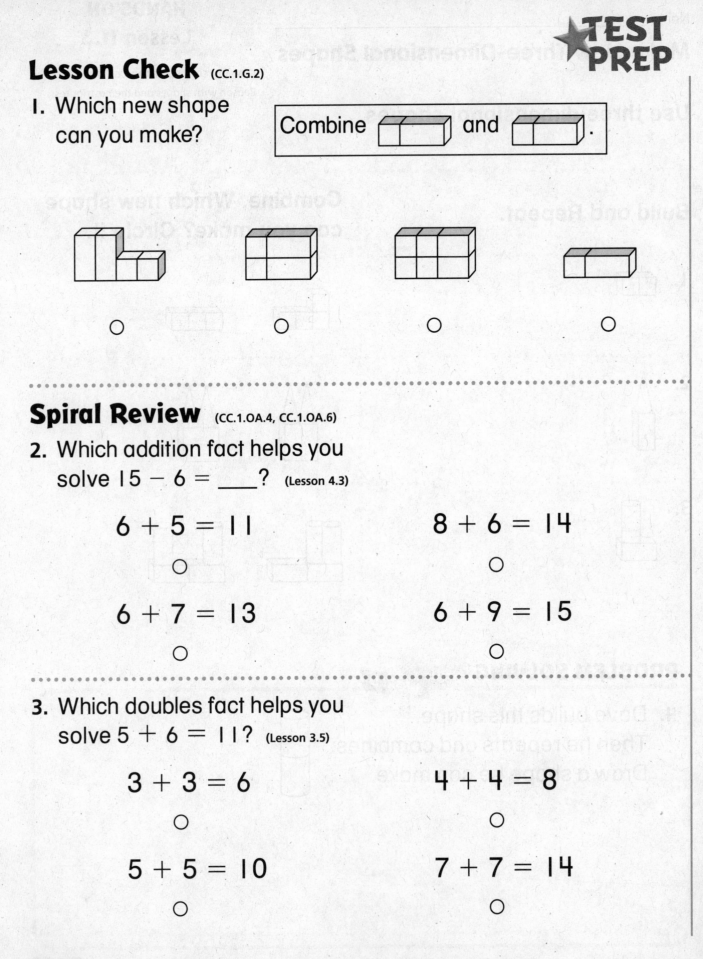 and [ ].

○   ○   ○   ○

....

Spiral Review (CC.1.OA.4, CC.1.OA.6)

2. Which addition fact helps you solve $15 - 6 =$ ___? (Lesson 4.3)

$6 + 5 = 11$
○

$8 + 6 = 14$
○

$6 + 7 = 13$
○

$6 + 9 = 15$
○

....

3. Which doubles fact helps you solve $5 + 6 = 11$? (Lesson 3.5)

$3 + 3 = 6$
○

$4 + 4 = 8$
○

$5 + 5 = 10$
○

$7 + 7 = 14$
○

Name _____

Problem Solving • Take Apart Three-Dimensional Shapes

COMMON CORE STANDARDS 1.G.2
Reason with shapes and their attributes

Use three-dimensional shapes.
Circle your answer.

1. Paco used shapes to build this robot. Circle the shapes he used.

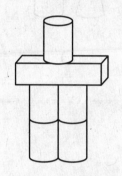

2. Eva used shapes to build this wall. Circle the shapes she used.

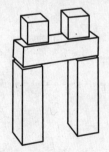

PROBLEM SOLVING REAL WORLD

3. Circle the ways that show the same shape.

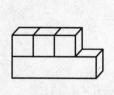

Lesson Check (CC.1.G.2)

1. Which shapes are used to make the picture frame?

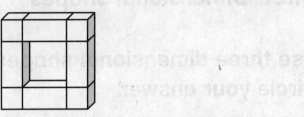

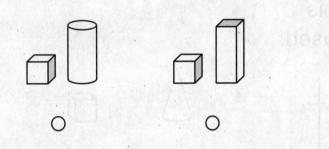

○   ○   ○   ○

Spiral Review (CC.1.NBT.3, CC.1.NBT.4, CC.1.NBT.6)

2. Which is true? (Lesson 7.3)

13 > 31   13 = 31   31 < 13   31 > 13

○   ○   ○   ○

3. What is the difference? (Lesson 8.9)

$$60 - 30 = \underline{\hspace{1cm}}$$

60   30   20   3

○   ○   ○   ○

Name _____

Two-Dimensional Shapes on Three-Dimensional Shapes

COMMON CORE STANDARDS CC.1.G.1
Reason with shapes and their attributes.

Circle the objects you could trace to draw the shape.

1.

2.

3.

PROBLEM SOLVING REAL WORLD

4. Look at this shape. Draw the shape you would make if you traced this object.

Lesson Check

1. Which flat surface does a cone have?

○ ○ ○ ○

---

2. Which flat surfaces could a rectangular prism have?

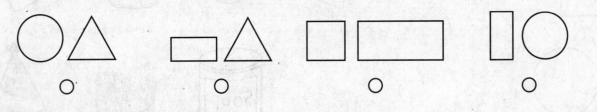

○ ○ ○ ○

Spiral Review (CC.1.OA.3, CC.1.OA.5)

3. Jade has 8 books. She gives some of them to Dana. Now Jade has 6 books. How many did she give to Dana? Which subtraction sentence answers the problem? **(Lesson 4.1)**

$9 - 3 = 6$ $9 - 2 = 7$ $8 - 3 = 5$ $8 - 2 = 6$

○ ○ ○ ○

---

4. What is the sum? **(Lesson 1.5)**

$$3 + 0 = \underline{\quad}$$

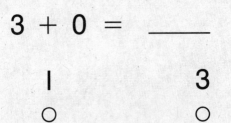

0	1	3	4
○	○	○	○

COMMON CORE STANDARDS CC.1.G.1, CC.1.G.2

Chapter 11 Extra Practice

Lesson 11.1 (pp. 457–460) ·

Use three-dimensional shapes.
Write the number of flat surfaces
for each shape.

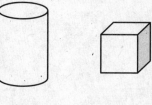

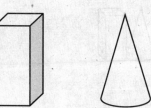

1. A cone has __ flat surfaces.

2. A cube has __ flat surfaces.

3. A cylinder has __ flat surfaces.

4. A rectangular prism has __ flat surfaces.

Lesson 11.2 (pp. 461–464) ·

Use three-dimensional shapes.

Combine.	**Which new shape can you make? Circle it.**

1.

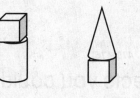

2.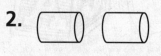

Lesson 11.3 (pp. 465–467)

Use three-dimensional shapes.

Build and Repeat.

Combine. Which new shape can you make? Circle it.

1.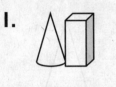

2.

Lesson 11.5 (pp. 473–476)

Circle the objects you could trace to draw the shape.

1.

2.

School-Home Letter

Dear Family,

My class started Chapter 12 this week. In this chapter, I will describe and combine two-dimensional shapes. I will learn about equal shares, halves, and fourths.

Love, _____

Vocabulary Builder

hexagon

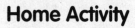

trapezoid

Home Activity

Use a napkin (square), a folded napkin (triangle), and an envelope (rectangle). Combine these items or other household items of the same shapes to make new shapes. Have your child name each shape used in the new shapes you made.

Literature

Look for these books in a library. Point out shapes and how they can be found in everyday objects.

The Greedy Triangle
by Marilyn Burns.
Scholastic,
2008.

Color Farm
by Lois Ehlert.
HarperCollins, 1990.

Carta
para la casa

Querida familia:

Mi clase comenzó el Capítulo 12 esta semana. En este capítulo, aprenderé sobre guras bidimensionales. Aprenderé cómo hacer guras más grandes que otras.

Con cariño, _____

Vocabulario

hexágono

trapecio

Actividad para la casa

Use una servilleta (cuadrado), una servilleta doblada (triángulo) y un sobre (rectángulo). Construya objetos usando estos u otros elementos de la casa con las mismas formas. Pídales a los niños que nombren cada figura usada en los objetos que usted hace.

Literatura

Busque estos libros en una biblioteca. Señale las figuras y muestre cómo se pueden encontrar en los objetos de la vida diaria.

The Greedy Triangle
por Marilyn Burns. Scholastic, 2008.

Color Farm
by Lois Ehlert. HarperCollins, 1990.

Sort Two-Dimensional Shapes

COMMON CORE STANDARD CC.1.G.1
Reason with shapes and their attributes.

Read the sorting rule. Circle the shapes that follow the rule.

1. **not** curved

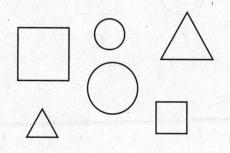

2. 4 vertices

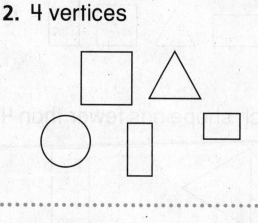

3. more than 3 sides

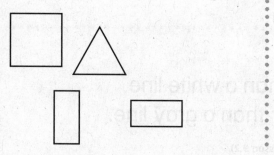

4. curved

PROBLEM SOLVING REAL WORLD

5. Katie sorted these shapes.
Write a sorting rule
to tell how Katie sorted.

_____

- -

_____

Lesson Check (CC.1.G.1)

1. Which shape would **not** be sorted into this group?

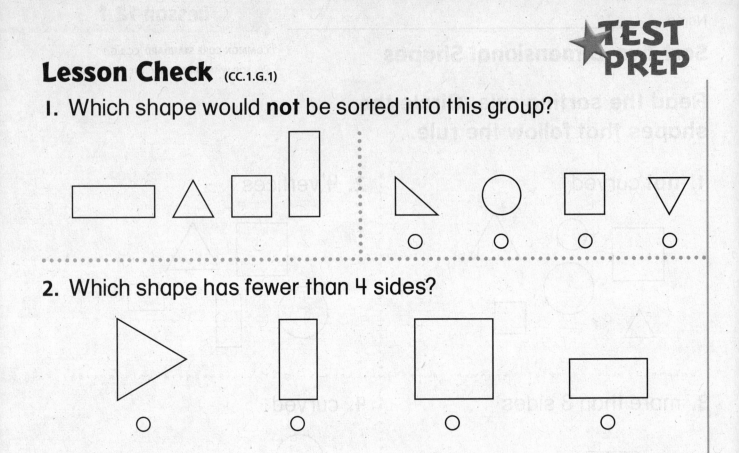

2. Which shape has fewer than 4 sides?

Spiral Review (CC.1.MD.1)

3. Clue 1: A black line is shorter than a white line.
Clue 2: The white line is shorter than a gray line.
Use the clues. Which is true? (Lesson 9.2)

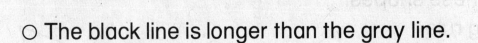

○ The black line is longer than the gray line.

○ The black line is shorter than the gray line.

○ The white line is shorter than the black line.

○ The white line is longer than the gray line.

Describe Two-Dimensional Shapes

COMMON CORE STANDARD CC.1.G.1
Reason with shapes and their attributes.

Use 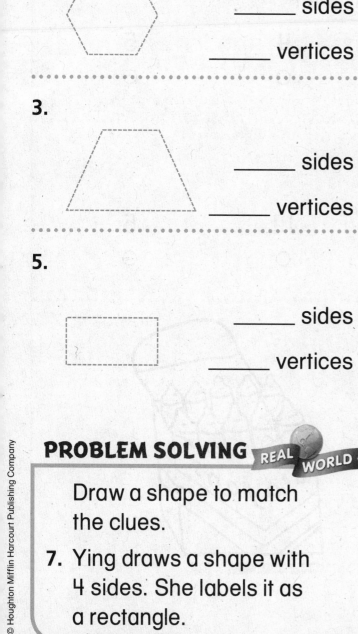 BLUE to trace each straight side. Use RED to circle each vertex. Write the number of sides and vertices.

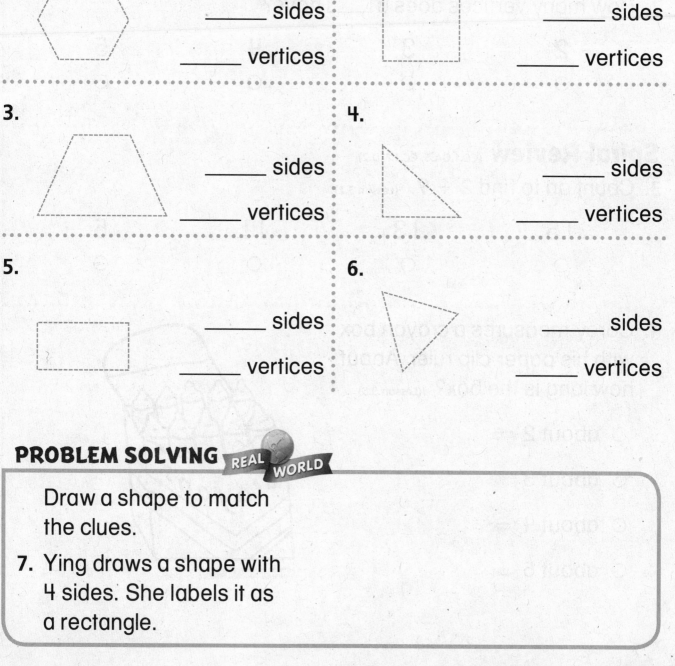

1.

_____ sides

_____ vertices

2.

_____ sides

_____ vertices

3.

_____ sides

_____ vertices

4.

_____ sides

_____ vertices

5.

_____ sides

_____ vertices

6.

_____ sides

_____ vertices

PROBLEM SOLVING REAL WORLD

Draw a shape to match the clues.

7. Ying draws a shape with 4 sides. She labels it as a rectangle.

Lesson Check (CC.1.G.1)

1. How many vertices does a triangle have?

   3   4   5   6
   ○   ○   ○   ○

2. How many vertices does a ☐ have?

   2   3   4   5
   ○   ○   ○   ○

Spiral Review (CC.1.OA.5, CC.1.MD.2)

3. Count on to find $2 + 9$. (Lesson 3.2)

   15   13   11   5
   ○   ○   ○   ○

4. Corey measures a crayon box with his paper clip ruler. About how long is the box? (Lesson 9.5)

  ○ about 2 ▭

  ○ about 3 ▭

  ○ about 4 ▭

  ○ about 5 ▭

Name _____

Combine Two-Dimensional Shapes

COMMON CORE STANDARD CC.1.G.2
Reason with shapes and their attributes.

Use pattern blocks. Draw to show the blocks. Write how many blocks you used.

1. How many △ make a ▱?

_____ △ make a ▱.

2. How many △ make a ◇?

_____ △ make a ◇.

PROBLEM SOLVING REAL WORLD

Use pattern blocks. Draw to show your answer.

3. 2 ▱ make a ⬡.

How many ▱ make 4 ⬡?

_____ ▱ make 4 ⬡.

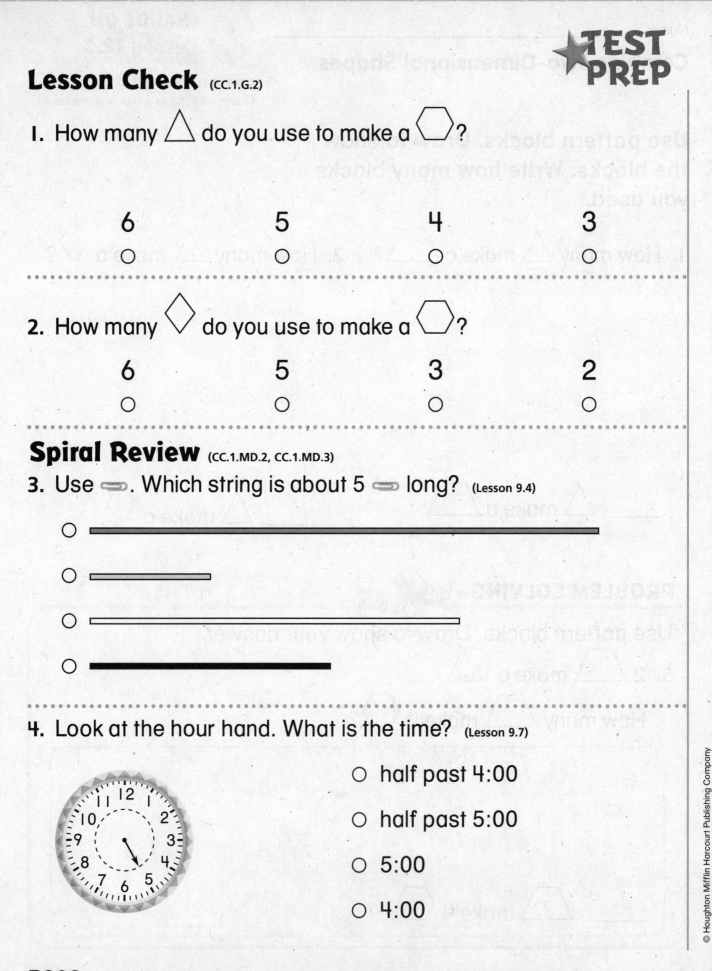

Lesson Check (CC.1.G.2)

1. How many △ do you use to make a ⬡?

6	5	4	3
○	○	○	○

2. How many ◇ do you use to make a ⬡?

6	5	3	2
○	○	○	○

Spiral Review (CC.1.MD.2, CC.1.MD.3)

3. Use ⬯. Which string is about 5 ⬯ long? (Lesson 9.4)

○

○

○

○

4. Look at the hour hand. What is the time? (Lesson 9.7)

○ half past 4:00

○ half past 5:00

○ 5:00

○ 4:00

Combine More Shapes

COMMON CORE STANDARD CC.1.G.2
Reason with shapes and their attributes.

Circle two shapes that can combine to make the shape on the left.

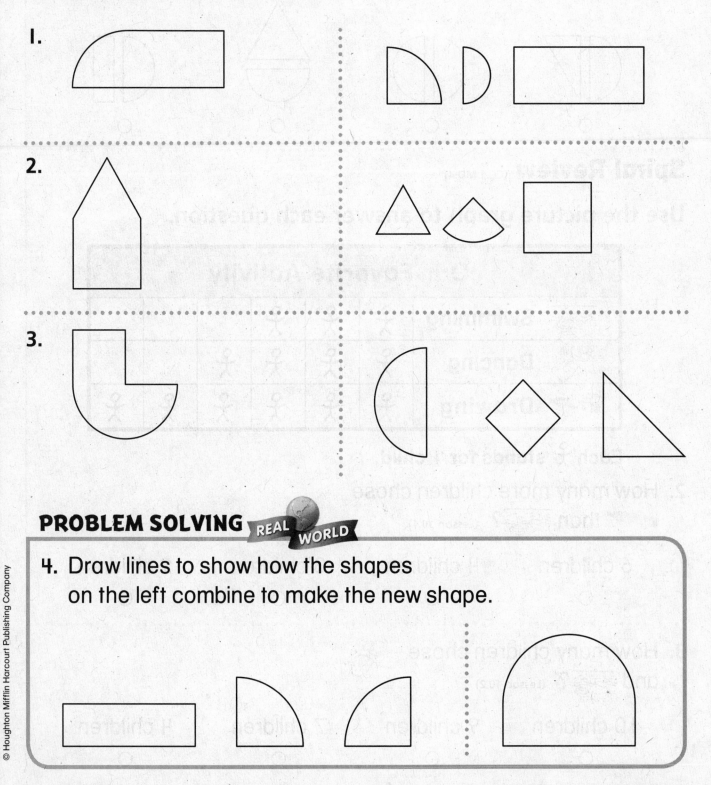

1.

2.

3.

PROBLEM SOLVING REAL WORLD

4. Draw lines to show how the shapes on the left combine to make the new shape.

Lesson Check (CC.1.G.2)

1. Which shapes can combine to make this new shape?

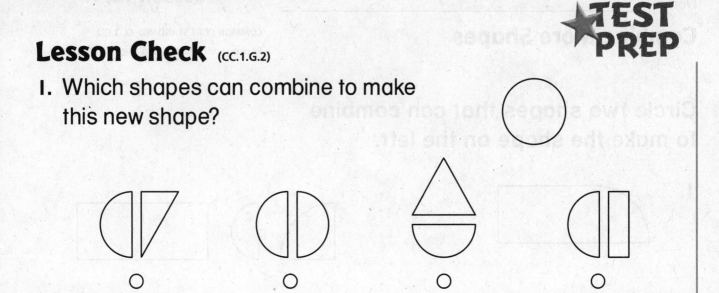

○   ○   ○   ○

Spiral Review (CC.1.MD.4)

Use the picture graph to answer each question.

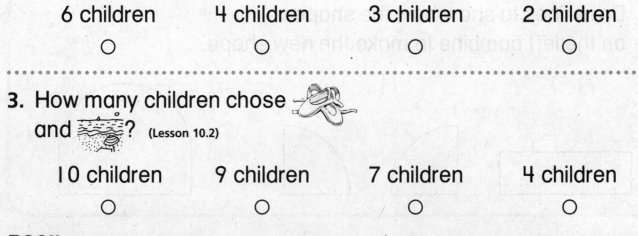

Our Favorite Activity						
🏊 Swimming	웃	웃	웃			
🩰 Dancing	웃	웃	웃	웃		
🖍 Drawing	웃	웃	웃	웃	웃	웃

Each 웃 stands for 1 child.

2. How many more children chose 🖍 than 🏊 ? (Lesson 10.1)

6 children   4 children   3 children   2 children
○   ○   ○   ○

---

3. How many children chose 🩰 and 🏊 ? (Lesson 10.2)

10 children   9 children   7 children   4 children
○   ○   ○   ○

Name _____

Problem Solving • Make New Two-Dimensional Shapes

COMMON CORE STANDARD CC.1.G.2
Reason with shapes and their attributes.

Use shapes to solve.
Draw to show your work.

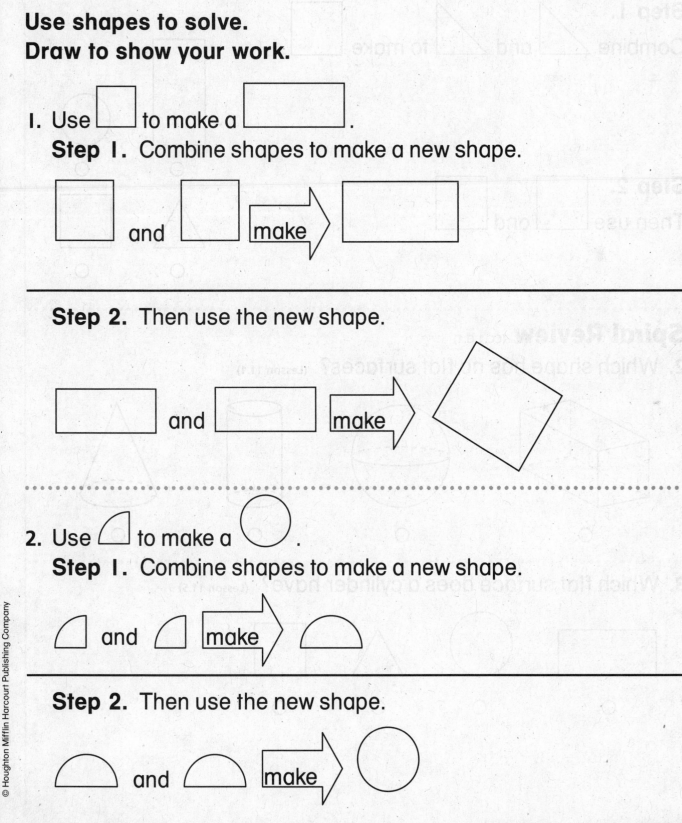

1. Use ☐ to make a ▭.

   Step 1. Combine shapes to make a new shape.

   ☐ and ▭ make ▭

   Step 2. Then use the new shape.

   ▭ and ▭ make ◇

2. Use ◹ to make a ◯.

   Step 1. Combine shapes to make a new shape.

   ◹ and ◹ make ⌒

   Step 2. Then use the new shape.

   ⌒ and ⌒ make ◯

Lesson Check (CC.1.G.2)

1. Which new shape could you make?

Step 1.
Combine △ and △ to make ▢.

Step 2.
Then use ▢ and ▢.

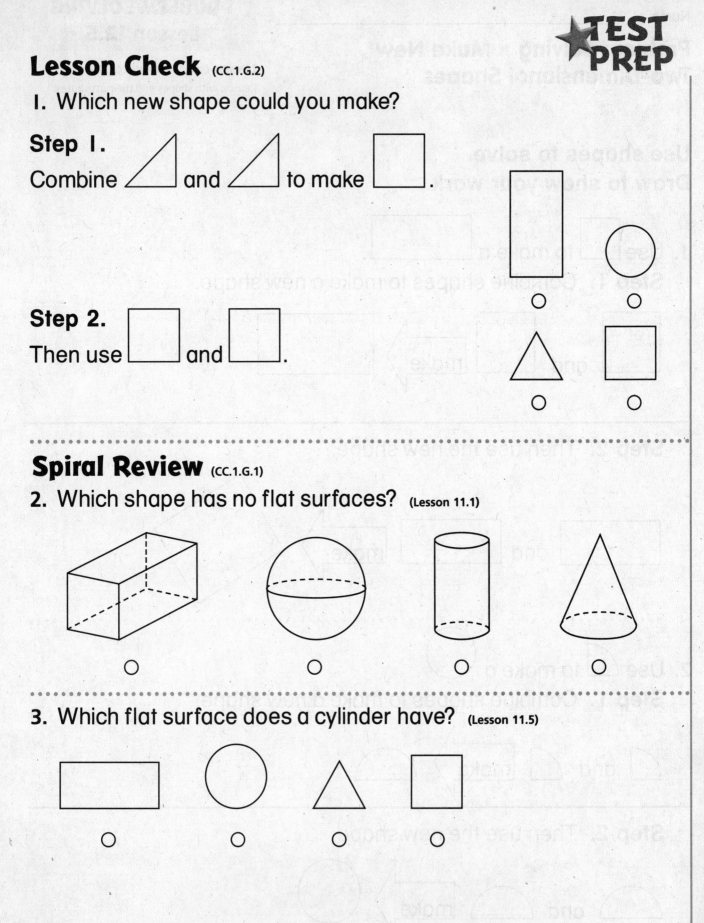

····················

Spiral Review (CC.1.G.1)

2. Which shape has no flat surfaces? **(Lesson 11.1)**

····················

3. Which flat surface does a cylinder have? **(Lesson 11.5)**

Find Shapes in Shapes

COMMON CORE STANDARD CC.1.G.2
Reason with shapes and their attributes.

Use two pattern blocks to make the shape.
Draw a line to show your model. Circle the blocks you use.

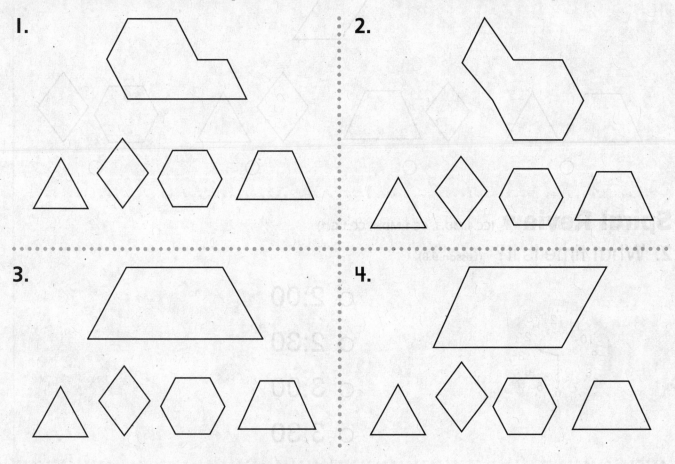

1.

2.

3.

4.

PROBLEM SOLVING REAL WORLD

Make the shape to the right. Use the number
of pattern blocks listed in the exercise.
Write how many of each block you use.

5. Use 3 blocks.

_____ _____ _____ _____

Lesson Check (CC.1.G.2)

1. Which two pattern blocks can make this shape?

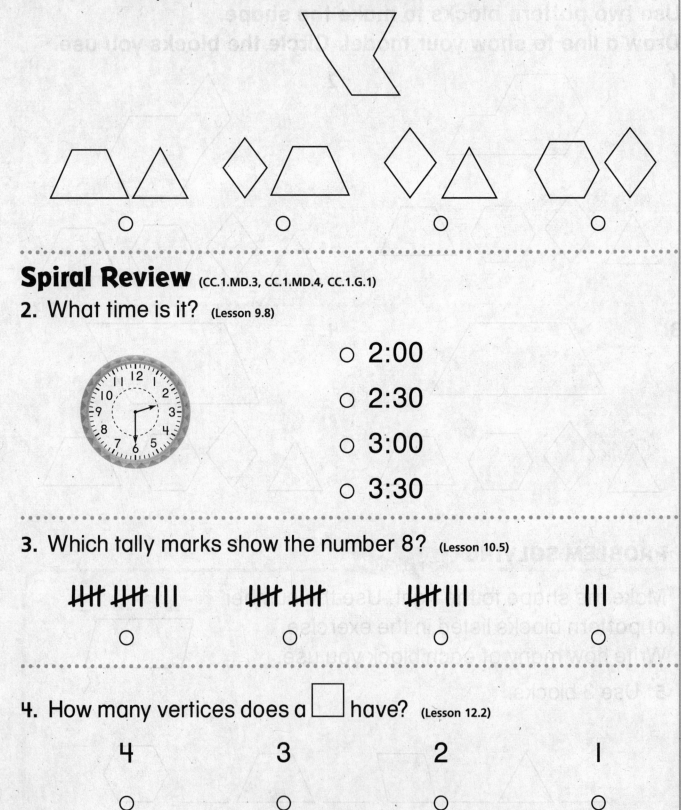

○   ○   ○   ○

Spiral Review (CC.1.MD.3, CC.1.MD.4, CC.1.G.1)

2. What time is it? (Lesson 9.8)

○ 2:00

○ 2:30

○ 3:00

○ 3:30

3. Which tally marks show the number 8? (Lesson 10.5)

〡〡〡〡 〡〡〡〡 〡〡〡   〡〡〡〡 〡〡〡〡   〡〡〡〡〡〡〡   〡〡〡

○   ○   ○   ○

4. How many vertices does a ☐ have? (Lesson 12.2)

4   3   2   1

○   ○   ○   ○

Take Apart Two-Dimensional Shapes

COMMON CORE STANDARD CC.1.G.2
Reason with shapes and their attributes.

Draw a line to show the parts.

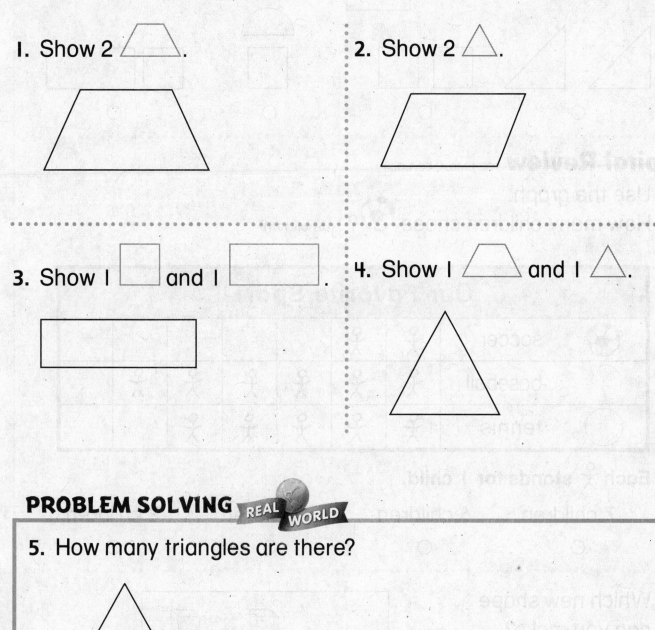

1. Show 2 ⬭.

2. Show 2 △.

3. Show 1 ⬜ and 1 ▭.

4. Show 1 ⬭ and 1 △.

PROBLEM SOLVING REAL WORLD

5. How many triangles are there?

_____ triangles

Lesson Check <small>(CC.1.G.2)</small>

1. Look at the picture.
What are the parts?

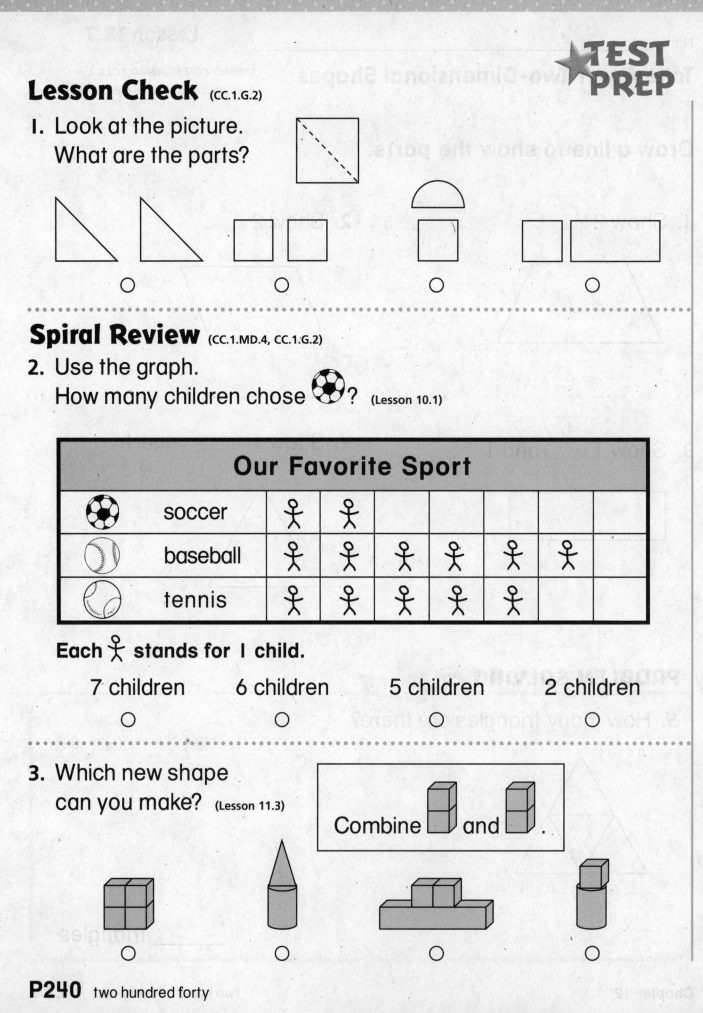

○   ○   ○   ○

Spiral Review <small>(CC.1.MD.4, CC.1.G.2)</small>

2. Use the graph.
How many children chose ⚽? <small>(Lesson 10.1)</small>

Our Favorite Sport

⚽	soccer	🧍	🧍					
⚾	baseball	🧍	🧍	🧍	🧍	🧍	🧍	
🎾	tennis	🧍	🧍	🧍	🧍	🧍		

Each 🧍 stands for 1 child.

7 children   6 children   5 children   2 children
○   ○   ○   ○

---

3. Which new shape
can you make? <small>(Lesson 11.3)</small>

Combine ⬚ and ⬚.

○   ○   ○   ○

Equal or Unequal Parts

COMMON CORE STANDARD CC.1.G.3
Reason with shapes and their attributes.

Color the shapes that show unequal shares.

1.

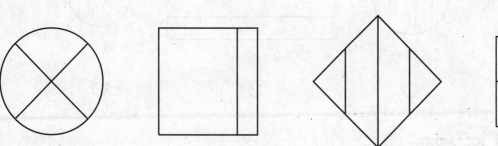

Color the shapes that show equal shares.

2.

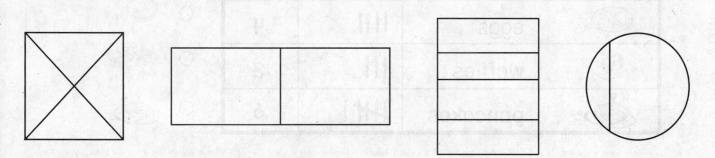

PROBLEM SOLVING REAL WORLD

Draw lines to show the parts.

3. 4 equal shares

Lesson Check (CC.1.G.3)

1. Which shows unequal shares?

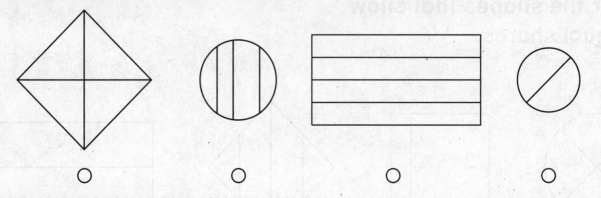

○   ○   ○   ○

Spiral Review (CC.1.MD.4)

2. Which food did the most children choose? (Lesson 10.6)

Our Favorite Breakfast		Total
🍳 eggs	IIII	4
🧇 waffles	III	3
🥞 pancakes	HHH I	6

○ 🥣
○ 🍳
○ 🧇
○ 🥞

3. Use the graph. How many children chose 🧸? (Lesson 10.3)

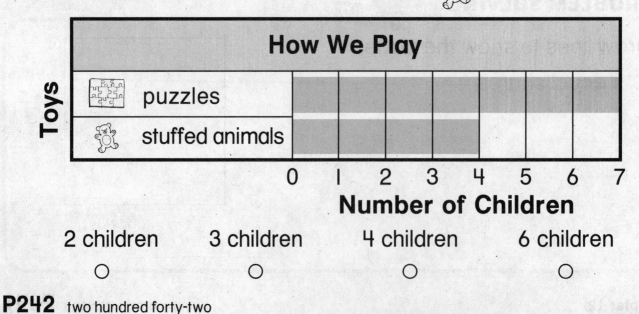

2 children   3 children   4 children   6 children

○   ○   ○   ○

Halves

COMMON CORE STANDARD CC.1.G.3
Reason with shapes and their attributes.

Circle the shapes that show halves.

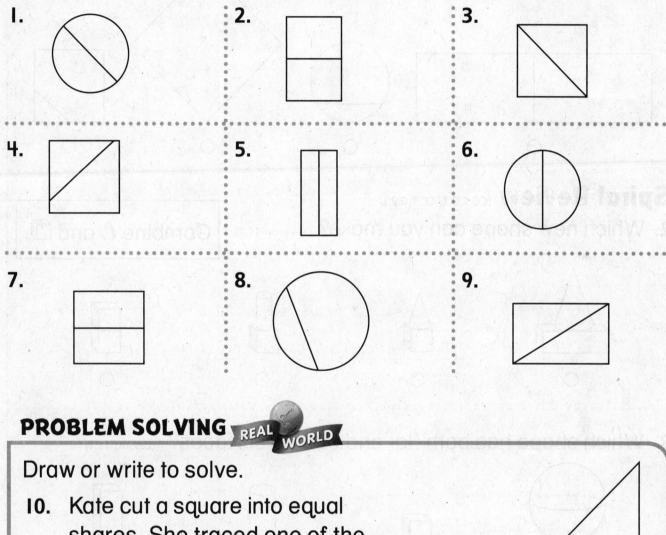

1.

2.

3.

4.

5.

6.

7.

8.

9.

PROBLEM SOLVING REAL WORLD

Draw or write to solve.

10. Kate cut a square into equal
     shares. She traced one of the
     parts. Write **half of** or **halves** to
     name the part.

_____

_ _ _ _ _ _ _ _ _ _ _ _

_____ a square

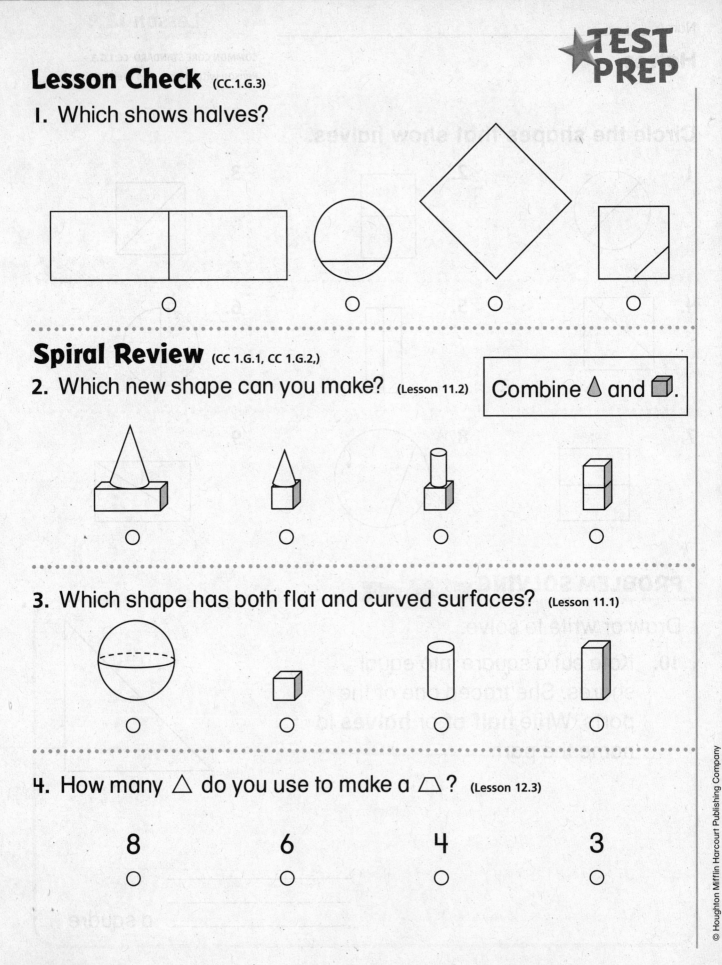

Lesson Check (CC.1.G.3)

1. Which shows halves?

○   ○   ○   ○

Spiral Review (CC 1.G.1, CC 1.G.2,)

2. Which new shape can you make? (Lesson 11.2)

Combine △ and ▱.

○   ○   ○   ○

3. Which shape has both flat and curved surfaces? (Lesson 11.1)

○   ○   ○   ○

4. How many △ do you use to make a △? (Lesson 12.3)

8   6   4   3

○   ○   ○   ○

Fourths

COMMON CORE STANDARD CC.1.G.3
Reason with shapes and their attributes.

Circle the shapes that show fourths.

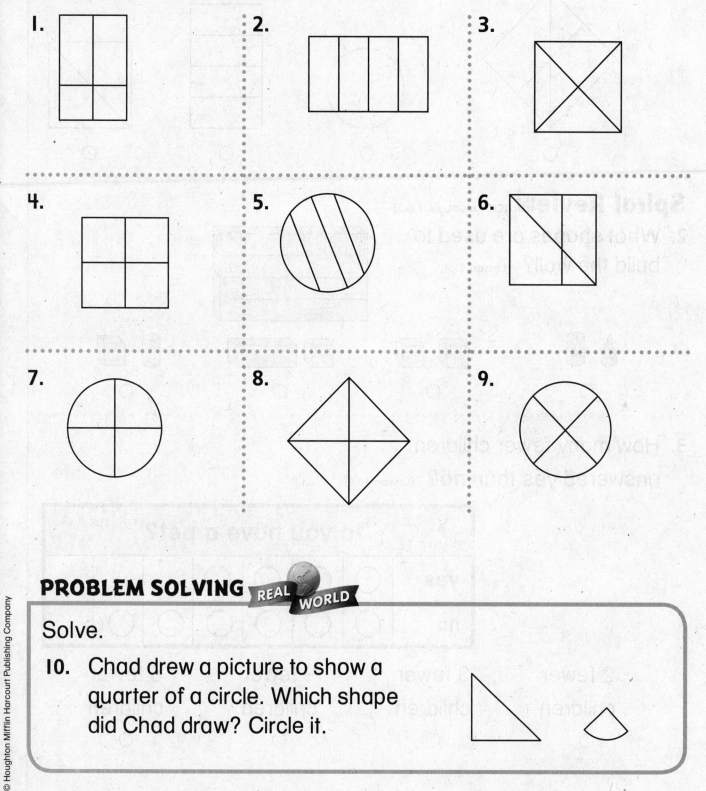

1.

2.

3.

4.

5.

6.

7.

8.

9.

PROBLEM SOLVING REAL WORLD

Solve.

10. Chad drew a picture to show a quarter of a circle. Which shape did Chad draw? Circle it.

Lesson Check (CC.1.G.3)

1. Which shows fourths?

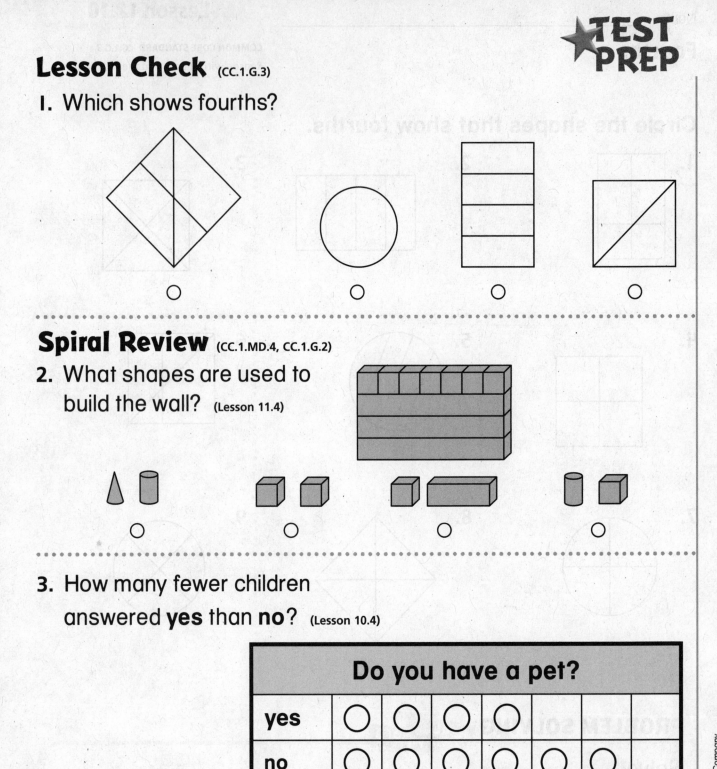

○   ○   ○   ○

- -

Spiral Review (CC.1.MD.4, CC.1.G.2)

2. What shapes are used to build the wall? (Lesson 11.4)

○   ○   ○   ○

- -

3. How many fewer children answered **yes** than **no**? (Lesson 10.4)

Do you have a pet?						
yes	○	○	○	○		
no	○	○	○	○	○	○

2 fewer children   3 fewer children   4 fewer children   6 fewer children

○   ○   ○   ○

COMMON CORE STANDARDS CC.1.G.1, CC.1.G.2, CC.1.G.3

Chapter 12 Extra Practice

Lessons 12.1 – 12.2 . . . .

Use 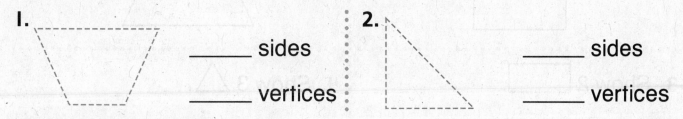 BLUE to trace each straight side.
Use RED to circle each vertex.
Write the number of sides and vertices.

1. _____ sides

   _____ vertices

2. _____ sides

   _____ vertices

Lessons 12.3 – 12.4 . . . .

Circle the two shapes that can combine
to make the shape on the left.

1.

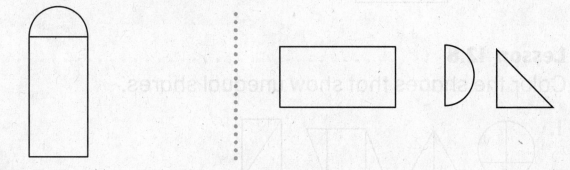

Lesson 12.6 . . . .

Use two pattern blocks to make the shape.
Draw a line to show your model.
Circle the blocks you use.

1.

2.

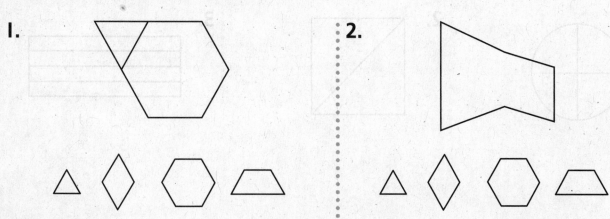

Lesson 12.7

Draw a line to show the parts.

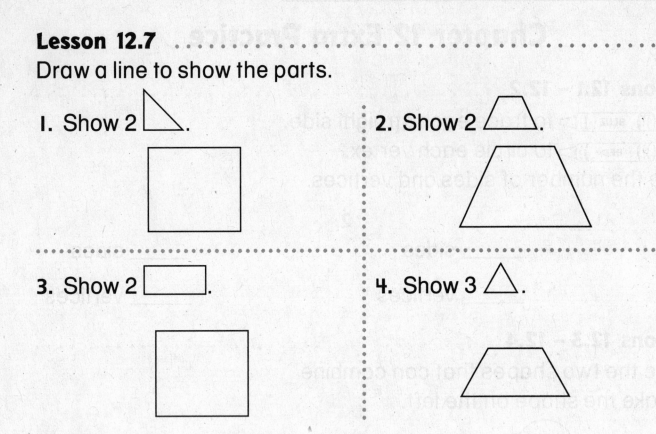

1. Show 2 △.

2. Show 2 ⬠.

3. Show 2 ▭.

4. Show 3 △.

Lesson 12.8

Color the shapes that show unequal shares.

1.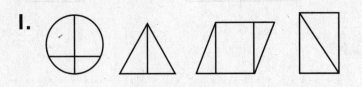

Lessons 12.9 – 12.10

Circle the shapes that show fourths.

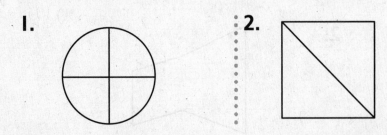

1.

2.

3.

Algebra • Ways to Expand Numbers

Essential Question How can you write a two-digit number in different ways?

Model and Draw

There are different ways to think about a number.

> 8 tens and 7 ones is the same as 80 plus 7.

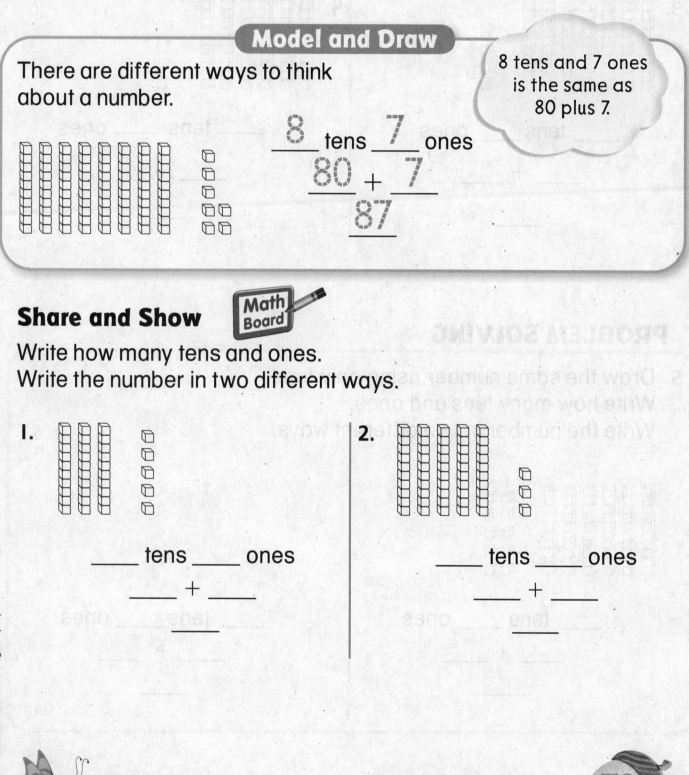

___8___ tens ___7___ ones

$$80 + 7$$

$$87$$

Share and Show

Write how many tens and ones.
Write the number in two different ways.

1.

____ tens ____ ones

____ + ____

____

2.

____ tens ____ ones

____ + ____

____

Math Talk   Does the 7 in this number show 7 or 70? Explain.

72

On Your Own

Write how many tens and ones.
Write the number in two different ways.

3.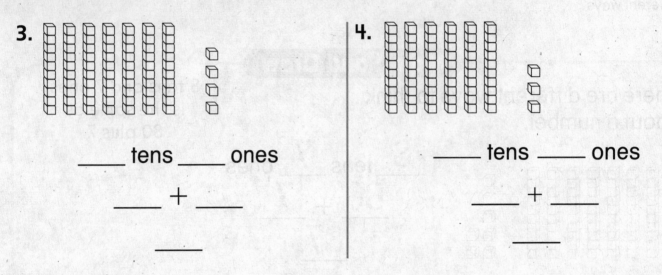

_____ tens _____ ones

_____ + _____

_____

4.

_____ tens _____ ones

_____ + _____

_____

PROBLEM SOLVING

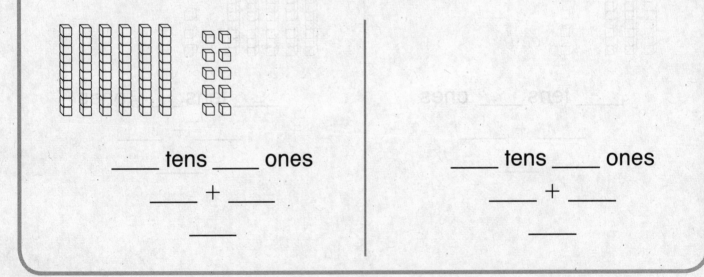

5. Draw the same number using only tens.
   Write how many tens and ones.
   Write the number in two different ways.

_____ tens _____ ones

_____ + _____

_____

_____ tens _____ ones

_____ + _____

_____

TAKE HOME ACTIVITY • Write a two-digit number to 99.
Ask your child to write how many tens and ones and then write the
number a different way.

© Houghton Mifflin Harcourt Publishing Company

Identify Place Value

Essential Question How can you use place value to understand the value of a number?

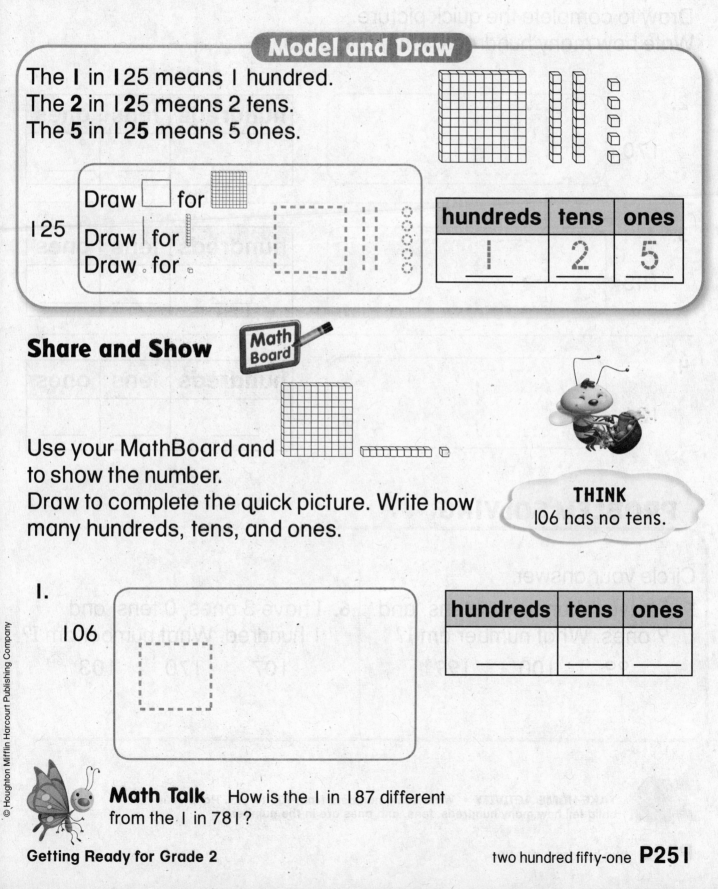

Model and Draw

The **1** in **1**25 means 1 hundred.
The **2** in 1**2**5 means 2 tens.
The **5** in 12**5** means 5 ones.

125

Draw ☐ for ▦
Draw | for |
Draw ∘ for ∘

hundreds	tens	ones
1	2	5

Share and Show

Math Board

Use your MathBoard and to show the number.
Draw to complete the quick picture. Write how many hundreds, tens, and ones.

THINK
106 has no tens.

1.

106

hundreds	tens	ones
___	___	___

Math Talk   How is the 1 in 187 different from the 1 in 781?

On Your Own

Use your MathBoard and ▦ ▭ ▫ .
Draw to complete the quick picture.
Write how many hundreds, tens, and ones.

2.

170

hundreds	tens	ones
____	____	____

3.

143

hundreds	tens	ones
____	____	____

4.

121

hundreds	tens	ones
____	____	____

PROBLEM SOLVING

Circle your answer.

5. I have 1 hundred, 9 tens, and 9 ones. What number am I?

    99   100   199

6. I have 3 ones, 0 tens, and 1 hundred. What number am I?

    107   170   103

TAKE HOME ACTIVITY • Write some numbers from 100 to 199. Have your child tell how many hundreds, tens, and ones are in the number.

Name _____

Use Place Value to Compare Numbers

Essential Question How can you use place value to compare two numbers?

Model and Draw

Use these symbols to compare numbers.

> is greater than
< is less than
= is equal to

45   **46**

I want to eat the greater number.

45 < 46
45 is less than 46.

Compare 134 and 125.

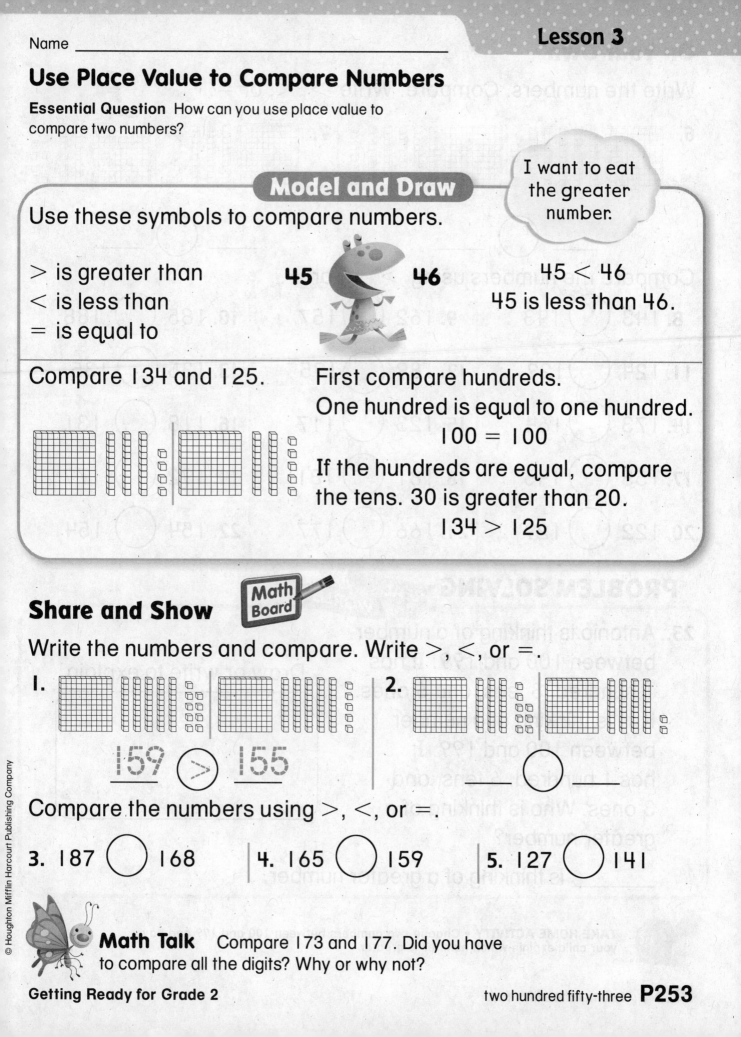

First compare hundreds.
One hundred is equal to one hundred.
100 = 100
If the hundreds are equal, compare the tens. 30 is greater than 20.
134 > 125

Share and Show

Math Board

Write the numbers and compare. Write >, <, or =.

1.   159 (>) 155

2.   ____ ( ) ____

Compare the numbers using >, <, or =.

3. 187 ◯ 168 | 4. 165 ◯ 159 | 5. 127 ◯ 141

Math Talk   Compare 173 and 177. Did you have to compare all the digits? Why or why not?

Getting Ready for Grade 2

two hundred fifty-three **P253**

On Your Own

Write the numbers. Compare. Write >, <, or =.

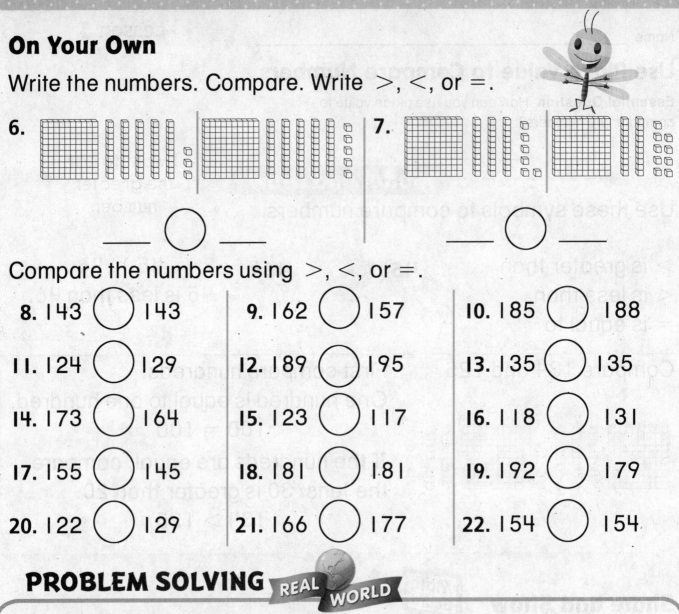

6. ___ ◯ ___   7. ___ ◯ ___

Compare the numbers using >, <, or =.

8. 143 ◯ 143   9. 162 ◯ 157   10. 185 ◯ 188

11. 124 ◯ 129   12. 189 ◯ 195   13. 135 ◯ 135

14. 173 ◯ 164   15. 123 ◯ 117   16. 118 ◯ 131

17. 155 ◯ 145   18. 181 ◯ 181   19. 192 ◯ 179

20. 122 ◯ 129   21. 166 ◯ 177   22. 154 ◯ 154

PROBLEM SOLVING REAL WORLD

23. Antonio is thinking of a number between 100 and 199. It has 1 hundred, 3 tens, and 6 ones. Kim is thinking of a number between 100 and 199. It has 1 hundred, 6 tens, and 3 ones. Who is thinking of a greater number?

Draw or write to explain.

_____ is thinking of a greater number.

TAKE HOME ACTIVITY • Choose two numbers between 100 and 199 and have your child explain which number is greater.

Name _____

✓ Checkpoint

Concepts and Skills

Write how many tens and ones.
Write the number in two ways.

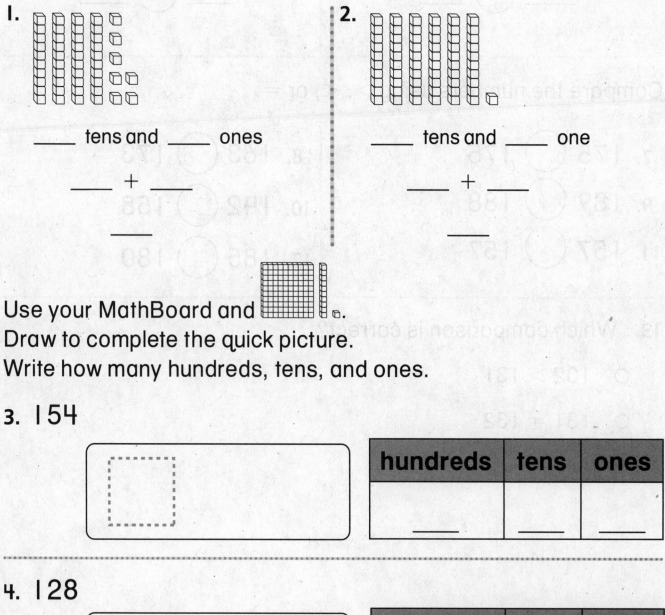

1. _____ tens and _____ ones

   _____ + _____

   _____

2. _____ tens and _____ one

   _____ + _____

   _____

Use your MathBoard and ▦▯.
Draw to complete the quick picture.
Write how many hundreds, tens, and ones.

3. 154

hundreds	tens	ones
_____	_____	_____

4. 128

hundreds	tens	ones
_____	_____	_____

Write the numbers and compare. Write >, <, or =.

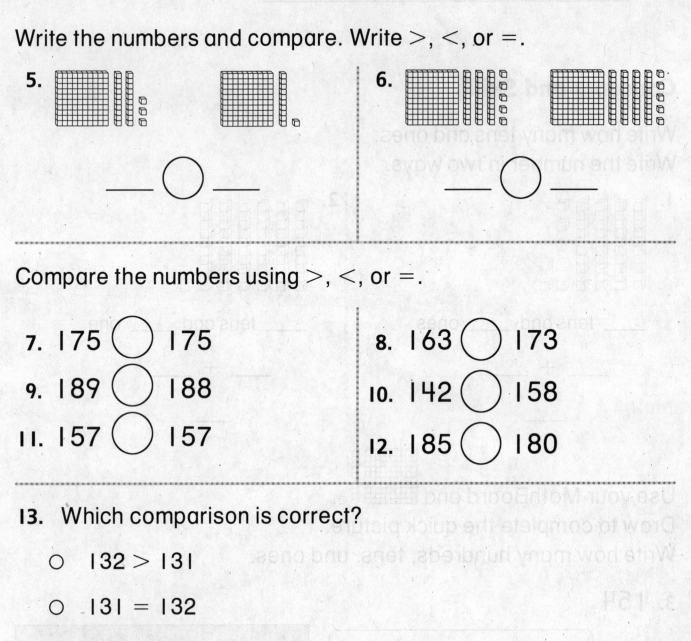

5. ___ ◯ ___

6. ___ ◯ ___

Compare the numbers using >, <, or =.

7. 175 ◯ 175

8. 163 ◯ 173

9. 189 ◯ 188

10. 142 ◯ 158

11. 157 ◯ 157

12. 185 ◯ 180

13. Which comparison is correct?

○ 132 > 131

○ 131 = 132

○ 131 > 132

Algebra • Addition Function Tables

Essential Question How can you follow a rule to complete an addition function table?

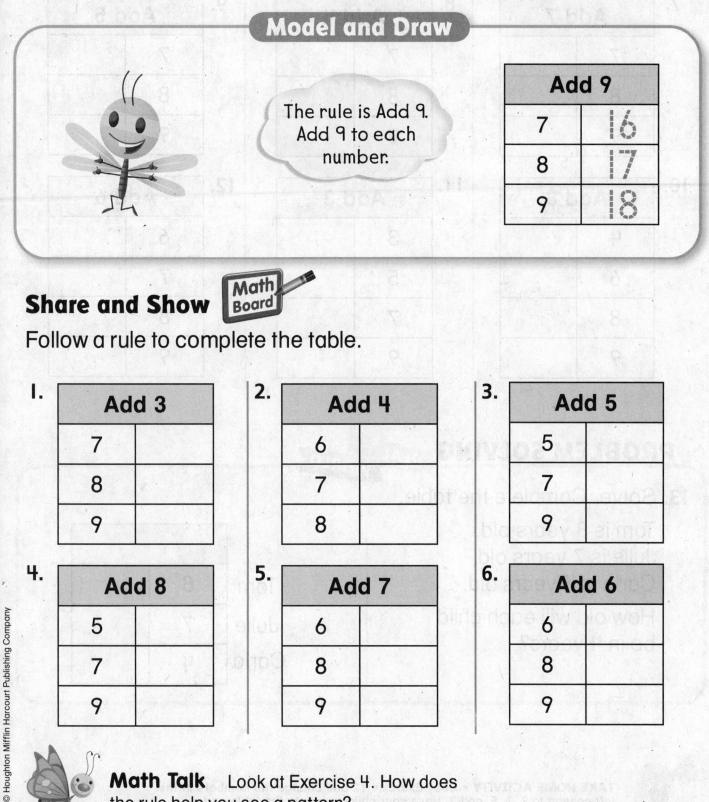

Model and Draw

The rule is Add 9. Add 9 to each number.

Add 9	
7	16
8	17
9	18

Share and Show

Follow a rule to complete the table.

1.

Add 3	
7	
8	
9	

2.

Add 4	
6	
7	
8	

3.

Add 5	
5	
7	
9	

4.

Add 8	
5	
7	
9	

5.

Add 7	
6	
8	
9	

6.

Add 6	
6	
8	
9	

Math Talk Look at Exercise 4. How does the rule help you see a pattern?

On Your Own

Follow a rule to complete the table.

7.

Add 7	
7	
8	
9	

8.

Add 4	
7	
8	
9	

9.

Add 5	
7	
8	
9	

10.

Add 8	
4	
6	
8	
9	

11.

Add 3	
3	
5	
7	
9	

12.

Add 6	
6	
7	
8	
9	

PROBLEM SOLVING REAL WORLD

13. Solve. Complete the table.

Tom is 8 years old.
Julie is 7 years old.
Carla is 4 years old.

How old will each child be in 4 years?

Tom	8	
Julie	7	
Carla	4	

© Houghton Mifflin Harcourt Publishing Company

TAKE HOME ACTIVITY • Copy Exercise 12 and change the numbers in the left column to 9, 7, 5, and 3. Have your child complete the table and explain how he or she used a rule to solve the problem.

Name _____

Algebra • Subtraction Function Tables

Essential Question How can you follow a rule to complete a subtraction function table?

Model and Draw

The rule is Subtract 7. Subtract 7 from each number.

Subtract 7	
14	7
15	8
16	9

Share and Show

Math Board

Follow a rule to complete the table.

1.
Subtract 3	
9	
10	
11	

2.
Subtract 4	
6	
8	
10	

3.
Subtract 5	
6	
8	
10	

4.
Subtract 8	
9	
11	
13	

5.
Subtract 7	
12	
13	
14	

6.
Subtract 6	
6	
8	
9	

Math Talk How can Exercise 2 help you solve Exercise 3?

On Your Own

Follow a rule to complete the table.

7.

Subtract 4	
11	
12	
13	

8.

Subtract 6	
7	
8	
9	

9.

Subtract 5	
7	
8	
9	

10.

Subtract 7	
13	
14	
15	
16	

11.

Subtract 8	
12	
14	
16	
17	

12.

Subtract 9	
12	
14	
16	
17	

PROBLEM SOLVING REAL WORLD

13. Solve. Complete the table.

Jane has 4 cookies.
Lucy has 3 cookies.
Seamus has 2 cookies.

How many cookies will each child have if they each eat 2 cookies?

Jane	4	
Lucy	3	
Seamus	2	

TAKE HOME ACTIVITY • Copy Exercise 12 and change the numbers in the left column to 10, 11, 12, and 13. Have your child complete the table and explain how he or she used a rule to solve the problem.

Name _____

Algebra • Follow the Rule

Essential Question How can you follow a rule to complete an addition or subtraction function table?

Model and Draw

The rule for some tables is to add. For other tables the rule is to subtract.

Add 1	
2	3
4	
6	
8	

Subtract 1	
2	1
4	
6	
8	

Share and Show

Follow a rule to complete the table.

1.

Add 2	
10	
9	
8	
7	

2.

Subtract 2	
10	
9	
8	
7	

3.

Subtract 1	
3	
4	
7	
9	

Math Talk   What is the rule for the pattern in
Exercise 1?

On Your Own

Follow a rule to complete the table.

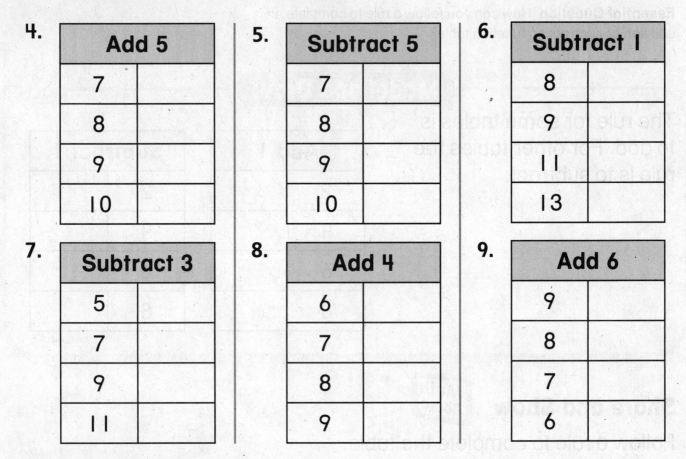

4.

Add 5	
7	
8	
9	
10	

5.

Subtract 5	
7	
8	
9	
10	

6.

Subtract 1	
8	
9	
11	
13	

7.

Subtract 3	
5	
7	
9	
11	

8.

Add 4	
6	
7	
8	
9	

9.

Add 6	
9	
8	
7	
6	

PROBLEM SOLVING

10. Find the rule. Complete the table.

3	
	8
7	10
	12

TAKE HOME ACTIVITY • Copy the table for Exercise 9.
Change the rule to Subtract 3. Have your child complete the table.

P262 two hundred sixty-two

Add 3 Numbers

Essential Question How can you choose a strategy to help add 3 numbers?

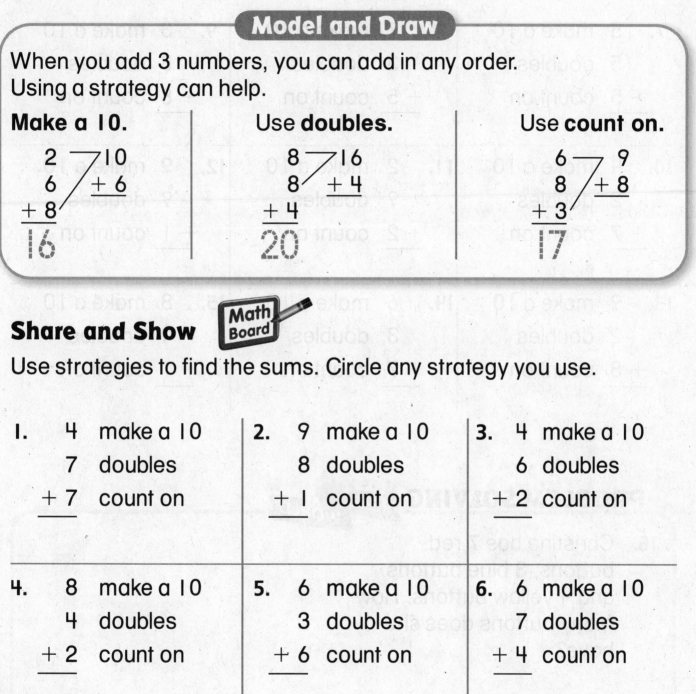

Model and Draw

When you add 3 numbers, you can add in any order.
Using a strategy can help.

Make a 10.

$$
\begin{array}{r}
2 \\
6 \\
+\,8 \\
\hline
16
\end{array}
\quad
\begin{array}{r}
10 \\
+\,6 \\
\hline
\end{array}
$$

Use doubles.

$$
\begin{array}{r}
8 \\
8 \\
+\,4 \\
\hline
20
\end{array}
\quad
\begin{array}{r}
16 \\
+\,4 \\
\hline
\end{array}
$$

Use count on.

$$
\begin{array}{r}
6 \\
8 \\
+\,3 \\
\hline
17
\end{array}
\quad
\begin{array}{r}
9 \\
+\,8 \\
\hline
\end{array}
$$

Share and Show

Use strategies to find the sums. Circle any strategy you use.

1.
$$
\begin{array}{r}
4 \\
7 \\
+\,7 \\
\hline
\end{array}
$$
make a 10
doubles
count on

2.
$$
\begin{array}{r}
9 \\
8 \\
+\,1 \\
\hline
\end{array}
$$
make a 10
doubles
count on

3.
$$
\begin{array}{r}
4 \\
6 \\
+\,2 \\
\hline
\end{array}
$$
make a 10
doubles
count on

4.
$$
\begin{array}{r}
8 \\
4 \\
+\,2 \\
\hline
\end{array}
$$
make a 10
doubles
count on

5.
$$
\begin{array}{r}
6 \\
3 \\
+\,6 \\
\hline
\end{array}
$$
make a 10
doubles
count on

6.
$$
\begin{array}{r}
6 \\
7 \\
+\,4 \\
\hline
\end{array}
$$
make a 10
doubles
count on

Math Talk Explain why you used the make a 10 strategy to solve Exercise 2.

On Your Own

Use a strategy to find the sum. Circle the
strategy you choose.

7.	5 make a 10	8.	7 make a 10	9.	3 make a 10
	5 doubles		3 doubles		8 doubles
	+ 5 count on		+ 5 count on		+ 8 count on

10.	4 make a 10	11.	2 make a 10	12.	9 make a 10
	2 doubles		9 doubles		9 doubles
	+ 7 count on		+ 2 count on		+ 1 count on

13.	9 make a 10	14.	6 make a 10	15.	8 make a 10
	2 doubles		3 doubles		4 doubles
	+ 8 count on		+ 7 count on		+ 1 count on

PROBLEM SOLVING REAL WORLD

16. Christine has 7 red
buttons, 3 blue buttons,
and 4 yellow buttons. How
many buttons does she
have?

_____ buttons

TAKE HOME ACTIVITY • Ask your child to choose 3 numbers from 1 to 9.
Have your child add to find the sum.

Add a One-Digit Number to a Two-Digit Number

Essential Question How can you find the sum of a 1-digit number and a 2-digit number?

Model and Draw

What is 54 + 2?

To find the sum, find how many **tens** and **ones** in all.

5 tens	4 ones		5 4
+	2 ones		+ 2
_5_ tens	_6_ ones		5 6

Share and Show

Add. Write the sum.

1.	72	2.	24	3.	41	4.	56
	+ 3		+ 1		+ 4		+ 2

5.	14	6.	33	7.	61	8.	93
	+ 4		+ 6		+ 8		+ 4

9.	31	10.	11	11.	40	12.	35
	+ 6		+ 7		+ 4		+ 3

Math Talk   How did you find the total number of ones in
Exercise 1?

On Your Own

Add. Write the sum.

13.	22 + 7	14.	53 + 3	15.	46 + 2	16.	71 + 8
17.	84 + 5	18.	93 + 4	19.	16 + 3	20.	37 + 1
21.	62 + 2	22.	23 + 5	23.	82 + 2	24.	44 + 4

PROBLEM SOLVING REAL WORLD

25. There are 23 children in the first grade class. Then 3 more children join the class. How many children are there now?

_____ children

TAKE HOME ACTIVITY • Tell your child you had 12 pennies and then you got 5 more. Have your child add to find how many pennies in all.

Add Two-Digit Numbers

Essential Question How can you find the sum of
two 2-digit numbers?

Model and Draw

What is 23 + 14?

You can find how many **tens** and **ones** in all.

	2	tens	3 ones		2 3
	+ 1	ten	4 ones		+ 1 4
	_3_	tens	_7_ ones		$\boxed{37}$

Share and Show

 Math Board

Add. Write the sum.

1.	82 + 12	2.	25 + 43	3.	15 + 14	4.	71 + 12
5.	36 + 21	6.	43 + 41	7.	57 + 32	8.	21 + 12
9.	12 + 12	10.	41 + 21	11.	32 + 41	12.	51 + 14

Math Talk How many tens are in 26 + 11?
How do you know?

On Your Own

Add. Write the sum.

13.	83 + 12	14.	73 + 21	15.	16 + 51	16.	23 + 43
17.	24 + 55	18.	67 + 21	19.	64 + 23	20.	51 + 24
21.	26 + 32	22.	51 + 25	23.	46 + 22	24.	34 + 45

PROBLEM SOLVING REAL WORLD

25. Emma has 21 hair clips. Her sister has 11 hair clips. How many hair clips do the girls have together?

_____ hair clips

TAKE HOME ACTIVITY • Tell your child you drove 21 miles and then you drove 16 more. Have your child add to find how many miles in all.

Repeated Addition

Essential Question How can you find how many items there are in equal groups without counting one at a time?

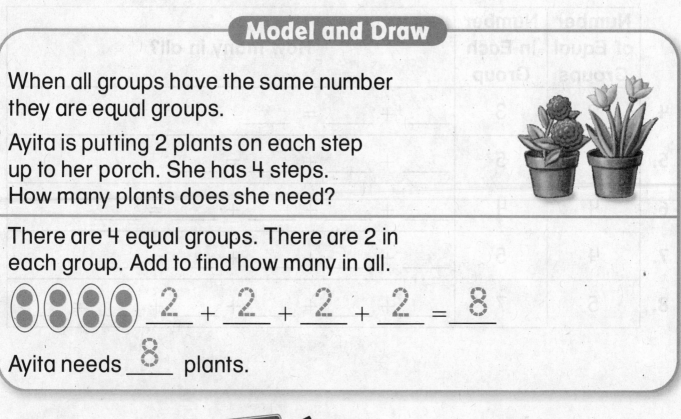

Model and Draw

When all groups have the same number they are equal groups.

Ayita is putting 2 plants on each step up to her porch. She has 4 steps. How many plants does she need?

There are 4 equal groups. There are 2 in each group. Add to find how many in all.

 __2__ + __2__ + __2__ + __2__ = __8__

Ayita needs __8__ plants.

Share and Show

Use your MathBoard and ⬤ . Make equal groups. Complete the addition sentence.

	Number of Equal Groups	Number in Each Group	How many in all?
1.	4	3	____ + ____ + ____ + ____ = ____
2.	2	5	____ + ____ = ____
3.	3	4	____ + ____ + ____ = ____

Math Talk   How can you use addition to find 5 groups of 4?

On Your Own

Use your MathBoard and ⬤. Make equal
groups. Complete the addition sentence.

	Number of Equal Groups	Number in Each Group	How many in all?
4.	2	3	____ + ____ = ____
5.	3	5	____ + ____ + ____ = ____
6.	4	4	____ + ____ + ____ + ____ = ____
7.	4	5	____ + ____ + ____ + ____ = ____
8.	5	7	____ + ____ + ____ + ____ + ____ = ____

PROBLEM SOLVING REAL WORLD

Solve.

9. There are 3 flower pots.
There are 2 flowers in each
flower pot. How many flowers
are there?

____ flowers

10. There are 2 plants. There
are 4 leaves on each plant.
How many leaves
are there?

____ leaves

TAKE HOME ACTIVITY • Use dry cereal or pasta to make 3 equal groups of 5.
Ask your child to find the total number of items.

Use Repeated Addition to Solve Problems

Essential Question How can you use repeated addition to solve problems?

Model and Draw

Dyanna will have 3 friends at her party.
She wants to give each friend 4 balloons.
How many balloons does Dyanna need?

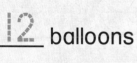

THINK $4 + 4 + 4 = 12$

_12_ balloons

Share and Show

Draw pictures to show the story.
Write the addition sentence to solve.

1. Ted plays with 2 friends. He wants to give each friend 5 cards. How many cards does Ted need?

_____ cards

2. Aisha shops with 4 friends. She wants to buy each friend 2 roses. How many roses does Aisha need?

_____ roses

Math Talk   What pattern can you use to find the answer to Exercise 2?

On Your Own

Draw pictures to show the story.
Write the addition sentence to solve.

3. Lea plays with 3 friends. She wants to give each friend 5 ribbons. How many ribbons does Lea need?

_____ ribbons

4. Harry shops with 5 friends. He wants to buy each friend 2 pens. How many pens does Harry need?

_____ pens

5. Cam plays with 4 friends. She wants to give each friend 4 stickers. How many stickers does Cam need?

_____ stickers

PROBLEM SOLVING REAL WORLD

Circle the way you can model the problem.
Then solve.

6. There are 4 friends. Each friend has 3 apples. How many apples are there?

4 groups of 4 apples

4 groups of 3 apples

3 groups of 4 apples

There are _____ apples.

TAKE HOME ACTIVITY • Use small items such as cereal pieces to act out each problem. Have your child check the answers on this page.

✓ Checkpoint

Concepts and Skills

Follow the rule to complete each table.

1.

Add 3	
2	
4	
6	
8	

2.

Subtract 7	
10	
12	
13	
14	

3.

Add 6	
10	
9	
8	
7	

4.

Subtract 6	
15	
14	
13	
12	

Use strategies to find the sums. Circle any strategy you use.

5.
$$
\begin{array}{r}
4 \\
3 \\
+\,4 \\
\hline
\end{array}
$$
make a 10
doubles
count on

6.
$$
\begin{array}{r}
3 \\
7 \\
+\,5 \\
\hline
\end{array}
$$
make a 10
doubles
count on

Add. Write the sum.

7.
$$
\begin{array}{r}
32 \\
+\,14 \\
\hline
\end{array}
$$

8.
$$
\begin{array}{r}
52 \\
+\,46 \\
\hline
\end{array}
$$

9.
$$
\begin{array}{r}
18 \\
+\,21 \\
\hline
\end{array}
$$

10.
$$
\begin{array}{r}
43 \\
+\,35 \\
\hline
\end{array}
$$

Use your MathBoard and 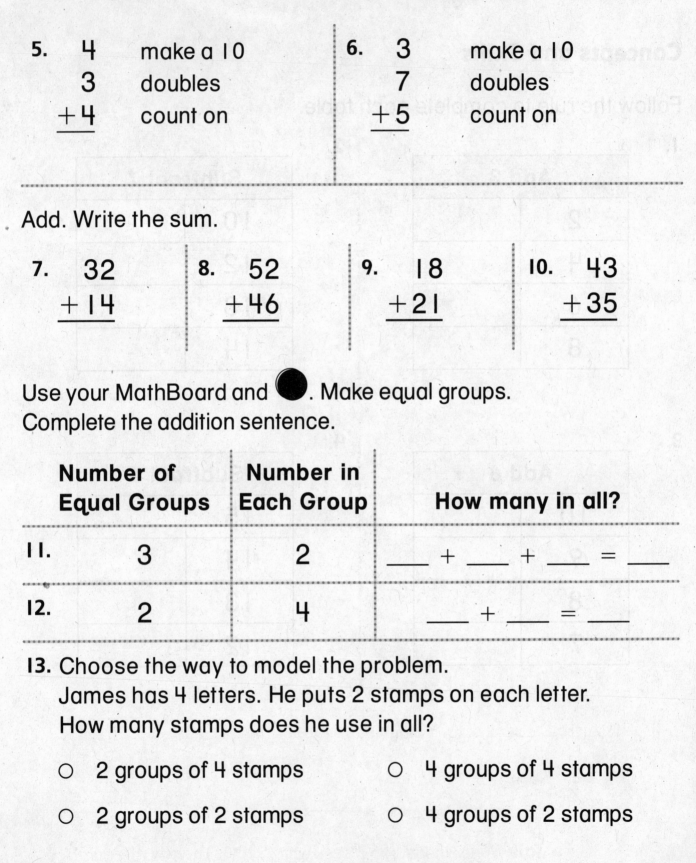. Make equal groups.
Complete the addition sentence.

Number of Equal Groups	Number in Each Group	How many in all?
11. 3	2	___ + ___ + ___ = ___
12. 2	4	___ + ___ = ___

13. Choose the way to model the problem.
James has 4 letters. He puts 2 stamps on each letter.
How many stamps does he use in all?

○ 2 groups of 4 stamps   ○ 4 groups of 4 stamps

○ 2 groups of 2 stamps   ○ 4 groups of 2 stamps

Choose a Nonstandard Unit to Measure Length

Essential Question How can you decide which nonstandard unit to use to measure the length of an object?

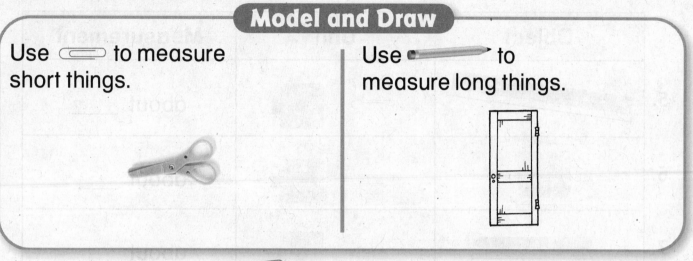

Model and Draw

Use ⬭ to measure short things.

Use ✏ to measure long things.

Share and Show

Use real objects. Circle the unit you would use to measure. Then measure.

Object	Unit	Measurement
1.	⬭ / ✏	about ____
2.	⬭ / ✏	about ____
3.	⬭ / ✏	about ____
4.	⬭ / ✏	about ____

Math Talk Alex measured a book with ⬭. Then he measured with . Did he use more ⬭ or ✏? Explain.

On Your Own

Use real objects. Choose a unit to measure the length. Circle it. Then measure.

Object	Unit	Measurement
5. 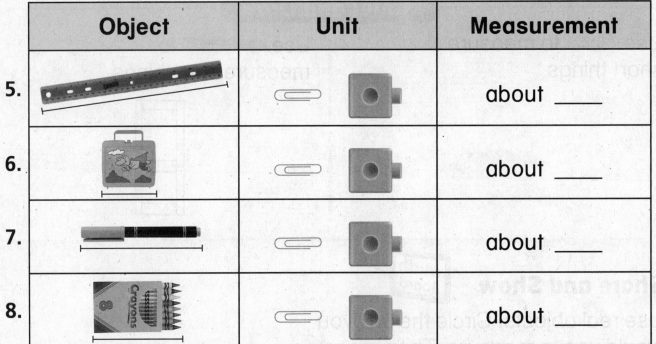		about _____
6.		about _____
7.		about _____
8.		about _____

PROBLEM SOLVING REAL WORLD

9. Fred uses 🎲 to measure the stick.
Sue measures the stick and gets the same measurement.
Circle the unit that Sue uses.

TAKE HOME ACTIVITY • Have your child measure something around the house by using small objects such as paper clips and then by using larger objects such as pencils. Discuss why the measurements differ.

P276 two hundred seventy-six

Name _____

Use a Non-Standard Ruler

Essential Question How can you use a non-standard measuring tool to find length?

Model and Draw

About how long is the pencil?

The end of the pencil and the end of the ⊂⊃ must line up. Count how many ⊂⊃ from one end of the pencil to the other.

about ___4___ ⊂⊃

Share and Show

About how long is the string?

1.

about _____ ⊂⊃

2.

about _____ ⊂⊃

Math Talk In Exercise 1, why must the end of the pencil and the end of the ⊂⊃ line up?

On Your Own

About how long is the string?

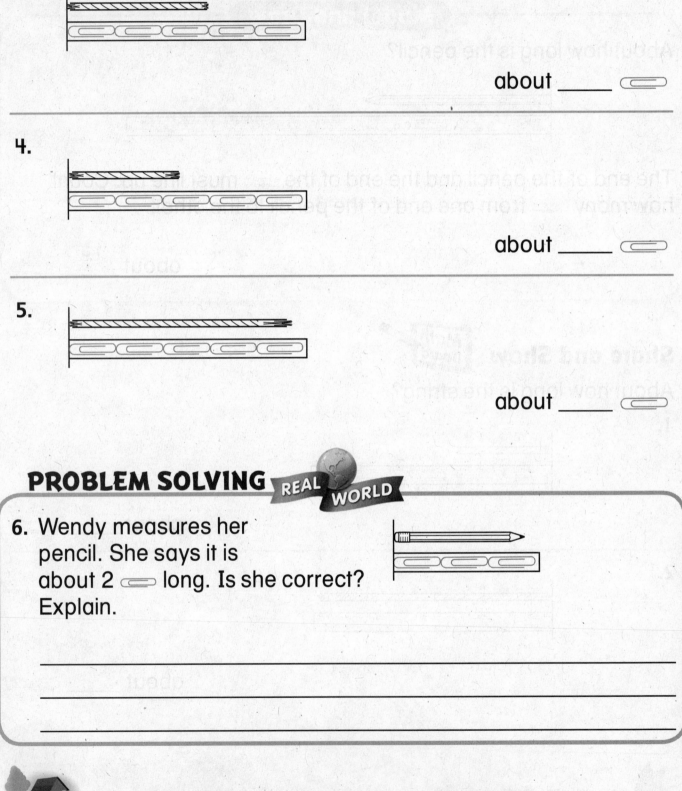

3.

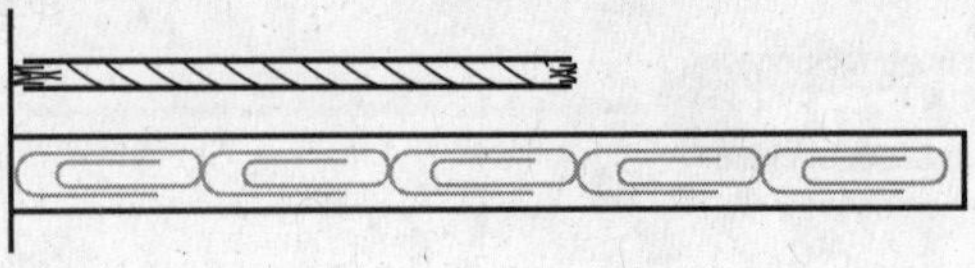

about _____ 

4.

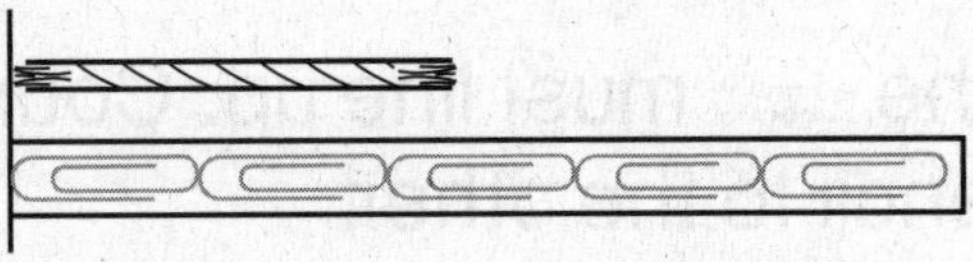

about _____ 

5.

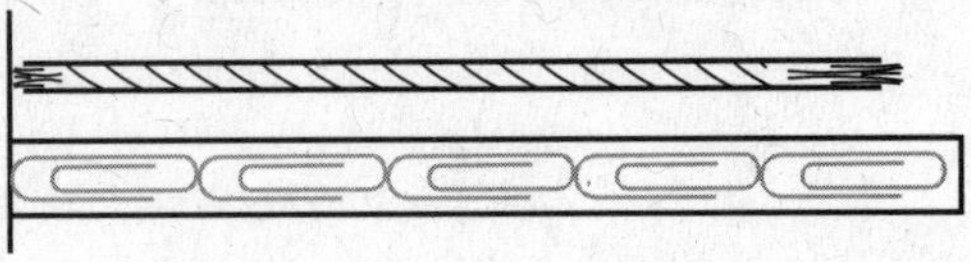

about _____ 

PROBLEM SOLVING REAL WORLD

6. Wendy measures her pencil. She says it is about 2  long. Is she correct? Explain.

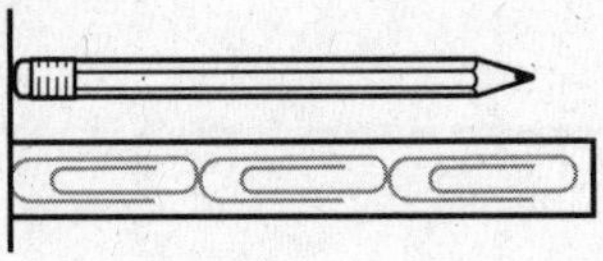

____

____

____

TAKE HOME ACTIVITY • Have your child use 20 paper clips to measure different small objects in your house. Be sure the paper clips touch end to end.

Name _____

Compare Lengths

Essential Question How can you compare lengths of objects?

Model and Draw

First, write 1, 2, and 3 to order the strings from **shortest** to **longest**.

Then measure with ▱.

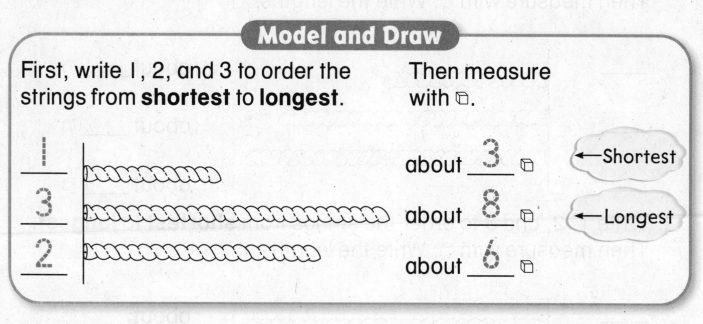

1 ⟨⟨⟨⟨⟨⟨⟨⟨⟩ about __3__ ▱ ← Shortest

3 ⟨⟨⟨⟨⟨⟨⟨⟨⟨⟨⟨⟨⟨⟨⟩ about __8__ ▱ ← Longest

2 ⟨⟨⟨⟨⟨⟨⟨⟨⟨⟨⟩ about __6__ ▱

Share and Show

Write 1, 2, and 3 to order the strings from **shortest** to **longest**. Then measure with ▱. Write the lengths.

I. ____ | ⟨⟨⟨⟨⟨⟨⟨⟨⟨⟨⟩ about ____ ▱

____ | ⟨⟨⟨⟨⟨⟩ about ____ ▱

____ | ⟨⟨⟨⟨⟨⟨⟨⟨⟨⟨⟨⟨⟨⟨⟩ about ____ ▱

Math Talk How can measuring with cubes tell you the order of the strings?

On Your Own

2. Write 1, 2, and 3 to order the strings from **shortest** to **longest**. Then measure with ⬡. Write the lengths.

_____   about ____ ⬡

_____   about ____ ⬡

_____   about ____ ⬡

3. Write 1, 2, and 3 to order the strings from **shortest** to **longest**. Then measure with ⬡. Write the lengths.

_____   about ____ ⬡

_____   about ____ ⬡

_____   about ____ ⬡

PROBLEM SOLVING REAL WORLD

4. Kate has these ribbons. Kate gives Hannah the longest one. Measure with ⬡ and write the length of Hannah's ribbon.

about _____ ⬡

TAKE HOME ACTIVITY • Give your child three strips of paper. Have your child cut them about 4 paper clips long, about 2 paper clips long, and about 5 paper clips long. Then have your child order the paper strips from shortest to longest.

Time to the Hour and Half Hour

Essential Question How do you tell time to the hour and half hour on an analog clock?

Model and Draw

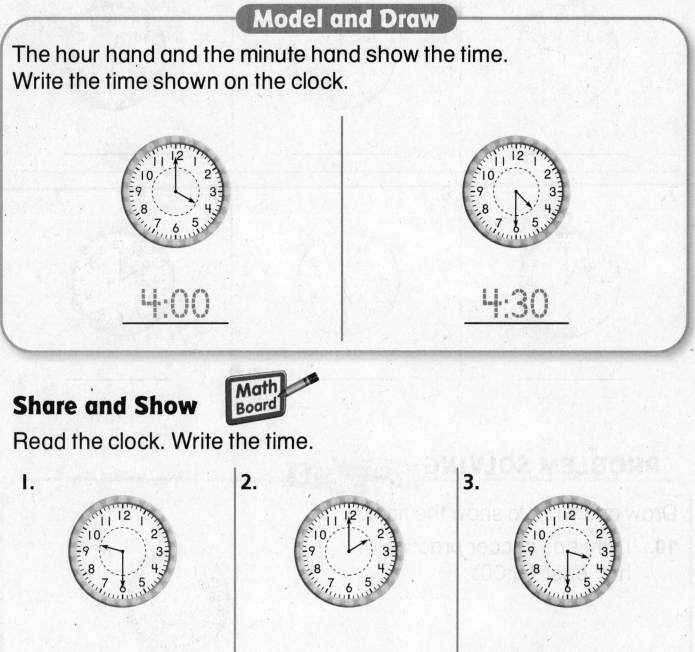

The hour hand and the minute hand show the time.
Write the time shown on the clock.

4:00

4:30

Share and Show

Math Board

Read the clock. Write the time.

1. _____

2. _____

3. _____

Math Talk   Why does the hour hand point halfway between 5 and 6 at half past 5:00?

On Your Own

Read the clock. Write the time.

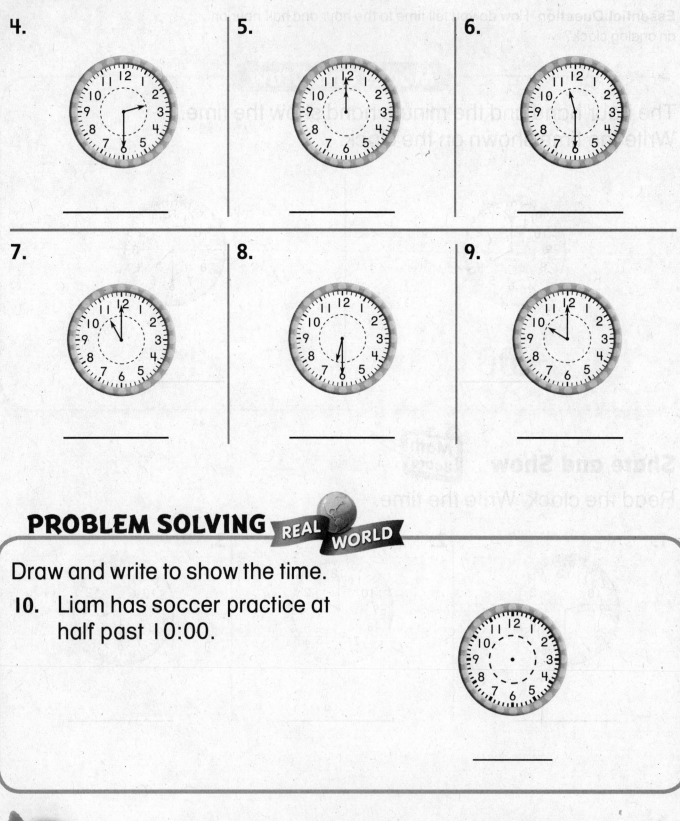

4. _____

5. _____

6. _____

7. _____

8. _____

9. _____

PROBLEM SOLVING REAL WORLD

Draw and write to show the time.

10. Liam has soccer practice at half past 10:00.

_____

✔ Checkpoint

Concepts and Skills

Use real objects. Choose a unit to measure the length.
Then measure.

Object	Unit	Measurement
1. 	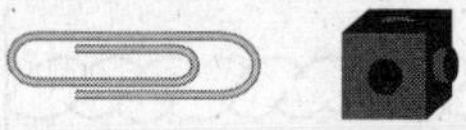	about ____
2. 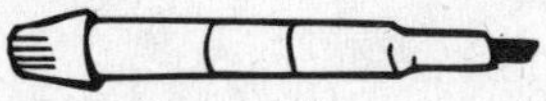		about ____
3.  MATH		about ____

How long is the yarn? Use the star ruler to measure.

4.

____ stars long

5.

____ stars long

Write 1, 2, and 3 to measure the
strings from **shortest** to **longest.**
Then measure with cubes. Write the lengths.

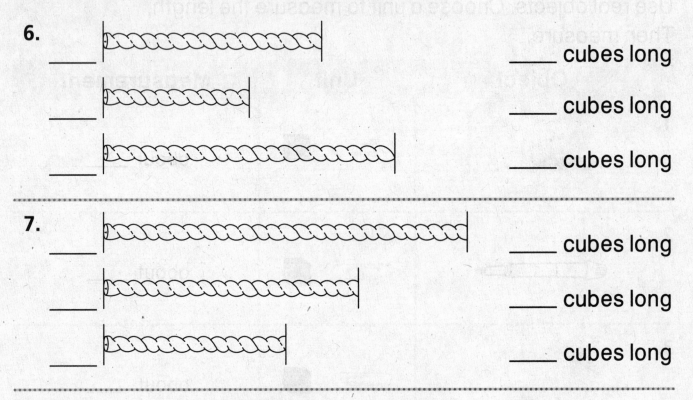

6. _____ ⟨string⟩ _____ cubes long

_____ ⟨string⟩ _____ cubes long

_____ ⟨string⟩ _____ cubes long

7. _____ ⟨string⟩ _____ cubes long

_____ ⟨string⟩ _____ cubes long

_____ ⟨string⟩ _____ cubes long

8. Read the clock. Choose the correct time.

○ 8:00

○ 8:30

○ 9:00

○ 9:30

Name _____

Use a Picture Graph

Essential Question How do you read a picture graph?

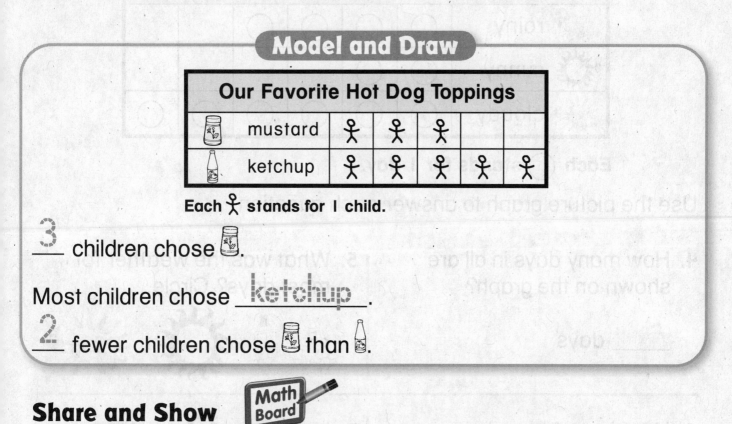

Model and Draw

Our Favorite Hot Dog Toppings					
mustard	�	�	�		
ketchup	�	�	�	�	�

Each � stands for 1 child.

_3_ children chose 🧂.

Most children chose __ketchup__.

_2_ fewer children chose 🧂 than 🍶.

Share and Show

Math Board

Our Sock Colors					
black	�	�			
white	�	�	�	�	�	�
blue	�	�	�		

Each � stands for 1 child.

Use the picture graph to answer the questions.

1. How many children are wearing 🧦? ____

2. What color of socks are most of the children wearing? _____

3. How many more children wear 🧦 than 🧦? ____

Math Talk How did you find the answer to Exercise 3?

On Your Own

Our Weather						
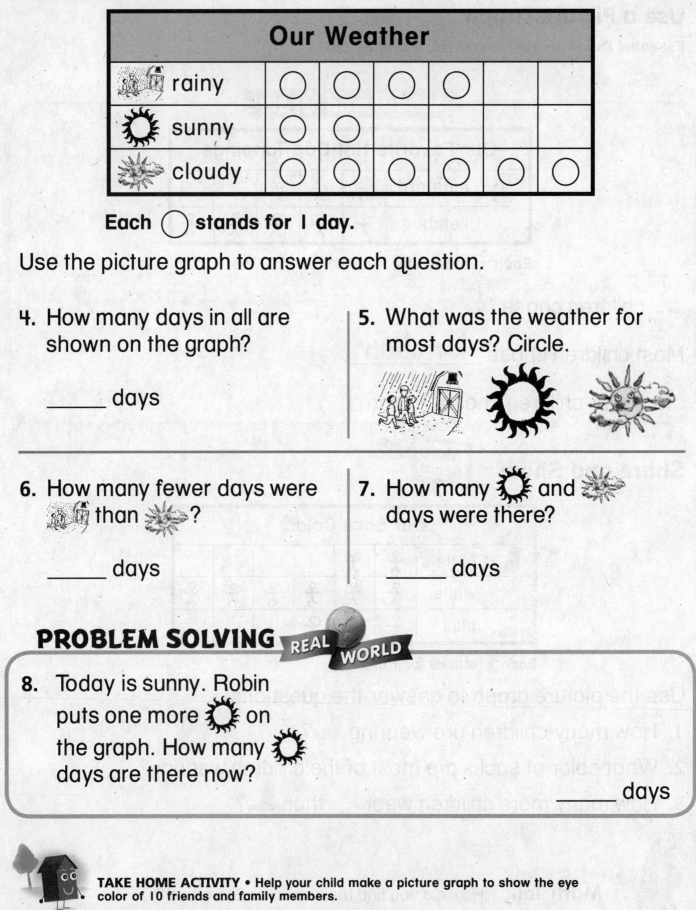 rainy	◯	◯	◯	◯		
sunny	◯	◯				
cloudy	◯	◯	◯	◯	◯	◯

Each ◯ stands for 1 day.

Use the picture graph to answer each question.

4. How many days in all are shown on the graph?

_____ days

5. What was the weather for most days? Circle.

6. How many fewer days were ☔ than ☁?

_____ days

7. How many ☀ and ☁ days were there?

_____ days

PROBLEM SOLVING REAL WORLD

8. Today is sunny. Robin puts one more ☀ on the graph. How many ☀ days are there now?

_____ days

© Houghton Mifflin Harcourt Publishing Company

TAKE HOME ACTIVITY • Help your child make a picture graph to show the eye color of 10 friends and family members.

Name _____

Use a Bar Graph

Essential Question How do you read a bar graph?

Model and Draw

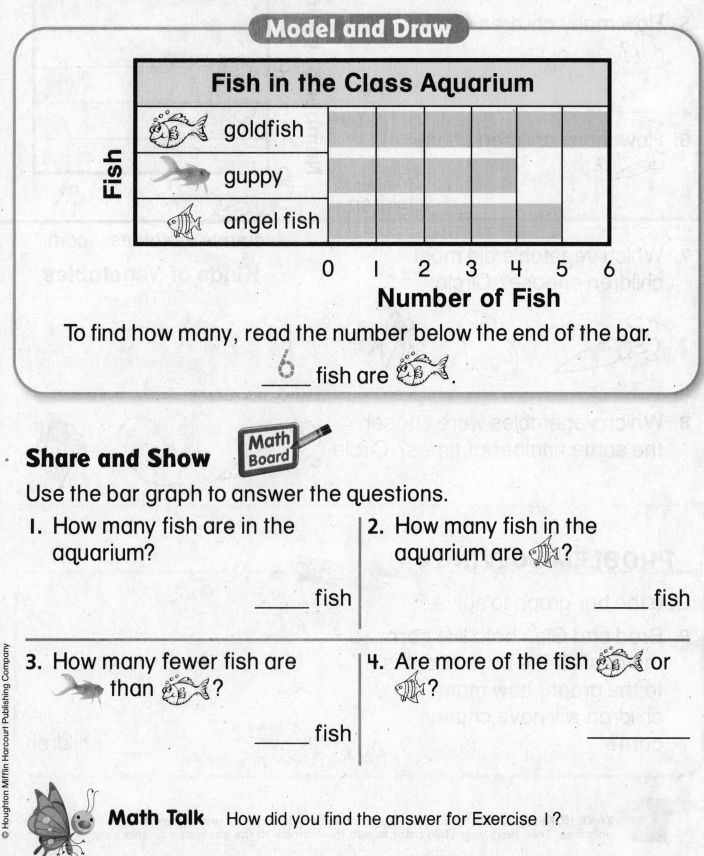

Fish in the Class Aquarium

Fish		
goldfish		
guppy		
angel fish		

0 1 2 3 4 5 6
Number of Fish

To find how many, read the number below the end of the bar.

___6___ fish are 🐟.

Share and Show

Use the bar graph to answer the questions.

1. How many fish are in the aquarium?

_____ fish

2. How many fish in the aquarium are 🐠?

_____ fish

3. How many fewer fish are 🐟 than 🐠?

_____ fish

4. Are more of the fish 🐟 or 🐠?

_____

Math Talk How did you find the answer for Exercise 1?

On Your Own

Use the bar graph to answer the questions.

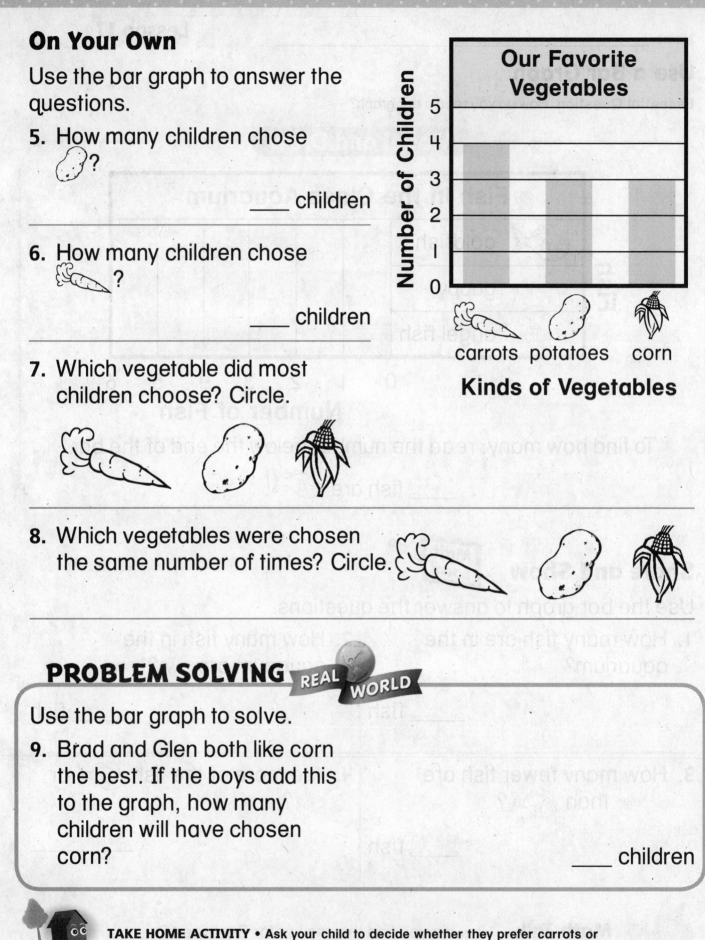

Our Favorite Vegetables

Number of Children

Kinds of Vegetables

carrots   potatoes   corn

5. How many children chose ?

_____ children

6. How many children chose ?

_____ children

7. Which vegetable did most children choose? Circle.

8. Which vegetables were chosen the same number of times? Circle.

PROBLEM SOLVING · REAL WORLD

Use the bar graph to solve.

9. Brad and Glen both like corn the best. If the boys add this to the graph, how many children will have chosen corn?

_____ children

TAKE HOME ACTIVITY • Ask your child to decide whether they prefer carrots or potatoes. Then have your child color to add their choice to the bar graph on this page.

Take a Survey

Essential Question How can you take a survey?

Model and Draw

You can take a **survey** to get information. Jane took a survey of her friends' favorite wild animals. The tally chart shows the results.

Favorite Wild Animal	
Animal	**Tally**
elephant	ЖІІ
monkey	ІІІ
tiger	ІІ

REMEMBER
Each tally mark stands for one friend's choice.

Share and Show

1. Take a survey.
   Ask 10 classmates which wild animal is their favorite. Use tally marks to show their answers.

Our Favorite Wild Animal	
Animal	**Tally**
elephant	
monkey	
tiger	

_____

2. How many children did not choose tiger?

_____ children

_____

3. Did more children choose elephant or tiger? _____

_____

4. The most children chose _____ as their favorite.

Math Talk Describe a different survey that you could take. What would the choices be?

On Your Own

5. Take a survey. Ask 10 classmates which color is their favorite. Use tally marks to show their answers.

Our Favorite Color	
Color	**Tally**
red	
blue	
green	

6. Which color was chosen by the fewest classmates? _____

7. Which color did the most classmates choose? _____

8. Did more classmates choose red or green? _____

9. _____ classmates chose a color that was not red.

10. Did fewer children choose blue or green? _____

PROBLEM SOLVING REAL WORLD

11. Jeff wants to ask 10 classmates which snack is their favorite. He makes 1 tally mark for each child's answer. How many more classmates does he need to ask?

Our Favorite Snack	
Snack	**Tally**
pretzels	II
apples	I
popcorn	IIII

_____ more classmates

TAKE HOME ACTIVITY • Have your child survey family members about their favorite sport and make a tally chart to show the results.

Identify Shapes

Essential Question How can attributes help you identify a shape?

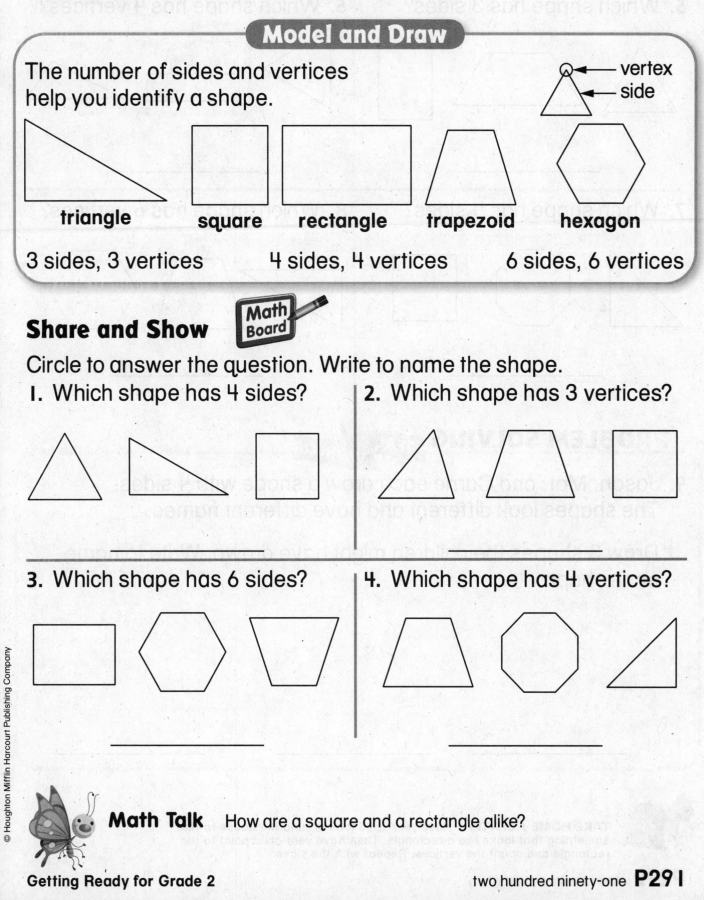

Model and Draw

The number of sides and vertices help you identify a shape.

← vertex
← side

| triangle | square | rectangle | trapezoid | hexagon |

3 sides, 3 vertices   4 sides, 4 vertices   6 sides, 6 vertices

Share and Show

Circle to answer the question. Write to name the shape.

1. Which shape has 4 sides?

_____

2. Which shape has 3 vertices?

_____

3. Which shape has 6 sides?

_____

4. Which shape has 4 vertices?

_____

Math Talk   How are a square and a rectangle alike?

On Your Own

Circle to answer the question. Write to name the shape.

5. Which shape has 3 sides?

_____

6. Which shape has 4 vertices?

_____

7. Which shape has 4 sides?

_____

8. Which shape has 6 vertices?

_____

PROBLEM SOLVING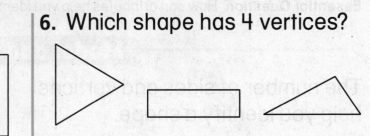

9. Jason, Mat, and Carrie each draw a shape with 4 sides. The shapes look different and have different names.

Draw 3 shapes the children might have drawn. Write to name each shape.

_____   _____   _____

TAKE HOME ACTIVITY • Have your child look around the house to find something that looks like a rectangle. Then have your child point to the rectangle and count the vertices. Repeat with the sides.

Name _____

Equal Shares

Essential Question How can you name two or four equal shares?

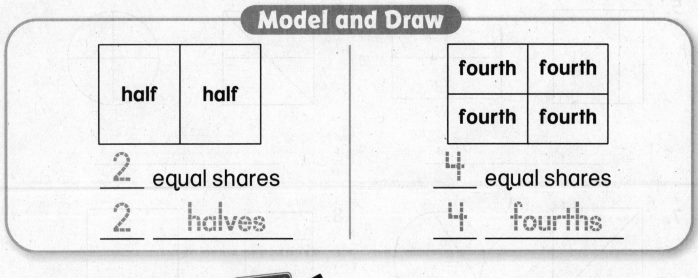

Model and Draw

half	half

__2__ equal shares

__2__ halves

fourth	fourth
fourth	fourth

__4__ equal shares

__4__ fourths

Share and Show

Circle the shape that shows equal shares. Write to name the equal shares.

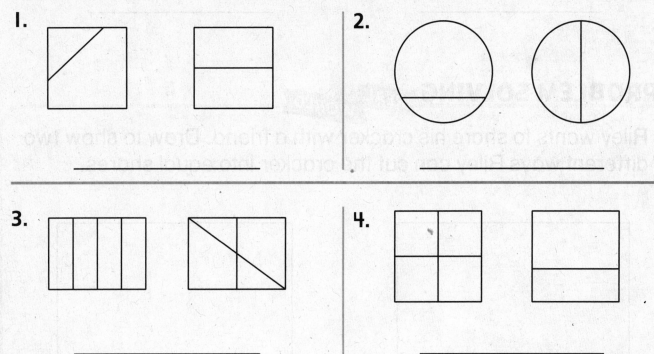

1.

_____

2.

_____

3.

_____

4.

_____

Math Talk Are all equal shares the same size and shape? Explain.

On Your Own

Circle the shape that shows equal shares. Write to name the equal shares.

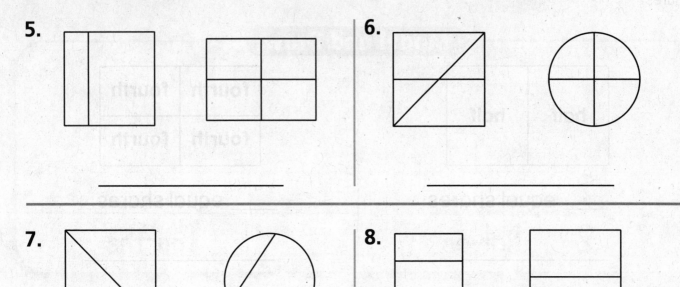

5. _____

6. _____

7. _____

8. _____

PROBLEM SOLVING REAL WORLD

9. Riley wants to share his cracker with a friend. Draw to show two different ways Riley can cut the cracker into equal shares.

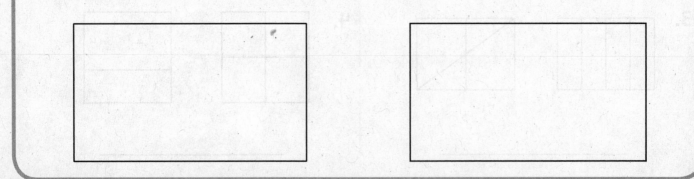

TAKE HOME ACTIVITY • Ask your child to help you cut a piece of toast into fourths.

✔ Checkpoint

Concepts and Skills

Use the picture graph to answer Exercises 1 and 2.

Our Favorite Fruit								
🍎 apple	☘	☘	☘	☘	☘			
🍌 banana	☘	☘	☘	☘	☘	☘	☘	☘
🍊 orange	☘	☘	☘					

Each ☘ stands for 1 child.

1. How many children choose an orange? _____

2. Which fruit was chosen most often? _____

- -

Use the bar graph to answer Exercises 3 and 4.

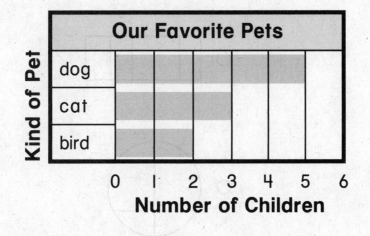

3. Which pet did most children choose? _____

4. How many more children chose a cat than a bird?

_____

5. Take a survey. Ask 8 classmates which sport is their favorite. Use tally marks to show their answers.

Our Favorite Sport	
Sport	**Tally**
baseball	
football	
soccer	

6. Did more children choose baseball or soccer? _____

Circle to answer the question. Then write the shape name.

7. Which shape has 4 vertices?

_____

8. Which shape shows fourths?

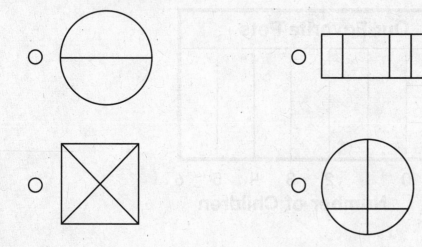